TODDLER DISCIPLINE

Effective Guilt-Free Strategies for Toddler Tantrums. Learn Positive and Kind Ways to Create Discipline In and Out of The Home to Help Your Child Grow Up Happy and Confident

MARIANNE KIND

Table of Contents

Part 1

TODDLER PARENTING

Tips to Help your Child Grow Up Happy and
Confident Without Difficult Behavior or Conflict

Introduction

Children are the apples of their parents' eyes, and parents just can't seem to get enough of their cuteness. They walk, make up their vocabulary, do things win their hearts, and leave them feeling proud of having created something so beautiful. Yes, parents, we are talking to you!

The concept of a Montessori preschooling is primarily focused on the early years' of formative development. The toddlers aging from 2.5 or 3 to 6 years are mainly the learners of this scientific-educational approach. This book will touch the Montessori method's historical significance and further delve into the essential aspects of this philosophy, which has a child-centered pedagogy and curriculum.

Subjects in the Montessori system, along with Montessori-specific lessons and exercises, are mentioned in detail to help provide a specific guideline to the parents and teachers alike to raise their toddlers at home, the Montessori way. The parent's role and the importance of educating the toddlers as preparation for life are essential ingredients for ensuring their proper development and enhancement as makers of men.

Furthermore, positive experiences at home, help your toddler avoid hindrances to growth, which are also a significant problem in untrained adults nowadays. The child's right to choose the purposeful work preserves their independence, confidence, curiosity, and inner satisfaction. It leads them towards the path of normalization, away from any possible deviations that may come their way otherwise. To provide your toddler with a nurturing, prepared environment is a crucial step in setting up a Montessori-friendly children's house to raise them in.

This is where a child's development milestones come into play. Child development milestones aim to make parenting for expecting and new parents slightly more straightforward as they set specific parameters of how much a child should develop within a particular timeframe. Think of it as a professional coach's way of timing their best athlete's running performance. They have to hit a few milestones to ensure a definite win. The same is the case with child developmental milestones.

Understanding a child's growth and development throughout the first years of parenting is imperative. As kids grow, they encounter multiple physical and cognitive challenges. However, the question of whether they are meeting the milestones as they should is what these developmental milestones answer.

Growth and development don't just entail visible changes in their appearance, weight, or height; it also includes milestones like emotional and social regulation, personality formation, communicating and speaking abilities, and sensory awareness. Monitoring and evaluating a child's developmental milestones is a significant means to measure how well they are developing. This makes for a useful guide to help parents, both new and existing, notice any delays or areas where their child should be growing but isn't. Think of these milestones as a list of items on a to-do list that you get to "tick off" or "check" once your child reaches it. It makes tracking their growth easier. If any of the developmental milestones are unchecked or missed, parents can notice that and seek advice or treatment, which is good because early detection is the best way to mitigate the effects.

Since every child is unique, one mustn't rely too much on these developmental milestones. Instead, look at them as a helpful reminder of what is considered appropriate for what age range. This is essential as many new moms get stressed when they notice that another child the same age is more active than theirs or that their child lacks the cognitive ability to make sense of things around them. Understanding milestones can go a long way in relieving anxiety.

CHAPTER 1:

What Is the Toddler Stage?

Toddlers are called toddlers because they are in that stage of development where they can't fully walk straight or are just learning. It is derived from the word toddle, which means to do the same. Toddlerhood begins when the child reaches the one-year mark. Scholars can disagree on when it ends as some suggest the developmental period ends when the child turns three, while others argue that it ends when the child reaches the four-year mark. Ideally, it ends when the child starts preschool, which isn't the same for every child. In some countries, children start school as early as three, whereas, in others, they don't go to school before five, like in most states in the U.S. From infancy, babies learn to form relationships with the people around them. Characters or features for that matter, but they do have intense hearing and smell senses. They can easily distinguish their mother's voice and smell when they are in their arms. Although crying is the only form of communication they know, they only nurture their skills as they grow older. As they reach toddlerhood, they are more expressive, understand several emotions like happiness, pain, or sadness, and recognize people better. This makes interactions more meaningful. In this first chapter, we shall look at the various socio-emotional developmental milestones toddlers achieve to gain valuable insight into how they form relationships and learn about discipline. Hopefully, this will enable parents to devise the right strategies that work best in developing their social skills and promote accelerated learning. However, before we begin, keep in mind that each child is unique in their way. Some are quick to pick things up, while others are slow learners. This means that not every child will start to talk and walk right after they turn one. Some may be more expressive or active than others. In behavioral development, we can expect our children to go through four different stages in the early years of their lives. The first stage is from birth until your child reaches one year old. This is primarily called the baby stage. Step 2 goes from 1 to 2½years old, called the younger toddler. Phase 3 is from 2½to to 4 years old, known as the preschool toddler. Finally, stage 4 from 4 years old up to 8 years of age or called the early school-age child. Within this said framework, children grow in size and behavior. Their behavior will change, but not necessarily for the better. This is where parents like you come in. For toddlers, having the ability to do things on their own finally, given their acceleration of freedom, this stage is exciting. For parents, toddlerhood is the perfect time to teach their kids early on of controls and limits. This will be all about learning to control their bodies and behavior.

Some of the following controls include:

- Control of behavior—learning that tantrums are not the right way to get parents' attention and influence them

- Control of bodily functions—such as being toilet or potty training

- Control over selfishness—learning that toys and food are meant to be shared. Even attention from parents and everything that he thinks belongs to him are to be shared.

- Control over frustration—it is like knowing and understanding that their so-called "freedom" does not always mean they can do things successfully. Perfect examples are feeding, bathing, and changing clothes.

- Control of separation anxiety—moving from close clinginess to being on their own at preschool and big school.

What Makes Toddlers Tick

Whether you think they are heaven-sent, immense treasure, terrible 2-year-old, or an explorer, all toddlers have one thing. They have these behavioral traits you never dared imagine existed. Some of these traits include:

Toddlers Have Little to Zero Sense

Ages 1 to 2 years old, toddlers are considered to have zero sense. It is because, during this time, all they got is maximum mobility and minimum sense. We all know that this combination is psychologically upsetting for parents like you. This is the stage wherein your toddler is unthinking and will do what he pleases—climbing up and down staircases, scattering toys, eating inedible stuff, and a whole lot more.

At this age, toddlers also get into trouble fighting with their siblings, and they do not know when to stop. Other unthinking behaviors include head-banging, spilling milk on bedsheets, and just messing around the whole house. For effective discipline, parents should know when it is best just to slow down or admit defeat. Unfortunately, admitting defeat is impossible for some, thinking that they should be the ones in control and in command. While this is true, there will be instances when it is better off just to rest your case. They often misunderstand these behaviors that they thought their children exist only to annoy them. They slowly forget the fun of having kids around and begin to focus on parenting as an exhausting task and routine.

Toddlers are Self-centered

This is a fact; toddlers only focus on their own happiness and needs. They do not have a care in the world simply because they are still young and do not understand what is going on.

Sharing of toys or politely asking for it will never happen if you have a toddler around. The idea of taking turns is quite foreign at this age as well. And although they love being around other children, they are more focused on being beside kids their age rather than being with them.

For parents, you don't have to worry; this behavior is normal. As the years progress and as your toddler matures, he will surely get through self-centeredness.

Toddlers Want Constant Attention From Parents

Most of the time, toddlers love to be the center of attention. If you notice, when your toddler is with another toddler or with several kids, the one who steals the limelight will indeed be hated. This example does not only extend to playmates but even to simple chores and activities such as cooking, a lengthy phone call, or even when their daddy suddenly hugs or kisses mommy.

Attention is essential to toddlers. Since they have little to zero sense, all they think and believe is that mommy or daddy is always there for them. But after a day of messy play, trying to keep the house in order in between games, and taking care of your toddler's needs, parents are already exhausted. What's more, is that you are not just going to do it for 24 hours, but for the rest of your life or as long as they need a Mom and Dad beside them.

The "No" Word

According to experts, toddlers only copy what they hear and see from their parents and learn to say "no" long before they know to say "yes."

Toddlers Have a Short Attention Span

Have a toddler sit on a chair with a toy or food on his hand, and he will last doing the activity only for 3 – 5 minutes. Three minutes if he finds it exciting and 5 minutes if he begins to be more curious about it. What does this mean? It means that they only live for the here and now.

Therefore, it is at this age when constant supervision, guidance, and praises come into play.

And so, if you have a toddler who whines all the time, who demands more stage position, who is self-centered, and has more power than sense, do not fret. Parents, these are all normal behaviors, so there is no need for blaming or for feeling unworthy or not good enough for your children. Just be the best Mom and Dad that you can be, and go with the flow.

CHAPTER 2:

Socio-Emotional Developmental Milestones at Age One

Most of the social cues toddlers pick up are from their parents, especially mothers. The "the monkey see, monkey do" stage where they don't understand the reasoning behind a behavior but still do it.

You can expect them to point and express their intentions in whatever vocabulary they have learned in the past year. You can do the same. To promote accelerated learning, point towards things you want them to know about or remember. Keep in mind that it is less likely that they will remember it as their memory isn't equipped to do that just yet.

Like that of their parents, grandparents, siblings, babysitter, or doctor, they will start greeting them with a smile or a 'hi' and willingly interact with them without supervision. Memorize their faces and voice. If they don't, this could be a red flag you need to talk about with your child's doctor.

They should also engage with you on a one-on-one basis, such as hand you things or take them from you. This again shows their eagerness to interact with you. They should also pick up the concept of taking turns, but this isn't a compulsion. Most kids have a tough time sharing their stuff with others.

They should also seek some independence, whether they have started to walk or not. They will want to explore things and move towards them to give their curious mind some explanation.

Socio-Emotional Developmental Milestones at Age Two

It is able to better assess the things around them and become more engaged and interested. They should be able to start parallel play by two. A similar space refers to a child playing alongside another child but not together. They may occasionally exchange or share things, but don't expect too much too early. They still need to learn to wait for their turn and share their toys or food with others. If they are already doing so, go ahead and praise their effort. Otherwise, they are ready to defend their toys the minute someone tries to touch them. Their social behavior stems from egotism because they have selfish thinking. Their desires direct their actions.

Moreover, this is the age when children start to engage with strangers with some confidence. They will wave at the cashier or smile at a passerby. Their reaction or response is a sign that they want to explore more and interact more. Not every child is this open and expressive about their desires, which means you need to encourage you. Inquisitiveness is a sign of intelligence. The more curious the child about the things around them, the more information they will take.

Socio-Emotional Developmental Milestones at Age Three

By the time they turn three, you might be starting to think about putting them into preschool. They are more talkative than ever before. They are full of energy, and the stability in their walking gives them more confidence to seek independence. Their social skills start to develop too as they interact with others more and more. They may even have a few friends they like to play with or share their toys with.

This means that they actively seek someone to play with them. Their attention span also increases, and they are more motivated to pretend to play. This is the right time when you, as their parent, have to provide them with ample opportunities to increase positive interactions so that they don't feel shy around strangers—the less traumatizing time when they start preschool as they will feel comfortable around others.

They will develop a basic understanding regarding safety rules such as why they shouldn't play with the knife, why they shouldn't tease the pet, or why they must stay away from the stairs altogether.

They will also start to listen better, which means you can request and order things from them. Reminders that don't seem like an order but rather a request.

They may experience sadness or anger firsthand. Encourage good social behaviors and how to deal with them without crying, whining, or throwing things. During such social complications, try to make them feel better by hugging or kissing them to show empathy.

Finally, their imagination will improve. They will start pretending-playing. They will concoct scenarios in their head. If they are into cars, they may develop a strategy like a traffic situation or a train that has gone over the rail, and an ambulance and fire-truck is headed to help them. When they reach this stage, start reading stories about the things they show interest. If they are into wildlife animals, read the animals' information helping each other out, obeying their parents, or portraying good basic manners.

We can use strategies and parenting tips that seem appropriate for a certain age. Parents can prepare themselves with the right tools and measures to develop excellent social skills to help them start preschool.

CHAPTER 3:

Within the Toddler's Mind

Every parent who has ever observed the serious, unblinking eyes of a kid has asked, "I wonder what she thinks?" Gaining an ever-increasing glimpse into your infant's active mind and how it functions is a fascinating aspect of infancy. The most significant reason these feelings are exposed to you is the increasing opportunity to connect. Here is a glance at some small child's thinking processes: Why is she so curious about everything? Curiosity is the key motivator for your little discoverer. A kitten does not turn on and off interest at will; it is her nature. She utilizes all her senses to seek to make sense of the world—what are stuff, what are they doing, how they function.

Curiosity is the explanation of why a 12-month-old uses her mouth and hands to discover anything within scope, which is when an 18-month-old is pulled like a magnet towards a sandbox. That is why a 2-year-old catches the cat's ears, pours out water from the sink, attempts to burrow through your cupboards, and beheads all the flowers through your yard. She cannot help herself—for the first time, at least. Nevertheless, she will know what is ideal and what is not. Is he feeling a sense of time? A kid cannot follow one clock or read a calendar. Typically, yesterday implies something that has occurred in the past, whether it was yesterday or six months ago. Tomorrow is a word all-purpose to the future. In reality, the notion of time a child has before the second or third grade does not match that of an adult. Your child lives more in the here and now. The way he marks the time is with daily routines. In addition, a 1-year-old understands there is breakfast, lunch, and dinner afterward. He knows that dinner will be in a short time, even if he has no idea how long "five minutes" or "fifteen minutes" is when he is hungry and sees you rattling pans in the kitchen. Naps help him to keep pace with the day too. Holding it as simple as possible brings your child tremendous reassurance. They allow him to know what will happen next in his day, offering the same comfort you would get from reviewing your schedule or staring at your watch. Support your child gage a sense of time by describing sequences: "After you play, I'll pick you up, have lunch, then take a nap." "After two more nights, we'll go on holiday."

How well she remembers? More than you could imagine. While many impressions of childhood are forgotten until we are adults, daily kids recall plenty for purposes that are not entirely known. They can associate certain events (such as the teller giving your child a lollipop when you go to the bank). They might start reminding themselves of the steps involved in finger painting or bedtime routine. Having a practice helps strengthen memories and builds an overall sense of security for your child. You should also motivate your child by posing him to use his recall skills: "What did we see at the zoo?" Kids prefer to recall things that deviate from what is usually planned. Therefore, instead of telling you about the lions and tigers and bears, your child might continue to talk about how he dropped his ice cream cone. Besides, Toddlers remember unusual events (such as a one-year zoo trip) more often than the routine details (say, if a zoo excursion is a regular thing). Study the day together at bedtime. By inserting information, help your child draw on his memories: "Yes, the ice cream has dropped. Just instead, we had a pacifier! "His capacity to arrange and store memories grows dramatically as your child's language skills develop. For e.g., you may hear your child speak about a large truck he had seen two weeks earlier. Alternatively, seeing a seashell could remind him of getting a beach holiday eight months earlier, using images also to protect memories. Hold snapshots of distant relatives available on the fridge frame, and even glance at family photos together.

How is his mind working? Toddlers are literal minds who are legendary. They lack a real understanding of the subtleties of words, meaning, and situation to see the complexities. When you say, "You are funny," your child can complain, "I'm not funny. My name is Sammy!"The child will develop more abstract thinking before age 2, as well; an illustration is the willingness to envision something that isn't there. Children reinforce knowing that things exist even if they do not remove artifacts and then go back to where they are placing them. Think of it as progressive peekaboo. Crackers can be found, for example, under the sofa cushions or blocks in a kitchen drawer. This lets a kid build confidence and an appreciation of the permanence of an object—"Is it really still there? "Exercising control is also a method of squirreling items away. Your child takes care of a tiny portion of her world in her own small way, as she chooses when. Besides, indeed, she can only wonder where those crackers are. Will he know quantity? Within his second year, your child gains knowledge of quantities simplistically. A 1-year-old can understand the concept of "more" and even "big" versus "little." By age 2, your child might be able to count as accurately as two might as possible. A few bright 2-year-olds can recite their numbers from one to 10. Yet, in fact, the capacity to actually identify more than two of anything is not mastered before age 3 or older. Counting songs (such as "Ten Little Indians") is fantastic fun for children and sets the foundation for a subsequent understanding of numbers.

The sense of humor of the Children may be simplistic, but it sure does exist. Has she developed a sense of humor? For example, satire and the stories of late-night comics go right over your child's ear. A sense of fun for a child is on the immature side. Yet there certainly is. A major game is a slapstick. Sound like sliding back, hearing your kid howl. Her weakness is confusion. E.g., when you make your nose an elbow or claim to put a shoe on your head, infants consider it hilarious. Sometimes you can use laughter to benefit, such as defusing a power struggle or amusing your infant when having her ready or diapered. One thumb rule: Always laugh at your wife, never at her. (Ultimately not until she will see you.)

Learning Fundamentals for Babies

A great deal of child-rearing expertise is gained at the job. Therefore, here are a few tips to burp, bathe, and diaper your newborn baby.

All babies, after being fed, will burp midway repeatedly. Burping enables unnecessary gas to exit and is swallowed through suction. The kid will keep filling faster if the air is stored in the belly; take in fewer at each meal. You can make your baby in different positions: with her looking over your shoulder, or while facing her down on your lap or sitting up. Try all of them to see which works better for your child. Using the one hand to firmly rub her back, use the other hand to protect your little one. Whereas if you decide to burp your child in the seated position, lean it forward, with your hand, to support her head firmly.

Sleeping

Starting at home on the first day, placing the kid in the cradle or crib on his back while he is groggy but still conscious. This way, without any support, he can begin to drop out. Do not fret if he is not falling asleep. You can rock him if he starts crying, but once he is calm, bring him right in the cot-before he sleeps. If he wakes up for his feedings in the middle of the night, leave the lights close to zero, and the feedings speedy and businesslike. If you start making it too pleasant, you may be encouraging more repeated feedings at night. He will have problems falling back to bed if it is too arousing.

Skin

Many newborns grow tiny white pimples on their nose and mouth, called **milia**, triggered by premature oil glands' blockage. Such whiteheads vanish under their own after a few weeks. There is no need to pinch clean. Babies can also grow baby acne, triggered by hormones in their mother's body that are already circulating.

The only remedy that is required is to wash the region three or four times a day with water and pat off. The pimples will disappear and leaving no visible traces in a few weeks.

Diapering

Should not use powdered pads until your baby is a couple of weeks old as it may irritate delicate skin. Alternatively, using cotton balls or a dry wipe immersed in hot water to wipe, and a warm towel or cloth to cover. Pass the powders and lotions (as lotions can irritate baby skin; the baby powder is carcinogenic and may be dangerous if babies inhale). If necessary, use cornstarch powder to keep the baby dry in warmer weather (still be careful to keep the powder distanced from her face so it will not be inhaled) and ointments only on a condition that your baby has a diaper rash. If his diaper is simply wet, no need to wash your baby at all; if it is dirty, clean extensively, always wiping from the front to the back (distant from the genitals) for hygienic reasons.

Cord Devotional Treatment

You don't need to bathe every day your baby in a shower during the initial week or two before her umbilical cord stub dries up and falls off. A few days, a fast bubble bath is all it needs. Besides, several doctors recommend the use of newborn skin only with water. Hold the umbilical stub, where necessary, safe, open to the sun throughout the day, and disinfect that with rubbing alcohol during each diaper change to keep it fresh and clean. When the skin across the belly button is dark, or the stub starts oozing, contact the doctor.

Communication and Babies

Babies begin communication from the first day they are born. There are critical times of rapid development before formal education ever starts when the brain is finest able to obtain speech (sound development) and dialect (understanding and using words). Their communication skills are more nuanced as young children mature. They try to recognize and use language to express their feelings and thoughts and to communicate with others. Parents, family friends, and caretakers are the most critical mentors and examples of engagement for infants. However, to make the best of this crucial moment, it does not require software, videos, or any other unique resources. Your day-to-day interactions with your kids help build their brains and enable the growth of communication.

Children develop differently, but most of them follow a natural timetable for speech and language learning. Interaction milestones are skill sets that children are expected to have by some age on average. These milestones build upon each other and help us know if the development stage is on track. Recognizing suitable communication milestones is beneficial for parents to promote their baby's development and seek assistance early if their toddlers do not meet them.

CHAPTER 4:

What Are They Learning and Trying to Learn to Do?

Recent advancement in brain science has demonstrated that babies' environment has a profound impact on brain-building and balanced growth. This initial phase of brain activity predicts how one feels and learns —both as children and adults— and how well.

During the 1st year of a baby's life, the brain is continually building its wiring network. Brain movement produces tiny electrical associations called synapses—the number of stimuli that a child experiences influences explicitly the number of synapses that develop. Repetitive and regular activation reinforces and renders the bonds lasting. We can lose some links that do not get used to it. For a young, growing brain, the early years are the "best time." This prolonged cycle of brain development and capability creation for networks happens only once in a lifetime. As careers and guardians, we have a small but rare ability to promote our children's brain circuitry development.

Here are some exciting details discovered by researchers:

- Children have a psychological desire and an ability to know.

- The fundamental networking of brain synapses is nearly complete within the first three years of accelerated brain growth.

- Children have a strong affinity for human appearance, expression, touch, and scent, over all others. Therefore, the baby's best gift is you, walking, running, handling, and talking to them.

- Fascinating stimuli may enhance excitement, focus, commitment, and learning enjoyment in increasing infants and babies.

- The more age-appropriate and engaging interactions, both physical and social-emotional, in which a child engages, the more circuitry will be designed to enhance learning in the future.

Children go through distinctive transitional stages as they mature from babies into young adulthood. There are numerous shifts in brain growth across each of these periods. What happens and is genetically determined nearly when these developments occur. Situational conditions and interactions within the community with critical entities significantly impact whether growing child profits from each developmental occurrence. Stages and ages are phrases used to outline essential periods in the timeline for human development. Throughout the vital developmental realms, including the physical, psychological, language, and communication-emotional, learning and success occur at a growing stage. The aim is to help parents recognize what happens in the brain and body of their child through each time, with the expectation that they may be able to offer the required guidance, motivation, direction, and strategies to allow a child to advance through each stage as quickly and effectively as possible depending on the particular collection of behaviors and desires of each individual.

Baby (Birth – 2 Years Old)

It can indeed be both difficult and fun to carry a child, especially for the first time. It is a process to grow the securities that will last a lifespan, giving the child the personal strength to build self-esteem and connect constructively to others. It is also the moment for parents to start learning who the new kid is. Each child is special, and parents must strive to recognize, appreciate, help, and foster each child's particular strengths and traits.

Toddler Development (18 Months-3 Years)

A new stage of testing starts when a kid takes its first steps. Children during this stage are free to roam around their environment. This is an opportunity to discover their settings deliberately. Language development is growing significantly, leading to the teaching of the names of points of interest, the capacity to ask for things. As they find their independence, yes, they grow the ability to say, "No! "The creation of what psychologist's term emotional control is a major problem during this developmental period. At this time, "Meltdowns" are regular. Still, parents may use the relationship formed through childhood to help them learn to amplify their emotional communication and begin to understand the complicated concept of delay of gratification. Although, they tend to be able to answer "Yes," spontaneously, children do require guidance, understanding how to embrace "Yes" from others. This is also a phase of rapid intellectual and social development, readying these children to start kindergarten, which includes collaborative interaction with peers while being able to compete emotionally and cognitively at the same time. A child's parent is in a situation to be a coach that provides the right mix of encouragement, support, and guidance. Parents will always function as the principal tutor for the mastering of fundamental skills and promote constructive exploration and testing with novel ideas and abilities.

Expressive and Receptive Communication Skills

Babies continue learning two types of communication skills from birth: receptive skills and verbal skills.

- Receptive communication is the potential of a baby to accept and comprehend a message from another person. Babies exemplify this skill by shaking their heads forward into your voice and reacting, often with speech patterns, to simple directions. Early on, such vocalizations will only be sounded; however, they will start to use expressive language as a baby nears their first birthday.

- Expressive communication is the ability to deliver a message through noises, monologue, signs, or writing to someone else. Instances of your baby's early remarkable achievements are crying, babbling, and using body language. Below are the general steps along the way for children from birth to age two to hearing, listening, speaking, language, and cognitive development. Keep in mind that development varies, and a single child may evolve better in one area than in the other. Your child may not have any of the skills mentioned before the age period is over.

First 0-3 Months

Baby will be making quiet coos and smiles at this age. Remember to communicate regularly with your baby so that they can look and learn!

4-6 Months

Although the kid is not yet developing sentences, they will be responding more to your conversation. They will start making consonant sounds as well, which are the foundations for full words.

7-9 Months

The baby's range of sounds will help it rise. They would even start remembering important words, including their own titles!

10-12 Months

That is when the infant usually begins using real terms! In addition to utilizing other communication devices, they can use simple, quick words like "mama" or "dada" to recognize their parents.

First Year

The language for the kid is increasing! They will understand many words, can use 5-10 (or more!) words alone, and respond to questions.

Second Year

The language skills of your toddler continue to advance at this age. They will start using two-word phrases by their second birthday, follow instructions, and enjoy listening to the stories.

CHAPTER 5:

Dressing Themselves, Food Preparation, and Toilet Training

R outine is the gold standard in the toddler world, and most of the parenting that we do occurs within the practice of routine daily maintenance. You'll find the right structural balance in these foundational routines to keep your toddler moving with the household's rhythm.

Getting Dressed

With young toddlers, sometimes, the mimicry starts early! Evelyn has zero hair, but loves to wave a hairbrush or my buzzing electric toothbrush over her head. Our daily dressing routines started to show in our toddlers' behaviors, with them extending arms and legs as shirts and pants are being put on. Mason was the easiest self-groomer, and we still joke about it today. This kid woke up every morning at 6 a.m. and came downstairs to our room wholly dressed. New underwear, jeans, shirt, socks, shoes, teeth brushed, hair combed—the whole enchilada. He was ready to go. Sure, he needed help to occasionally refresh his teeth or redo his hair, but he has his style and owns it. As young as they are, kids may still have specific clothing needs thanks to sensory-related issues or just plain old preferences (for our Ava, that meant nothing itchy and no denim, so welcome to Leggings-town!) This age group doesn't put up much of a fight.

Without the dexterity and strength to put on their clothes, they're at your mercy. Dressing young toddlers in layers makes it easier to adjust to temperature changes as the day goes on.

Older toddlers often become capable of getting themselves undressed for bath or bed, as well as getting dressed in simpler outfits. They'll also begin developing strong opinions on these outfits. Choose Accordingly. Once they're able to dress, consider outfits that match their abilities. Avoid buttons or tough zippers.

Be Attentive

Being available (not preoccupied) and standing by your toddlers while they dress is a great thing, but you should remind them that you're just there in case they need you.

Take the Time

When a toddler knows that you or your partner is in a hurry or need to get something done quickly, they'll resist and do the exact opposite. Try to give yourself plenty of time.

Regulating Your Own Emotions and Moods

Go ahead; we'll catch-up

Toddlers don't know how to hurry, so rushing them will just frustrate you. Consider where you're rushing to. Can you be a few minutes late? When you choose calm, the whole family dynamic will follow suit.

Teachable Parent Tools to Deploy

Be a clothing buddy. Help your kids gain confidence and get dressed alongside them. I laid both of our outfits on the bed and put the pieces on, one by one, with colorful commentary!

Prep Your Clothes

To plan, every Sunday, we do laundry. We also pull outfits for everyone, with underwear, socks, and accessories included in small metal bins labeled "Monday" through "Friday." The days are color coordinated for the younger ones, so if we say "Mason, go get the orange bin," he knows it is Tuesday.

Once your toddler can dress and undress, it's best to give them no more than two choices. We allow the kids to help choose their outfits on Sundays for the week, so there isn't a fight. If they're not feeling the clothes we chose, they can switch out the bin for a different day. Who doesn't love eating? Well, when your little table-mate is tossing your homemade pesto sauce to the dogs and offering you a slobbered-on a hunk of garlic bread, you might think differently.

I'm a veteran of food combat, and I've bounced back from serving spaghetti marinara over a beige carpet. Despite the mess, eating is one of the most joyful times. Setting kids up to enjoy food and "eat the rainbow" now ensures they'll be well-rounded eaters later. Using the following tools to make eating fun, you'll make it less of a struggle for you and your littlest gourmet.

Eating

We all choose our parenting battles, and Jen and I decided it was important to us to make sure our kids had developed palates. Even trying to raise little foodies, we still run into issues. Ava does not eat cheese, Charlie won't eat any leafy greens, and Mason won't touch avocados. Having a picky eater is a huge universal frustration, so what do you do? Remember, those small successes in this marathon help tremendously. It can be easiest to take the three or four foods your toddler latches on to and continue to serve them, and there's a time and place for that route, but it's certainly not always. We decided to tackle this issue head-on.

Evelyn developed an oral aversion after being force-fed antibiotics, so she views eating as intimidating. We're reacclimating her by showing her it's a fun process, so she's allowed to play with her food—feel it, squeeze it, and, yes, throw it. We talk to her about "kissing" her fish crackers and raisins, so when she licks her lips, she understands there's something good there. It is exhausting, for sure. But raising toddlers who have healthy palates will typically guarantee they won't be the adult ordering a steak and potato dinner "with no parsley and hold the salad."

Your toddler doesn't understand that you're trying to help establish good eating habits—they only care about the frozen yogurt pop. Food that's inherently bright and well-plated makes us want to eat more—even toddlers. They're more apt to partake if they like what they see.

Most everything hits the floor at this stage. They do well with purées but keep them progressing. Finger foods work best because toddlers get to feel them, and kid-safe animal-shaped toothpicks are great for picking up food. But the first time your gleeful girl grabs a spoon or a kiddie fork, don't expect amazing results; Evelyn uses her dirty fork to brush her hair.

They're still getting the hang of chewing, so watch them closely. Food should be bite-sized for their mouth, not yours. Keep cubes (olives, chicken, broccoli) no larger than the size of your pinky nail. When babies are first experimenting, they eat like little squirrels, "munching" with the front of their mouths, whereas toddlers learn to move food to the back and to chew. With age comes dexterity and the use of a spoon or fork. Consider starting a healthy dialogue around food, aiming for specifics over generalities, like "This carrot will help you see in the dark," or, "This blueberry will give you a strong brain!" over "This is yummy!"

The amount of food you think they need may be very different from the amount of food they feel like they need. Start with very small portions fit for little tummies and let them ask for more. It's best for kids to eat until they're full, not necessarily until they clear their plates.

Eat together if you can, sit down as a family every night. It doesn't matter if you have one kid or nine or sit in the kitchen, at a picnic table outside, or around the coffee table. Just. Sit. Together. And serve your kids what you eat, at least for dinner. Don't assume that they don't like it. On a family cruise, we learned our kids were willing to try unfamiliar things and complex flavors: Ava loved chicken tikka masala, Charlie would eat any kind of seafood, and Mason could devour spinach enchiladas. Don't cheat your Tod out of exciting, necessary experiences by keeping menus limited. Fly new food under the radar. If there are "tried and true" items on the plate, slipping in something new might go unnoticed. A nutritionist friend recently told us that anxiety causes an increase in stomach acid, leading to fullness feelings. Having something familiar on the plate leads to less anxiety surrounding mealtime.

I can't pinpoint a specific age for when it's appropriate to potty-train your kids—it's different for everyone. The best way to assess whether they are ready is by communicating and reading their signals, including:

1. Can they express when they're wet?

2. Do they hold their diaper?

3. Can they mimic your toilet use?

4. Do they attempt to wipe while you're changing them?

5. Are they drawn to a training potty or capable of sitting and staying on it?

Toilet Training

I'm not an expert; however, I'm a dad who's researched potty-training, worked in the parenting space for a decade, and been through this rodeo four times.

Scientifically speaking, a toddler between twelve and eighteen months has very little bladder control, so training them early isn't so much about training them, it's about training you.

With our family, little hints were clutch. Evelyn cried every time she peed or pooped in her diaper, so her discomfort signaled to us that she's ready to transition. Mason attempted to use the potty on his own. They would also approach the adult potty and pull at the seat or try and mimic our actions—standing up, sitting down, and pulling on the toilet paper roll. We've had two training potties; the first is a simple red seat "bowl" that sat lower. Our second, a Fisher-Price sing-along version, played a song every time it was used, which encouraged them to keep using the potty. The tricky part about being able to determine whether your kids are ready is to acknowledge their state of mind. The idea of sitting on a potty could be overwhelming (from a sensory perspective) or exciting (from an independence standpoint)—it's all uncharted waters.

She is acknowledging ownership over something as crazy as the potty can go a long way. I like our Evelyn, and your Tod starts to approach the training potty, you'll know she's almost ready to start training. Seeing Evelyn unroll yards of toilet paper is frustrating, but we know she's growing used to the many moving pieces of the bathroom!

At this more advanced stage, disposable training pants like Pull-Ups help bridge the gap between being ready to potty-train, but not having the control to hold it while sleeping.

Go for the Stand-alone

A stand-alone potty with or without a dump-able (no pun intended) insert a must. We also purchased a smaller toilet seat insert that clips onto the regular one to keep smaller tushies from falling in.

Pop a Squat, buttercup

We began by introducing our toddlers to sitting down on the potty to pee or poop. Pee was generally what happened first, but if we got a poop, bonus!

Eat first, Potty second

Our pediatrician explains that it can trigger their need to go to the bathroom when a toddler eats or drinks. Consider using that timing to get your little one used to use the potty.

CHAPTER 6:

How Can Routine Help Your Child?

We know that it isn't easy to set up a routine in the lives of children in practice, especially with the rush of everyday life, irregular hours, and lack of time. Although the family must adopt some habits and rules in the little ones' daily lives. A routine for children, from an early age, helps them to grow more confident and independent.

Little ones like to know what will happen during their day. After a nap, knowing that is the snack or that, before bed, is the story, provides a sense of security. This makes the little ones feel less anxious. Over time, the routine can even cause your baby to develop absolute mania, such as sleeping with the same blanket or just eating certain foods. It's the way they must feel in control, in this world still so foreign to them.

Benefits for Moms and Dads

For parents, pre-established routines also bring many benefits. First, because they feel more secure, the little ones tend to accept the farewell moments better. For example, the time to leave the playground or say goodbye when parents go to work does not become so difficult because they understand that they will return. Thus, from an early age, the little ones will realize everyday life schedules and rules. When they grow up, they become children and adolescents with a greater sense of organization and responsibility, establishing study and bonding schedules, such as helping the family in household activities. Besides, routines also help organize the life of parents. Having established programs for meals, naps, showers, and games makes the whole family manage better and have more time to enjoy the moments together.

Know-How to Be Flexible

It's useful to remember that the excess is never acceptable and hence not worth turning the house into a barracks! You need to know the time to be flexible so that the routine does not become something negative. On weekends, for example, you can sleep a few more hours or have lunch later. The important thing is to set schedules and create healthy habits that make the environment more organized and comfortable for everyone!

Bedtime

Bedtime is the first routine idea of the little ones, and they need to know the difference between day and night. Naps during the day should always be in a clean environment, without disturbing noises or changing the house's routine.

For night sleep, parents need to perform "sleep hygiene" as a ritual. It can be a relaxing bath, followed by a story. The room should be dimly lit and free of noise.

Time to Feed

It is healthy to have family meals, all seated at the table, and tasting varied foods. Take the opportunity to talk and realize that your little one is growing. You can also enjoy setting up a new menu for the following week.

Establish Schedules

It's beneficial for children to have schedules to wake up, carry out activities, play, and sleep. Following the program makes the child get used to it and establishes a routine. You can assemble for your little one a timesheet with drawings, showing the order of your day, which will bring more security to them.

Organized Spaces

Having an organized environment will help the little ones. For this to happen, they must know that:

- After playing, they should store their toys

- Used clothes should be placed in the basket

From an early age, the little ones can and should help with the housework. After all, they are also part of the house!

What is the Importance of Routine for The Child?

The establishment of the routine is vital for the child and their adult life. The adult you will depend on your experience as a child. Childhood is when you establish a strong sense of self, and routinely reinforces a positive self-image. In this sense, the routine benefits can be summarized as: For the child to feel safe, they have to acquire positive and healthy habits from the beginning. Children don't know the order of things when they are born, and so it is adults who must teach them to organize their lives through schedules associated with routines, that is, through activities they must do every day in the same way.

The repetition of rituals helps the child assimilate an inner scheme that makes the world predictable and safe.

What Do Habits and Routines Mean for Children?

The routine is a personal custom established by your coexistence and does not allow modification. That is, it is inflexible, safeguarded some particular situations that are beyond our control, such as unforeseen events. The habit is a stable mechanism that creates skills and can be used in various situations, such as putting on seat belts. Practices are customs, attitudes, behaviors, or behaviors that imply learning. The well-used and used habit allows us to face everyday events.

Habits and routines contribute to constancy and regularity, useful mechanisms, and fundamental for both family and school life.

What are the Consequences of Lack of Routine for The Child?

Not having a basic routine brings behavioral problems that can be considered inconvenient by an inexperienced professional; at school, the child may present difficulties that are often also perceived as Learning Disorders. In addition, the child becomes disorganized, giving more work than usual. The construction of the personality can also be affected since the routine has limits and rules necessary and fundamental for constructing the character of the person. Children crave control, just as adults do. Without a performance, they may feel that they have none, and this can result in anxiety and tantrums.

How Can We Establish A Healthy Routine for Children?

First, be aware of what each child can do at the age they are. Give autonomy forever. Do not raise your children as if they were princes or princesses. They need to learn early on that they are ordinary people just like any other. Time to sleep, wake up, play.

Create habits and rules: brush your teeth after meals, do the chores first, and play later.

Teach them to organize their own objects and toys.

Always speak the truth so that the child does not learn to lie at home.

At mealtimes and on homework, the TV, tablet, and mobile phone should be out of the child's reach so as not to compete with what needs to be done.

Teach your children that you, as parents, are the people of authority at home. Be in charge, but don't forget to be flexible and remember that you're growing tiny adults. You must be the people of affective and authoritative reference to your children. Do not delegate to others the education and rearing of your children. The real presence of the parents is fundamental to the development of the child. Stay tuned to the way they talk, how they dress, how they behave. Your children observe your ways of being and adopt your habits as their own. Sometimes the behavioral problem that the child presents originates from the home itself.

Follow the evolution of your children in school, and in the face of difficulties, seek help as soon as possible. Take care of your children's self-esteem! Please do not call them by nicknames or negative words. This affects the self-esteem and emotional growth of your children. Set small tasks so that the children also contribute to the proper functioning of the house.

And remember, a well-educated child from an early age will be a responsible and happy adult in the future!

CHAPTER 7:

The Brain of a Toddler and How It Works

There is a lot to learn about the brain of your toddler. In a word, it is simply amazing. As a new mother, it may seem like there is so much you need to know about your dearest one. This is true. However, it can be a more relaxing and beautiful journey for you as long as you have the right knowledge about how they think and act and how this phase is most crucial to the rest of their lives.

There has been quite some research on how toddlers think and why they act the way they do. This is worth studying as they can sometimes come out as totally different people from all we have seen and admired in the movies. Toddlers are all fun and more. By knowing how the function of their internal organs, you can be able to raise them into becoming sufficient individuals that you would be most proud of in the future.

According to research done along these lines, what a child achieves in his first three years of cognitive abilities, would take about sixty years or more for an adult to complete. This is because, as an adult, our sense of reasoning and absorption of both facts and abstract elements are well advanced compared to a child. In other words, the toddler's brain works differently from that of an adult. From about age two till age six, there are many marked differences in how things are perceived and assimilated in comparison with later years.

Many theorists have thus, described the brain of a toddler as a sponge––and rightly so too. This conclusion is based on the point that they take an enormous amount of information from the environment and the world around them. What happens in the case of toddlers is that they absorb everything in their environment. It is worthy of note that the rate of this absorption is indiscriminate, continuous, and effortless. It clearly shows that a toddler does not select what to absorb and what to leave out by saying it is indiscriminate. He or she takes in just about everything. Unlike the adult that can point to what not to allow in, the toddler takes them all in. This absorption is continuous too. This means that it continues all through this very delicate stage of their lives. Then, it is equally effortless. They do not exert any effort or force at it. After all, they are laughing, crying, having fun, playing around, or something like that. There is no profound moment where you can point to the time when they are absorbing per se. Even if there are times when they are glued to the TV, it surely does not last for long before their attention moves to something else. But you see, all this while, they were absorbing so much without them even knowing. Little wonder it is so effortless!

In essence, toddlers relate to their environment far differently than adults do. They do not just see things and recall them afterward. They absorb them, such that what they see becomes part of their very core. This is all-natural to them.

Another thing worthy of note is that toddlers develop a considerable percentage of their core brain structure between ages 0 and 5. From ages 0 - 3, children tend to absorb information both unconsciously and unknowingly. This is typically called the unconscious stage. This is the stage where they learn to sit, stand, walk, use their hands, and even speak. They do all of this through mimicry. That is, these basic faculties are developed through mimicry. Toddlers will naturally imitate what they see; as they grow up to begin to make more independent choices. This early stage is so crucial for toddlers to move on to more complex growth stages, or better put, more advanced stages of growth.

There are behavioral patterns exhibited by toddlers that show off how they think. These impulses are stimulated by neurons that are controlled by the brain. Hence, they are worth studying. Asides the fun that a toddler brings to the table each day, they typically engage in approximately 57 billion struggles called power struggles every day.

Again, this behavior is normal and essential for the appropriate development of the child. There are some practical things to focus on relating to the brain of a toddler and help them live out this period of their lives. Note that individual facts to be here will be most valuable in knowing how to get your toddlers to learn through the process of their growing up.

The first thing to note is that toddlers, because of the level of formation of their brains, do need you to tell them many times what you need them to do. This already gives off the truth that handling toddlers need a generous dose of patience, and tons of extras in your handbag, in the kitchen, the dining, everywhere!

As adults, we have what is called "executive function skills." These sets of skills are responsible for our ability to focus our attention on something. It is also what is responsible for our being able to remember whatever instructions we choose to retain. It is the same set of skills that is responsible for how we control impulses. Needless to say that even as adults, we sometimes are not able to hold our emotions together, how much more toddlers who have not yet developed these skills at all. This is the reason they need to hear the same instructions over and over again. For example, a child can begin to color the walls because they are trying to have fun. That action may not be suitable for mum and dad as they have to incur some damages later. Now, telling a toddler that they should stay off the wall once can never do the trick. How can it? He or she does not see the reasons to stay off, nor can they—until you keep telling them again and again while letting them know that you are not happy about their actions (we shall get to that shortly), then they can begin to step back.

Someone used the illustration of the Grand Canyon. On one side is your toddler, who wants to color the wall. On the other side is why he or she should not do it because of the effects it might have. Getting your toddler to see why he or she should not make a mess of the wall, just like getting to the other side of the Canyon, would be no small effort.

Imagine building a bridge that long and, more importantly, strong enough to get over to the other side!

This is what your continuous use of words, telling your toddler the same thing over and over again, is seeking to achieve. One trial cannot do the job, certainly not with the bustling impulses within them.

It means you would have to tell them to keep off the wall a thousand times over (or hopefully less) to begin even to consider it! It would take much time, which in this case is many words to build the bridge and help them find the connection; that they need to keep off the walls (you know you would have to provide an alternative for them anyways, where they can color).

So far, the new mother's point is to see her toddler as having very vibrant and active impulses that the child cannot control just yet. However, by repeating the same things repeatedly, you are helping them in many ways. First, they can see that the look on your face may be disapproving anytime you correct them. As they keep noting this with each time you update them, they will eventually stay off because mum said not to, and more vividly. After all, they do not want to see that look on her face.

Another angle to view this is that toddlers learn better through experiences. It would take a lot, which is true, many life experiences to successfully create the connection you seek in your toddlers' brain.

Lastly, these connections made possible through experiences would lead to the formation or development of the toddler's executive function skills when they age. To recap, repetition is not only essential but helpful for your toddler. It would require patience to keep at this. The rewards are great for your toddler. The happiness would be tremendous for you too, because the intent of raising a child is for him or her to grow up a steady and complete human. Hence, it is key to remind your toddler. It is essential to guide and comfort them. This is because every single experience would help build the bridge they all need at this tender stage of their lives.

What then happens if a mother loses patience along the way? It is crucial to ask this question because it is true that your toddler needs the experience to learn.

So, when tempers are almost up on your side as the mum, just take a deep, deep breath. Another thing that can help you to picture the Grand Canyon and visualize that your words are genuinely laying more and more boards across.

There is something else to call your attention to—your toddler feels negative emotions like adults do—feelings like anger, sadness, anxiety, powerlessness, frustration, confusion, etc. What is different is that the adult brain now knows how to handle these situations (although the mode of handling this may differ across different individuals, let alone if they are successful at it).

In essence, toddlers cannot stop to think over before taking their actions because that part of the brain that allows them to do this is not yet developed. They will, with time, but for now, they will pretty much show forth any and whatever feeling that takes center stage. Like, when they feel any negative emotion, it takes them over completely. Even for your toddlers, these feelings could be quite raw, new, and even confusing— so they need you more at this time to help them.

How can a mother help her precious one when the negative feelings come rushing in and take over? Another way is to label their present emotion. You could use a reflection or mimic their expression. Mimicking their presentation is an excellent way to get their attention at the time. For example, if your toddler is stomping his foot and refuses to stop, you can also begin to stomp yours and keep an expression on your face, similar to what is on his. Then when his eyes are on you, take a deep breath —this would encourage him to take him too. So, you are helping him breathe by breathing. After this, he is now calmer to hear you talk. You can then say something like, "you seem to be angry. What was it you wanted?" Also, by putting words to their emotions, you could, for example, when your toddler begins crying uncontrollably because you cut his cheese in half when he wanted it full, say the words that his emotions are carrying.

CHAPTER 8:

Overcoming Tantrums and Challenges

Temper tantrums are periods of drama and intense emotion; it's essential the toddler quickly learns that their temper tantrums won't get them control over things otherwise you. There are two ways you'll achieve this (a) by ignoring their behavior wholly or see their naughty action and suggesting that once they have finished, you'll ask them about it.

Tantrum Triggers

You can avoid some tantrums by minimizing the situations that set a toddler off. These include:

- Extreme fatigue (skipped nap, late nights)

- Not getting what she wants fast enough

- Being unable to verbalize desires

- Hunger

- Sickness

- Physical inability to try something

- Having an excessive amount of expected of her for her age or developmental stage

- Big life changes (new sibling, new sitter)

- Little life changes (popped balloon, time to go away playground)

- Too much to try to (too many errands, classes, playdates)

With practice, you'll quickly defuse things so that you'll discuss it with them calmly and quietly.

Temper Tantrums

They are beginning at around 15 to 18 months (sometimes earlier). The important reason is developmental; your child realizes that things aren't the way they want to be. He still wants to be nurtured and coddled sort of a baby, but he also craves an older child's autonomy. Alongside this sense of push-pull comes several other influences that will drive him to the brink within the blink of an eye fixed.

A tantrum is your child's way of claiming, "Enough! Help!" She expresses her frustration within the only way she knows how: with screams, flailing limbs, dramatic contortions, or collapsing during a heap. Tantrums are perfectly normal, and you are not likely to form it through toddlerhood without experiencing one or even 100.

Tantrums peak around age 2. They taper off as your child approaches 3, as her verbal skills and physical control increase, and she or he learns more appropriate ways to channel her displeasure and outrage (though they will persist right up to kindergarten).

Prevention Advice

The simpler and more pressure-free your toddler's days are, the calmer they're going to unfold. Search for ways to streamline the morning rush, for instance, like letting your child attend sleep in fresh play clothes the night before, keeps your expectations realistic, too. Never mind if her shirt isn't tucked in or her hair isn't combed. Please don't attempt to haul her around on six different errands on Saturday morning. Also, helpful: increasing your tolerance; ask yourself if a disturbing behavior (or uncombed hair) makes a difference if it isn't hurting anything and doesn't set a dangerous precedent, let your child have her way. But don't abandon all restrictions during a misguided effort to bypass tantrums. It's believed that persistent tantrums are especially common within the homes of oldsters who are overly permissive. Firmness lets a toddler know what the bounds are, so he doesn't need to test you the maximum amount.

Your Best Response

Most parents wish desperately that they might make it stop immediately. Unfortunately, you can't. Your best strategy is to be neutral and supportive; the calmer you're, the quicker the tantrum will pass.

Sometimes it helps to intervene; you'll be ready to distract a young toddler, for instance, and squelch the cries quickly. Some children answer hugs or caress soothing works because your child has lost control of herself, which is frightening for her. She feels liberal to yell and run through her frustration within your arms' relative safety and luxury. Don't attempt to reason together with your child.

Long-winded

Explanations about why she feels the way she does, or why she can't have something she wants, will fall on deaf ears they'll only further enrage your child. Generally, the less you say —during and after the tantrum— try to or have something you've already nixed. Giving in teaching her that a tantrum may be a great way to urge what she wants.

Often, it is best to try anything to remain nearby, a reassuring presence. But let the tantrum burn itself out. Chronic tantrum throwers are often surprised to be ignored within a couple of minutes. They'll calm themselves and advance to something else.

Public Tantrums

In addition to an equivalent factor that fuels a tantrum within your front room's middle, a couple of other things may cause people who explode publicly. For instance, social pressure, like once you bring your child to a celebration, can push a toddler over the sting. Parents, too, feel added pressure in some social situations (a baptism, visiting a replacement school) once they sense, rightly or wrongly, many judgmental eyes are upon them; otherwise, you might want so badly for your darling to act sweetly ahead of Grandma that you simply unconsciously telegraph your anxiety to your child—maybe you fuss about his clothing or dirty face quite usual, or cluck a couple of too many warnings before time kids also act up publicly to urge your goat they know that you respond more quickly or feel less sure of yourself when there's an audience—meaning they'll have a far better chance of winning their way.

Prevention Advice

Prep, your child, before you go somewhere so that the experience isn't unnervingly alien. Before you enter a toy store where you want to devour another child's birthday present—always a dangerous mission— remind your child that you only won't be buying him a toy that day. Say, "It's Susie's birthday were buying her a toy; you will see many things that you want to possess, but you cannot this point. I'll need your help finding something Susie will like, but we'll need to leave the shop if you begin to cry or scream." Be fully prepared to follow through on this warning.

In outlining your expectations, be as specific as possible a toddler doesn't know what "Please be good" means. You would possibly remind him to use his quieter indoor voice, for instance. Time outings around naps and mealtimes to ensure your child's good humor suppose your toddler is fussy, tote, and food and drinks.

Once you reach your destination, make your child feel comfortable. For instance, at a toy store, you'll bring one among his toys inside to carry while you shop; you should not buy him a toy to bribe him to cooperate him feeling involved by describing what you're doing and thinking. Let him help you make choices—even nominal ones, like which thanks to turning the cart. At a celebration, pay him special attention to warm him up before you explode and mingle with the different grownups. Carry him, bring his favorite blanket, and pack any age-appropriate entertainment, like a favorite toy.

Your Best Response

If ignoring the tantrum for a couple of minutes doesn't work, take your child to a secret place (a corner of the shop, your car). Remain neutral and let her regain self-control. But don't rush or chastise your child. Once she's calm, return to your activity as if nothing ever happened. There is no got to rehash the incident. She barely understands it herself. A reminder of the trigger may start the cycle everywhere again if she's having a tough time and has melted down, be prepared to abandon your activity, chalk it up to life with a toddler.

Whining

Why it happens: Whining—a.k.a. Whimpering, bellyaching, fussing, moaning 'n' groaning—is a natural developmental step midway between crying and talking well. Babies haven't any choice but to call to urge you to feed or change them. Toddlers believe this same plaintive sound, mixed with their growing vocabulary, to precise their discontent and signal their wants like temper tantrums, their relative lack of control over their world means they will find plenty to be unhappy about. However, what starts legitimately quickly enough, becomes a nasty habit if left unchecked, which will take years to outgrow. (Guess what, most whiny adults were like as children.)

"Bad" Words

Parents of verbal children are thrilled once they begin to string together their first sentences. But pride swiftly turns to mortification when words like poop, doo-doo, stupid —and worse— escape those beautiful lips. Kids age 2 and under are parrots; they repeat most anything, especially when the words are funny-sounding alliterations (wee-wee, poo-poo). Ignore such talk without comment. At this age, your reaction, whether amused or angry, inspires toddlers to continue using juvenile swearwords.

Kids whine because it works; it is a classic catch-22: Parents concede to whining because once they respond, the annoying sound stops. Alas, kids then keep it up whining on future occasions because they see that it yields great results. The parents' and, therefore, the child's behaviors reinforce one another. All kids whine—at least sometimes, and a minimum of until they're taught better alternatives. Handling this behavior, the proper way early in life can nip more problems later.

Prevention Advice

You can't anticipate all of your toddler's needs, of course. She's getting to whine, a minimum of a touch. The more her basic needs are met — being fed and rested, getting much your attention— the less of a drag whining is apt to be. Some children simply need tons of attention.

You may find that if you stop what you're doing and indulge your child live or read her a book for just a brief while, she'll be more likely to play by herself afterward. Another tip: Say no to your child's requests; only you mean it. Parents often deny simple, reasonable requests—to read another book and play outside —because they're preoccupied or tired. But if you become a chronic naysayer, you're more likely to possess a toddler who whine.

Your Best Response

A whine is, admittedly, a formidable opponent. It's grating. It seems like fingernails on a chalkboard. And it goes on and on. Rather than getting cross, attempt to consider your child's whining as a warning siren. Consider these possible causes and address them accordingly (note that a lot of of those situations also can cause temper tantrums, which, like whining, stem from an inability to precise oneself):

- **Illness**. If your child is unusually whiny, check her fitness.

- **Neediness**. Five minutes is sort of a lifetime to a toddler, especially if he's waiting to possess a physical need met (such as thirst or getting his coat zipped). Your job is to show your child a more acceptable way of phrasing his request. Label his attempt, so he understands why you're annoyed: "I hear whining." Then redirect: "As soon as you'll inquire from me calmly, I'll get what you would like." If your child isn't using many words yet, you would possibly help him with an easier redirection: "You want juice? Say, 'Juice, please.'" Even if your child can't enunciate the words well, ask him to settle down (or, if possible, to undertake to mention the word); then, when he makes the trouble, quickly reward him with praise and, therefore, the juice. It provides a funny demonstration to show your child the difference between what a whine and a traditional tone of voice sound like.

- **The gotta-have-it syndrome**. Faced with the countless temptations of a toy store, for instance, a child's notion of what constitutes his immediate needs skyrockets to incorporate everything in view. New sights and sounds entrance toddlers. They often reach out and beg to research, once you don't decide to concede, the simplest tactic is to ignore this type of whine flat-out.

- **A desire for attention**. Funny how your child's needs suddenly escalate the minute you're on the phone or within the midst of another task that diverts your attention from her. The hour before dinner is another ordinary whine time. Your child is bidding for your attention. However, it is best to ignore her until she will use a formal tone of voice or act calmer.

- **Fatigue**. Crabbiness picks up when kids are tired. Flare-up times for whining: morning rushes, missed or late naps, bedtime, or the months during which your child is outgrowing a nap but still occasionally needs it. View sleepy whines more empathetically than you would possibly at other times. Say, "You sound worn out" or "I skills that feel." check out the general situation to ascertain if you'll make any improvements: Does your child attend bed early enough? Would he enjoy quiet time instead of a dropped nap?

- **Your failure to follow through on a promise**. What parent hasn't skilled some urgent request with the words "I'll be there during a minute"? Or "Let's do this later." Or "Eat your dinner first, then you'll have cake." apart from a young child's difficulty in grasping time, a drag can develop when parents don't follow through. The kid was told one thing, but something else happened. It doesn't matter if you've forgotten or been distracted. The effect is to perpetuate your child's insistence. A toddler who knows that promises will invariably be administered, on the opposite hand, learns to develop trust and, therefore, attend patiently. If you say, "I'll be there during a minute," make certain that you simply can follow through that swiftly, or don't make the promise.

Biting

Whether your child is that the biter or the bitten, it's small comfort to understand those sinking little teeth into a lover's soft flesh is pervasive toddler behavior. Because it is so primitive and painful, however, most parents worry. Rest assured that biting doesn't suggest your child is antisocial or a Dracula within the making.

Children begin to bite people soon after their first teeth appear. The behavior is most every day among 1-and 2-year-olds. Sensitive children who are impulsive or easily upset are especially susceptible to biting. The practice is typically outgrown during the preschool years, as children learn more socially acceptable ways of expressing themselves.

The first bites could also be accidental. Babies often gnaw to alleviate teething pain. They also use their mouth to explore the planet. If you are breast-fed, you'll remember your baby's shock biting your breast when her new teeth came in. And she, in turn, probably noted your response, whether it had been an exclamation of pain or a surprised "Hey!" Early biting persists when children discover they will use the behavior to urge their parents to increase. It's fun.

One-year-olds often an utter pleasure, like once they get too aroused during wild play. Like a baby's first curious nips, biting can escalate as a toddler learns that it inspires a moment reaction, and sometimes a stew when another child is involved. Remember that negative attention appeals to a toddler even as very much like positive.

Stress may intensify the impulse to bite, for instance, and a toddler could also be during a new care situation or tired from an overscheduled day. Some experts believe that biting is increasing among toddlers because they're under increased stress from long days at child care, sometimes without adequate stimulation or guidance.

Prevention Advice

You can't entirely prevent bites, but you'll reduce their frequency. Avoid sending your child mixed messages by nibbling his fingers or toes live. Roughhousing, generally, isn't a realistic idea for a toddler browsing a biting spell. attempt to minimize the chances of your child feeling overwhelmed, for instance, by providing age-appropriate toys and keeping an eye fixed on things when he's with a playmate. (See the checklist "Minimizing Day Care Bites.") If your child becomes a chronic biter, take a step back to think about his overall day.

On occasions, once you notice that he's channeled feelings of anger or frustration in additional socially acceptable ways, make sure to comment and congratulate him. The long-term goal is to show your child self-control so that he's ready to resist the urge to attack by biting.

Your Best Response

React to a biting incident immediately but calmly. Pull your child aside (if another child is involved) and say, "No biting during a firm voice, biting hurts people." you'll mean the opposite child's reaction: "See how sad Adam feels?" Don't overreact the kid who's been bitten should get the lion's share of the eye (from you also as from his mother), not the biter. When your child regains control, underscore, "Remember, no biting," and send him back to play.

What not to do: Never bite a toddler back "to show you what it seems like." It only sends the kid a confusing message: "Is biting okay, then, if Daddy does it?" neither is it effective to use such old-fashioned remedies as making the kid taste hot-pepper sauce.

Even patiently and persistence, reforming a biter can take a short time. But you'll begin to ascertain longer periods elapse between incidents.

Screaming

All toddlers scream sometimes, and the first high-volume howls are usually accidental as your child discovers all the various things that her voice and lungs can do. She may learn quickly that an honest holler is often even simpler than a whine to capture grownups' attention and make her wishes known (and, more important, heeded). To a power-loving toddler, the throw-back-your-head-and-shriek method may simply feel better, too. When it's skilled over time, screaming becomes a chronic habit.

Prevention Advice

You can't stop an occasional scream, but you'll take steps to keep a toddler from shrieking. A scream is often so ear-splitting that it's tempting to mention, "Hush already! Here's your toy [or book, or cookie]." But you ought to never concede to a screamer, regardless of how irritating the sound. Nor do you have to scream back. Yelling simply communicates that it's okay to boost the decibel level.

Best Response

Stay calm. Tell your child that you simply can't understand what she wants when she's screaming: "It hurts my ears once you talk so loud. When you're quieter, I can listen." Ignore her until she calms down. Teach your child other effective ways to use her voice. See if she will mimic you whispering or singing instead. Explain the concept of using an inside voice (normal speaking tones) and an outside voice (which are often louder). Later, you'll simply warn, "Inside voice, please," instead of the more negative "No yelling!"

Supermarket Squalls

As a baby, your child was a fine shopping companion, content to take a seat placidly within the little seat at the front of the handcart, and receive his fellow shoppers' compliments. He may smell doughnuts within the bakery section or spy a display of bright plastic toys within the middle of the cereal aisle. This cornucopia of temptations is just too great to ignore. Being belted into a seat compounds your child's itchiness. What's more, you get to touch everything and steer the cart, so why can't he?

Prevention Advice

Few parents can escape grocery shopping with a toddler in tow, you'll be ready to minimize such trips, however, by trading off child care together with your partner or a lover so that the opposite can shop solo. Once you can't escape bringing along a toddler, you'll still have a good, productive outing. The trick: Keep him engaged, involved, and happy. Set yourself up for fulfillment by timing a shopping trip when your child is rested.

For example, early Saturday morning is best than five-thirty on a weekday on your way home from work and daycare. Resist the impulse to march through the aisles as quickly and efficiently as possible. Instead, take a couple of extra minutes to offer extra attention. It'll prevent time at the end of the day.

Keep up a running narrative of your excursion. "Let's see, what's next? we'd like bread. With bread we will make sandwiches and French toast. What's your favorite sandwich?" Find ways your child can assist you, too. Let him hold the shopping list or coupons.

Schedule grocery outings when your child is rested. Snack time may be a good selection because you'll let him eat something,

Maybe bread or animal crackers (ideally, an item stocked within the first few aisles) while you shop. Remind your child of the mission: "We are here to shop for the food on Mommy's list so we will have goodies to eat for dinner. We will not buy everything that you simply see or want. But if you cry or whine, we'll head home empty." Some parents allow their child to form confident coveted choices during the excursion, like the cereal or snack cracker you'll buy. Others let the kid select one special treat within the store, like a fresh cookie.

Praise your child for his good behavior on successful outings. Use specific terms: "I sure liked how you set the items within the cart and ate your snack quietly. And you used such a relaxed inside voice. You were a true helper."

Your Best Response

What if, despite your best efforts, the grocery gremlins get your child? The most transgressions include tantrums (especially the gimme-gimme variety), tossing items out of the cart, and trying to flee the cart. Keep your cool, to avoid escalating the strain.

Sometimes a positive spin helps: "If you stop yelling [stop throwing, sit still], then we will keep shopping and appearance for the type of cereal that you simply like." Distraction helps, like offering a snack. Or engage the child: "Look, apples! are you able to find the most important red ones?"

The safest place for her is securely strapped within the front seat. Remember that toddlers are lightning quick, so don't turn your back for long, or walk down the aisle far away from the cart. The amount of youngsters injured by shopping carts is on the increase, mostly because parents are in too great a rush to strap toddlers in.

CHAPTER 9:

Inspirational Activities

Montessori education integrates many activities that hone the child's skills and help him engage more in his/her interests while fostering independence and love of learning.

Here are ten inspirational activities to promote the principles of the Montessori Method:

1) Promote the Development of Body Harmony through Exercises in Precision

Let the child do what he/she is interested in. Their creativity naturally seeks to be expressed. Adults are supposed to help the child find ways to cultivate those interests and within a safe environment.

Understand that children are naturally drawn to the details. There are so many instances where parents, teachers, and other adults are surprised when a toddler or preschooler points out something that they haven't noticed.

This natural tendency to focus on details can be used to help teach children. For example, teaching handwashing can be made more interesting by giving step by step instructions. Start with where to get the materials for handwashing and close with where to put things back in their proper place.

Another method is when teaching them exercises that require fine-motor skills. For example, teaching fidgety toddlers can be made more exciting and fun by telling them to pour water without touching the water container to the glass. Make them focus on detail, and they will give their undivided attention to the activity.

Teach children as accurately as possible. Never skip or omit steps just because it is time-consuming to teach a young child. When children accurately perform activities, they can refine their motor skills.

Some of the most Montessori-recommended activities to involve children include setting up the table, serving food for meals, washing the dishes, and clearing up after meals.

2) Promote Independence in Learning by Letting Them Do Things Independently, Like Washing Their Hands After Activities

One of the core principles in Montessori is teaching children to be independent. Many parents, educators, and caregivers think that they are doing children a big favor by serving them. Serving them all their needs and doing things for them is counter-productive.

Children are naturally curious and want to try new things. Babies naturally bring items into their mouths to find out more about them. They reach out for things, grasp, grab, and play with them; they are all ways for children to learn while developing their motor skills and mental capacities.

Just think of how a baby learns to crawl, then walk and run as he/she grows older. The parent always carries him/her everywhere or puts him/her in a baby carriage.

Therefore, it is critical to allow children to follow their nature to learn and hone skills necessary for them to grow, mature, and develop their skills, talents, and capabilities.

Parents and educators can help by not serving the child, but by providing the child opportunities to practice and to pursue their interests. Their primary responsibility is to teach children how to be independent. That includes providing opportunities for children to develop their physical motor skills. These opportunities also allow children to develop their intellectual, emotional, and social skills.

Montessori classes teach more than academics like math, language, and science. Classes also include teaching and providing children opportunities to sharpen their skills and develop their interests.

It is not surprising to see toddlers able to wash their hands and help out with cleaning up the table after meals. They also know where to get the things they need and where to put these back after use.

Patience to teach young children. It will require giving time to be with the children to guide them while they learn. But remember that while you need to let them do it themselves—you have to supervise them.

For example, adults will have to stay with the child while the child learns to pour water. Letting the child do this without supervision can lead to safety issues, like slipping and possible injuries due to spills.

3) Do Not Limit the Child Based on a Pre-conditioned Concept

One of the keys to promoting independence and the development of skills is providing opportunities for the child to practice the skills. Many parents think that their child is still too young to do something. For example, some parents think that their 3-year-old is too young to learn to wipe down a table after eating. Montessori proved that no child is too young to learn skills, especially practical life skills, like cleaning up after one's self.

Adults should show confidence in the child's ability. If a child shows a willingness to learn or to do something, let them. Just be nearby to lend assistance if needed or if something is about to go wrong.

For example, if a child wants to get a glass of water from a water dispenser, let the child do so for himself/herself. The adult should show where the child can get the cup and how to use the water dispenser. Be nearby and ready to step in if the cup is about to overflow because the child has yet to develop skill in estimating when to stop the water flow. Adults also need to realize that children find a sense of pride and self-confidence.

4) Intervene Only When Necessary

Montessori Method is big on independence. Children work independently, but that does not mean there is no supervision present. Montessori educators are always there, observing the children.

Intervention is minimal because children are given opportunities to work things out for themselves. Teachers do not say, "That's wrong. Here's the right way to do it." Instead, children are allowed to find out for themselves where things went wrong.

The brain is naturally wired to find solutions. By letting children work independently, their brains are being trained to seek creative solutions for themselves.

This approach helps children develop creative thinking and problem-solving skills. They find their own methods of approaching problems, from perspectives that cater to their individual processes. This is more effective in teaching children than having them memorize things. This Montessori Method allows children to be active in the learning process and not mere absorbers of information.

When a teacher observes that a child made a mistake, no punishment or harsh rebuke is given. Instead, the teacher respects the child. The teacher helps the child realize what is wrong and the steps that led to the mistake. Then, the teacher allows the child to think for himself/herself on how to remedy the mistake. Activities such as those involving Knob Cylinder blocks are perfect for this.

The only time a teacher must absolutely step in is when safety is in question. The teacher must intervene in a decisive, firm manner when the child is observed doing something that might harm him/her or others.

5) Respect the Child's Autonomy

Respect for the child is utmost in the Montessori Method. Children are never forced to do something they do not want to. If a child wants to spend the morning period resting or merely observing other students, teachers allow that. There are no good results here. The child will find the school to be a bad experience. The teacher's insistent prodding will only cause the child to be more adamant in not doing any schoolwork. Forcing a child to listen to lessons won't result in any learning.

6) Include Nature

Let the child experience nature. Montessori is not about keeping children within the four walls of the classroom. It aims to develop the whole child. This includes letting the child feel oneness with nature. This is still part of providing the child opportunity to feel part of the community, including being part of the greater earth community.

Montessori also believes that being out in nature can rejuvenate the mind as well as the body. Parents are advised to bring their children outside and let them play and discover the world around them. Let the children run, crawl or roll in the grass. Let them touch the trees, leaves, the grass and the ground. This helps them develop discrimination of various textures, sizes, types of objects. There is also that refreshing feeling that only being out in nature can give and cannot be found inside the classroom.

7) Let the Child be Familiar with Social Security

Let him forms a relationship with other living creatures instead of waiting around to be given everything they want; they are given tasks that help them realize their place in society. Tasks like watering the plants and feeding pets may seem simple, but these have a considerable impact on a child. These activities help them develop compassion for other living creatures.

These teach them that there are living things that depend on them. If they do not water the plants or feed the animals, these creatures will die.

With this realization, children learn about long-term thinking. They learn to connect that what they do today is related to what happens the next day.

These activities are based on the instincts of the human soul - caring for others. A child has a nurturing instinct. Montessori knows that this child's part is just as important to cultivate as problem-solving skills or reading skills.

8) Never Speak Bad Things to and About the Child

Focus on developing and strengthening the positive aspects of a child. Ever force something that is not in the child's nature. Instead, focus on what the child is interested in and what the child shows the capacity for.

The teacher should observe the child and look for talents and strengths. Seek to include activities that allow for development. For example, a child shows a knack for visual arts. The teacher should provide more activities where the child can hone this talent. An example may be to take the child out in nature and ask the child to draw what he/she saw.

Focusing on the positives of the child's nature leaves smaller opportunities to notice the defects. This works for both the teacher and the child. When the teacher chooses to focus on the child's positive aspects, the teacher becomes less critical and more patient in dealing with the child. For the child, seeing that lessons and activities focus on his/her interests, he/she becomes more engaged, active, and focused.

Teachers, caregivers, and parents should always remember to never speak of the child in a negative way. This holds whether the child is present or not. Negative words are powerful. A single negative comment can do so much damage to a child's mental health and emotional state. It can single-handedly destroy a child's fragile sense of self.

Teach Cooperation

Cooperation can yield many prospects for the child's growth, but it requires a lot of hard work and skill. You're cooperating with the child, who is just a toddler and needs your affectionate companionship at all costs. You cannot be robust, neither you can induce horrific compulsions among them. But you must nourish the fundamentals of care and start by listening to them. You can observe their notions, and you can stay connected with their memories in a longer run. However, the question arises that what can be the potential methods of inducing cooperation in the children? Well, the answer is as follows:

Ways to be cooperative with the kids

Following are the ways to be cooperative with your kids

Taking Turns

While we are taking turns, we are boosting team management and cooperation among the toddlers. We need to understand that the baby is all growing up, and they are imitating the notions of all the elders in a respected manner. They need to understand that while growing up, the life pattern can be hazardous, and the one, who can become cooperative and compassionate, can only yearn to be successful. An example can be portrayed here to understand the thinking of the child. While they are playing blocks and or creating a puzzle, let them do their modes alternatively. It would be best if you took turns while you're building blocks for them, and then you have to see what they do in return. So, taking turns means that you have to be a team player, and you have to be cooperative with them at all costs.

Explain Your Reasons for Limits and Reasons

A controlled environment is very pertinent to reflect good progress in society. It is the only way through which success and sustainability can be achieved in the team.

In this way, the house will be in order, and they will perpetually perceive management and order. Hence, this model of cooperation can be very useful for the soul and heart of the child, and you need to induce this method in all ways necessary.

Take Time to Problem Solve

You should take time to see if the kids are capable of solving the dilemmas that come in their life. Problems like the breaking of a glass, the absence of any material, and the overall loss of any prodigal thing can be termed as examples.

Thus, when such dilemmas appear, the parent must ask the child many minutes and questions. Like what seems to be the problem, baby, how can the problem be solved, is there any potential solution? If so, then what is the alternative to it. When the child finds answers, and if the answers are polite and keen, then please do encourage.

This encouragement will give collective clout to the children, and hence, the child will be able to yield more love for the parent.

Do Chores Together Start at an Early Age!

You need to encourage your child to do chores with you mentally. This means that if you're washing the dishes, you must allow your child to share the work burden with you. If you're washing your car, then you must bring your child into the work as well. Moreover, any burden of a work, which is being conducted and shared by you, must be allowed to be executed by your child as well. In this way, the child will learn how to cooperate with the parent and will come one step closer to the field of house-living. If you do not do it and do not allow the child to host you; properly, then you will see the negative results of their upbringing. Therefore, you must see your child get the very best of housework and do all your best in making the child look cleaner and more efficient.

Giving More Praise for Cooperative Efforts

If your child is doing something cooperatively, then do please them and give them thumbs up. Otherwise, they won't reconcile with you. The child can do a lot of work once they are given a boost and some mental encouragement. They can thaw their weaknesses and can convert them into happiness. They can see the role of their efforts progressively and can make the uttermost of the house routine. If you see others' cooperation, please do let your child learn the art of collaboration as well. Giving them more praise will clear all the mental barriers in their head about parenting, and they will come one step near you in many aspects. Thus, more recognition can lead your child to the cooperation they deserve.

Always Be Suggestive

Never be compulsive or orderly to your children. Always look to it that they have a caring parent that is suggesting them to do more and more things. If you find a mistake in them, then correct them genuinely and never let other things come in the way. Once you do bad things for the child, you will ultimately be surrounded by issues.

Your child will become paranoid, and you'll make a mess of your life. Therefore, suggestions to your child will always lead to more innocence and cooperation in the child.

Give Your Child Choices While Maintaining the Rules

You are maintaining the order in your child, but at the same time, you want them to be cooperative. So, under such circumstances, it is very pertinent that you're suggestive of your child's actions and let the child be on the same path with you. For instance, before bed, if you want your child to follow the rules, ask them politely if they have brushed their teeth, and are their diapers clean. These cute and innocent questions will liberate the child from tension, and they will cooperate more.

Explain Them the Situations in a Calm Manner

Explain to them the reasons why low expectations come in the way. And do not yell at them while you're doing so. If, by chance, they cannot clear any exam, then it isn't your obligation to defame them. Just be a kind parent and let them understand the possibilities of life in an affectionate manner. Try to suggest more cooperative tactics that will enable them to yearn enjoyment. So, the explanation of challenging situations in an easy way will make your child more cooperative and substantial.

Play Games with Them

Games like cricket and football are very significant to boost creativity and subjectivity in the kids. If you hold a bat and hit your child's ball, the child will learn cooperation by all means necessary. Even if you're playing the game of football with them and running alongside them and telling them how to kick, then you are cooperative, and the child will be more productive to your advice and learning. Therefore, play as much of the games you want to play with them, and in the end, you'll end up being very affectionate with them. Splendid methods make the child know the cooperation platform and feel proud if you're doing so.

Always Ask Permission Before Joining

Always ask your child permissions if you're about to join them and see what the child can do. If your child is playing the match of cricket and watching them, try your best not to disturb them; if you're washing the dishes and the child is watching movies, ask their permission to join them. These examples assert your cooperative and affectionate behavior with the child and, eventually, lead the child to a better end. But if you are arrogant and stubborn enough to scold them vociferously, then you must not expect any kind of cooperation from the child. Because the child will be very stubborn for you, and they won't learn the art of collaboration.

Sharing Is Caring

If you're a busy guy and have a strict schedule on your time, try your best to comply with your child. Understandably, the child will not get your routine, and with innocent questions and a jolly mood, everybody can calm down. For instance, the child can get to the bottom of your routine, and you're having a tough time dealing with them so, in such a circumstance, you must adhere to all the disciplinary steps that can navigate obedience in your child and hence, you need to share things with him, to achieve cooperation from their side. Hence, they will care for you if you share your routine with them.

So, with such ways and measures, the term cooperation can be easily put forward to the students and children.

CHAPTER 10:

Self-discovering

The Montessori Method of teaching has a unique aspect in it that is known as self-discovering. It is an indulging process due to which an individual can manifest new things in themself. These things are not explained before to the individuals, and by the passage of time, they tend to discover something in them as a result of active effort and brainstorming. With its specialized gadget of a broad curriculum, the Montessori method allows individuals to find self-discovery modes in them. The following are some of the children's tactics and frameworks while they are self-discovering themselves.

Through the years, discovery through Montessori has proven to be an excellent and effective way for children to learn. As the children go through the Montessori classroom's different learning areas, they know the concepts and skills they need to enrich their education. As you watch any child go into such a classroom, you will marvel at how they can learn without much help from their teachers.

Decision-Making: Allowing Children to Make Their Own Choices

Decision making and a child's choice are integral elements of the Montessori method. As the parent, you're aware that you act as a guide, merely a way-shower and support system for your child's journey.

Allowing your child to choose their course of action and activity engagement opens up new pathways for individual skills, talents, and gifts to shine through.

If the choice is taken away and they are made to conform to a rigid structure and 'one way' way of doing things, they are less likely to step fully into their self-expression and special personal qualities. Everyone is unique, and Montessori aims to bring this to the forefront.

Visual Learning

Visual learning is learning through visual representations, such as images, written material, video, or whiteboards. Visual learning involves taking in a range of sensory information through the sense of sight.

Auditory or Musical Learning

Auditory learning is learning through sound. Auditory learners process information and concepts best when heard or listened to. They are also the types of learners who learn best using rhythm or melody; thus, they are also known as musical learners.

For instance, musicians learn best by listening to a specific musical piece. Then they try playing the same amount from memory.

These learners may also learn more effectively when there's music playing on the background or when they're whistling, humming, toe-tapping, and doing some musical or rhythmic action while learning.

Kinesthetic Learning

Kinesthetic learners understand and process information best when actively engaged in it, such as through touch or using their bodies and movement to acquire knowledge.

These learners love interacting with the world around them since it is how they learn. They are scientific, and they enjoy hands-on learning, which is perfect because Montessori is all about hands-on activities.

Linguistic Learning

Linguistic learners are the ones that learn best when they're able to use linguistic skills such as speaking, listening, writing, and reading. It's even better when they're able to learn through a combination of these different skills and methods.

Naturalist Learning

Naturalist learners are the ones that learn best by experience and working with nature. When you think about naturalist learners, an image of a scientist may come to your mind. This would be entirely accurate because a lot of scientists are naturalist learners. They love to observe the world around them; they love experiencing their world, and they learn more effectively through experimentation.

Teach Compassion

Teaching compassion through activities and exercises which involve love and respect for animals and ecosystems is a great and effective way to enhance your child's empathic nature.

Many children are already naturally empathic - it is the world and some of the societal practices and structures in play that make them less so. We are born with a natural sensitivity and compassion towards sentient creatures, and this is often displayed through many acts of kindness shown by the children. Feeling genuine sadness and empathy towards animals, questioning the process of eating them, and feeling plants and other nature on a deep level are all common occurrences.

The Montessori framework is ideal for developing this natural compassion and connecting to a child's empathic nature.

Practicing Kindness

Practicing and acknowledging kindness in the classroom or environment you have created for learning and activity is another way to develop empathy. This can be done by offering praise, where appropriate, and words of support and encouragement, such as 'that was nice of you,' 'that was very thoughtful and considerate,' or 'it was very kind of you to do this.' Remember, you are a guide for your child or children, so supporting efforts through verbal recognition will further increase the kindness and compassion they are already exhibiting. Try and not to overdo it, though, as too much attention to the natural kind and empathic displays can have the opposite effect, bringing focus to your child's pride and praise instead of the acts they are engaging in.

Being Respectful

It is very accurate to suggest that learning, by example, is one of the most effective ways to learn. Showing respect and treating your child as a young adult, or an equal is possibly one of the most powerful ways to be an example of empathy. Showing respect to objects, learning material, things in your environment, and other humans, plants, and animals will directly influence your child or children.

Self-Care

When students or toddlers come into the Montessori School, they are taught to self-care themselves. They are trained to learn the most favorable aspects of themselves, and by doing so, they care for themselves. Dynamically, the children understand that what is meant by self-respect, self-mannerism, and self-dignity is that they would not shout loud or make obscene gestures.

Moreover, the toddlers are given independent environments, where they can grow sustainably. The toddlers can get a huge amount of understanding for themselves, and thus, for more extended means, the toddlers can get to care themselves profusely. Thus, the much-anticipated aspect of love is self-care, and self-discovering helps the infants grow more effectively.

Caring for the Environment

The toddlers are taught to care for the enviromnent. Although they are very young and need to be careful while they chose the right environment to stay, the Montessori School regards the ideal features for their children. In the initial months of school, the toddlers are taught how to clean the environment by showing them the cleaning art. They are given some woolen cloths so that the children can easily tide the nearby dirt with full zeal. Hence, the caring of the environment is a chief aspect of self-discovering for the toddlers, and it is taught nowhere but by the Montessori School.

Development of Motor Skills

Motor skills are essential for a child to come across. These skills give the horary values of a good citizen and a punctual human being. These skills further enhance the aptitude of young schoolers and give them a reason to succeed in life. These skills include walking, climbing, running, and jumping. Children tend to discover their athleticism through these skills, and in the future, they get more successful while doing it. Thus, the development of motor skills is yet another aspect of self-discovery, and it is given by the Montessori School in all the possible manners holistically.

Language Learning

Language learning is yet another exciting art that needs to be accumulated by the students at all rates possible. This is a conversational approach that needs to be given to all the toddlers in the initial phase of their lifelines. They are taught how to converse on pictures. They are trained to name the objects; the students' singing is related to the students' cognition. Thus, numerically, people can discuss the importance of self-discovering. The mode of self-discovering is accelerated when language learning is more acceptable. Therefore, the Montessori School shares its pride in fostering more and more productive avenues for the classmates.

Social Skills

The Montessori School teaches social skills to infants about how they need to behave with the colored babies and how to be compatible with people in various ways. Social skills give the students more enhanced capabilities to reach more progress in their mental skills and other developmental skills. From a young age, they learn the edifices of tolerance, mutual acceptability, and sympathy. In social skills, the toddlers and infants are taught how to shake hands and how to be more convincing for others to be with them.

Language Development Activities

Object and Sound Comparison: From around your home, gather a selection of items that your child is very familiar with and can name. These can either be household items or play toys. Sandpaper Letters: The letter blocks are easy to make if you would not invest in a premade set. Trace and cut out the entire alphabet on pieces of sandpaper. Each letter should be a few inches in height. Ensure that the script you use is consistent throughout and stick to either upper- or lower-case letters. Once you have the letters cut out, adhere them to small boards of a contrasting color. Most Montessori schools prefer to start with lower-case cursive.

Movable Alphabet Word Formation: While it is possible to use a simple set of refrigerator magnets for this activity, it is advised that you either purchase or make a particular set of the moveable alphabet, with one color designated for consonants and the other for vowels.

The color differentiation helps the child to recognize the different roles of the letters.

Chalk Letter Writing: Sometimes, Montessori activities are so simple that they seem almost too obvious. When you encounter these activities, take a moment to think about what other ways your child's educational experience can be enriched by participation.

Phonetic SoundBox: This is an activity using the phonetic soundbox aimed toward the older child that is getting closer to independent reading. Find several items from around your home that have short spellings with sounds that can be easily decoded. For example, pen, tag, cup, dot, etc.

Mathematical Development Activities

Sandpaper Numbers: Nearly identical in presentation to the sandpaper letters used above, sandpaper numbers will teach your child how to write numbers and reinforce each visual representation's name correctly. The numbers used should be zero to nine; however, zero should not be introduced until the child has had an opportunity to learn and understand none. This seems pretty basic, though, to a young child associating order and quantity to a visual number, it can be challenging to grasp nothingness.

Spindle Box: For this activity, you need a spindle box and a complete set of spindles. This is also one of those pieces of equipment that can easily be created if you do not wish to purchase one. All you need is a long box, with enough dividers to separate the box into compartments numbered zero through nine. You will also need enough small rods for the child to place the appropriate number into each slot.

Number Rods: Number rods are excellent for introducing a variety of mathematical concepts and are an excellent investment for your Montessori home school as you will have continued use of this product for at least a couple of years. A good number rod set will include instructions for several activities, the most basic of which is a simple ordering exercise that will help introduce the rods' concept to your child.

CHAPTER 11:

Sensorial Activities

S ensorial exercises sharpen up the toddler; visual, auditory, tactile, olfactory, and gustatory. Toddlers are predominantly open to refining their intentions from the early age of two, thus the importance of integrating the Montessori sensory activities into their lives. The materials for these activities should be prudently designed to meet the basic principles set out by Dr. Maria Montessori. The Montessori sensory materials aim to sharpen the toddler's senses to isolate and categorize materials distinctively in his/her environment. As a result, toddlers are offered the chance to refine their intelligence regarding the surrounding.

The Montessori materials for refining the senses of toddlers are specifically designed to.

Help the toddler to concentrate on isolating and identifying one quality at a time.

Help the toddlers in making their own corrections through the control of the error feature of the material.

The materials are physically attractive to call in the toddler's attention and help maintain focus and concentration.

The sets of materials are usually complete to help the toddler go through the exercise to completion without pausing to find a missing part.

The materials are meant to turn theoretical ideas into essential concepts.

Sensory Activities for Toddlers

Note: for the activities in this section, toddlers are defined as toddlers under five. Nonetheless, the activities are not for a specific age group only. Monitor your toddler on what he/she likes and can do with ease because they develop at different paces.

The Coin Boxes

The coin box, or alternatively a domino box, enhances the hand-eye coordination of toddlers. The material is designed with closing and opening slots and a hole in the top lid. Toddlers are encouraged to fit particular objects in the box, which is opened when full to remove the objects. The disappearing and reappearing of the objects in the box refine the child's concentration while the exercise of fitting items into the hole improves accuracy.

Straws in a Cup

This activity involves putting colored straws in different containers, and the toddler is invited to empty one at a time then put the straws back. To upgrade this exercise, a Montessori teacher is encouraged to use colored containers so that the toddler can sort the straws according to colors when putting them back into the boxes.

The Texture Basket

The texture tray or basket is an innocent activity that draws toddlers' attention into isolating materials' texture. You must assemble different materials within the house for the exercise and put them in a tray or basket. Invite the toddler to feel the items by turning them over their hands and help them identify and isolate soft, in one basket, and challenging, in a different basket. Note that you should use simple words for this exercise.

Sound Cylinders

Sound cylinders are stress-free and the most magnetic materials to make and use. Toddlers are always delighted to hear the different sounds produced by the cylinders. For the activity, use a control cylinder (say a yellow cylinder) to make the first sound by shaking it. Proceed to the next cylinder (say red). Shake the second cylinder and ask the toddler to differentiate the sound from the first one. If the sound made is the same, the cylinders are put in one tray. Different sounds are placed in separate trays. Invite the toddlers to shake the cylinders and sort them according to the sound they make.

Color Marbles

This activity helps learners to differentiate colors. Toddlers are invited to sort the marbles according to their colors and putting them in a matching container. Consider using primary or straightforward colors like red, yellow, white, and blue. Remember to read out the colors of the marbles and the containers to them as you match them in the presentation. Once all the items are sorted, please place them in a basket and invite your toddlers to sort them. Additionally, you can upgrade this activity by increasing the range of colors and playing the color hunt game. You ask the toddler to point a particular color in the house.

The Grain Box

This activity involves providing a variety of grains in different texture and size. Pool different grains, like rice, beans, sand, stones, beads, etc. in a tray, basket, or box. Invite the toddler to feel the texture, isolate the color, or isolate by size. For safety purposes, bear in mind the age of the toddler and the grain provided. Always keep watch when carrying out this activity.

Spooning Ice

This activity is best suited for a hot day. You must provide ice in a bowl, an empty bowl, and a pair of tongs or a spoon. Show the toddler how to scoop and lift ice with a knife or tongs from one bowl into the other. Invite the toddler to try their hands on the activity. You can also ask the toddler to feel the bowl's temperature with ice and the empty bowl by wrapping their palms around the bowl. This activity can be upgraded once the ice has melted by transferring the water from one bowl into the other using a syringe.

Sorting by Shape

For their activity, you should begin with a sample pack of simple shapes. For a start, provide the same conditions in the same color. At this point, your toddlers can sort according to color. Advance by mixing the colors, but maintaining the shapes. As you progress, introduce tracing the shapes on a piece of paper or board. For the presentation, name the conditions as you sort them first before inviting your toddlers to do the same.

Fabric board

This activity is very crucial in introducing texture to toddlers. The exercise involves presenting different fabric squares of different textures and inviting the toddler to feel the difference.

The textures are described in simple words like rough, soft, and silky, etc. The toddler is expected to match the fabrics with a similar texture.

A homemade fabric board is made by cutting a piece of Styrofoam placard into a good size that fits into your basket or tray. Next, you glue different fabrics on each placard.

Simple Puzzle

This activity is essential in helping toddlers to decode size and shape. The best puzzle for starters should be a 1-3 shape puzzle. The unknown can be done by cutting a placard into one form (say triangle), then drawing a mystery in shape. Cut out the drawn lines. Using a different piece of paper, drawn a rough draft of the puzzle to be used as a control. Invite the toddler to set up the cut pieces to form a complete shape seen on the control paper.

The Pink Tower

A complete pink tower consists of ten cubes of different sizes. For this activity, invite your toddler to help you carry the cubes to your play station. Starting with the most massive cube, construct the tower by piling the next most enormous cubes on top until all the cubes are used. If they can't identify the next most massive cube, help them by pointing out the cube.

Knobbed Cylinders

The knobbed cylinders are meant to help the toddler differentiate height and diameter. Each block consists of roughly five cylinders decreasing in height and diameter. Show the toddler how to carry the cylinders from one station to the other, from the biggest to the smallest, to help them arrange the cylinders inside one another. Once the entire block is done, replace the cylinders in their original station.

Hanging Ball Activities

The set of activities in this section involves the use of a suspended ball. The ball is suspended to save you the time of chasing after missed balls as the exercise goes on. Set up the activity by putting a ball in a net and tying it with a rope. Suspend the ball on a hook, making sure it is at chest-level to the toddler.

Racket and Ball

Help your toddler hit the suspended ball using a ratchet. The point is to let the ball swing back and forth without missing a hit. Make the activity more challenging by using smaller balls and ratchets.

Push and Catch

The exercise requires the toddler to push the ball and catch it as it swings back without missing or letting it bang against their body. This helps in refining concentration by carefully watching the ball hang from and to the hands. Upgrade to a more challenging series by asking the toddler to clap between the catch and the push.

CHAPTER 12:

Hand-eye Coordination Ball Games

Rolling a Ball

For this activity, sit opposite to your toddler. Have them sit with legs apart facing you. Roll the ball towards the toddler and ask them to catch the ball before it hits the body. The activity requires the toddler to watch the rolling ball prudently and synchronize the hands into stopping the ball before it reaches the body.

Ball Relays

This activity is suitable for many kids. The process requires that you provide a basin or basket full of balls. Make the kids line up behind each other and place an empty basket or basin at a reasonable distance from them. The exercise is picking a ball and running to the empty basket to put it there. Once the kid has put the ball in the basket, they run back and lines up behind the other kids. This arrangement ensures that every kid has a turn to pick a ball, run, and put in the other basket before coming back. Alternatively, the kids can line up in between the baskets with each kid keeping their position permanently. The kid closer to the basket with balls picks a ball and passes it to the next kid until the ball reaches the last kid that puts it in the empty basket. The activity goes on once the other basket is full. To introduce more challenges, you can increase the distance between the toddlers and ask them to toss the ball to each other or pass it overhead.

Tossing and Passing a Ball

This activity requires a lot of focus and concentration from the kids to toss the ball overhead to one another without missing a catch or overpassing the ball. Position the kids at a distance from each other. Give them a ball and ask them to toss it to each other. Increase the challenge by making circles on the ground and asking them to stay in the rotation when throwing and catching the ball.

Ball to Wall Toss and Rebound

This exercise follows the toss and catches activity. Once the kids can pass the ball and see it successfully, you move on to the wall-toss. Here, you show the toddler how to toss a ball against a wall and wait for the rebound. The toddler is expected to catch the ball as it rebounds. Keep a record book to note down the number of successful tosses and witness before the ball falls down. Always encourage your toddler by offering a present every time they break their record.

Toss and Catch

One of the best hand-eye coordination activities is tossing the ball up in the air and catching it again. The exercise becomes more challenging when you introduce a circle that the toddler must maintain standing in when tossing and catching the ball. Additionally, as your toddler makes progress, encourage to launch higher.

Threading and Lacing

Another activity that enhances hand-eye coordination is stringing beads or lacing up cards. To start, use beads with larger holes and reduce the holes' size as the toddler makes progress.

Beads in a Straw

You are expected to present colored straws and small beads of different colors. Help the toddler fit the dots in a straw of the same color.

Tasting Bottle

This game is fundamental in helping a toddler to isolate the four significant tastes: salty, sweet, bitter, and sour. The game also helps improve the responsiveness of the toddler to understand the connection between palate and scent. The activity involves presenting different bottles, each containing a different taste. The game is to taste the contents of the bottle and identify the taste.

Smelling Jars

Just like the taste bottles, the smelling jars are presented containing different scent. The toddler is invited to smell each pot and differentiate the odor in each jar. This activity helps in building the ability of the toddler to isolate the aroma.

Matching Thermic Tablets and Bottles

The game is aimed at refining the thermic sense of the toddler. The materials required are a set of thermic tablets in a box. For the presentation, remove all the pills and place them on a tabletop. Invite the toddler to feel the temperature of each with the back of the hand. Due to the difference in heat conductivity, the tablets will have a varying temperature range according to the material they are made of. For the game part, you can ask the toddler to close the eyes and feel one table. Ask the toddler to find a tablet that feels the same without opening the eyes. Once done, have the toddler open their eyes and see if the tablets have been sorted correctly.

Maracas and Clatters

Put some maracas and clatters in an enclosed container. Invite the toddlers to shake the box as they listen to the sound produced. You can put on some soft music for the toddlers to shake the maracas and clatters along as they dance to the tunes.

CHAPTER 13:

Things That Won't Screw Up a Toddler

The things that won't screw up your toddler are more numerous than you might imagine. We will explore below a few of the things parents fear might mess their kids up, but which are, in fact, good for them and are crucial to developing a healthy concept of self and the world around them.

Saying No

Telling your toddler, no won't ruin them. Often, children do things, say things, or ask for something they're not allowed to have to test the boundaries. Of course, little Max wants you to give in and buy him the giant Lego set, but he's not going to hate you if you don't. He might tell you that he hates you, but that is an entirely different thing from actually hating you.

Consistency in your naysaying will save both you and your child time bargaining and cajoling and help them move on to other subjects. When a child knows that no means no, it saves both of you time and hassle, and can lead to doing and saying things that can nurture a loving relationship.

Be careful of saying no too often and without reason. Some parents fall into the habit of saying no without any real sense. Davy, a father of six kids under the age of ten, admits that sometimes he says no simply because he's tired and left alone, even though he knows that he should say yes. "When the boys want to play touch football in the yard, I know I should play with them and be a good role model for them. Not every time, of course, but more often than I do."

If they want to play in the street, street danger is a legitimate reason to tell them not to. If they want to play in the yard and ask you to come out with them and there isn't a reason that this will screw them up in any way, say yes.

When Max wants to play trucks in the yard, and you can't think of a reason why you're telling him no other than that, you're the parent, and you said so, that might be an indication that you should be saying yes instead. After all, interactive playtime is significant to a toddler's development.

Discipline

A toddler is not too young to receive punishment for wrongdoing. In fact, the sooner you teach them that their actions have consequences, the less you will have to discipline them in the future.

One of the keys to effectively disciplining a toddler is to choose a punishment that fits the crime. Grounding a toddler doesn't make any sense. The point of discipline is to teach Norah that her actions have consequences, and what she does affects what happens to her. If she scribbles with markers all over her bedroom wall, hand her a scrub brush and help her clean the border off. The most effective kinds of consequences are natural consequences. When she realizes that scrubbing the crayon off the wall is hard, she'll think twice before coloring it next time she takes her crayons out to make art. Mona used grounding as her primary means of disciplining her three-year-old. She'd tell him to stop throwing his toys, and when he didn't listen to her, she'd say to him that he was not allowed to watch TV for a week. While this strategy might work on an older child, a toddler won't understand the correlation between throwing toys and no TV. When it comes to disciplining toddlers, it's best to keep the punishment in line with the crime, as well as dish it out immediately. Rather than grounding a child for throwing toys, try a time out or taking away the toys for a day.

Not Giving a Constant Barrage of Choices

A toddler doesn't have abstract reasoning skills. Particularly if you live in the upper-middle-class suburbs, helicopter parents, who constantly hover over their kids, protecting them from any negative emotions and offering them a giant spread of lunch meat from which to choose their lunch, are becoming strangely normal. Out of fear of having their child experience hurt and disappointment, these parents strive to give their children the best they can always. No sacrifice is too big. This sounds noble, but what they don't realize is that giving a child a constant barrage of choices, like more than one dinner option if they don't like something, either runs the risk of over-stimulating them or it reinforces their already very selfish worldview.

Whim doesn't learn how to deal with their frustration and disappointment. Also, a child who is presented with a steady stream of choices runs of the risk of becoming over-stimulated and having a meltdown.

The person who spread the myth that children have fragile self-esteem that needs to be protected has never seen a toddler at all costs. A toddler is incredibly self-absorbed. When you give them many choices, you're reinforcing their view of themselves as the universe's center. Good decision-making is obviously a skill that you want to teach him, but don't take it to ridiculous heights, or they will get overwhelmed and then start to assume that they are always entitled to having a choice in everything.

Delayed Gratification

Patience can be taught as early as infancy, but it's definitely not too late to learn as a toddler.

One way that you can teach your child to be patient is to let them pick out a treat when they go shopping with you, but don't let them eat it as soon as they get to the car. Instead, have them save it for their snack time later. A child who learns how to be patient early on in life will be a more patient adult. The problems that a lot of American children are having in school and at home stem from not being taught how to have patience.

Learning the art of delayed gratification can be one of the most useful, long-lasting lessons you can teach your child to keep from screwing them up.

CHAPTER 14:

How To Stimulate Good Behavior In Children

S timulating a good behavior in children is one of the best ways to impose limits without applying punishments regularly. The only problem is how to do that. In most cases, our little ones tested our limits and seemed to do anything not to obey.

Here are ways to stimulate good behavior:

Be the Example

Being an example in our children is the most effective way to teach anything - both good and bad. When it comes to motivate good behavior in children, it is no different. Here are a few examples of what you can do for your child to learn. Catch your child's attention when you split snacks with your husband or when you have to wait in the bank queue, pointing out that adults also have to share and stay too.

Realize The Good Behavior

If you are like any parent in the world, when your child is behaving well, you leave him playing alone and take advantage of the time to do anything you may need to. But when your child is misbehaving, you direct all your attention to him to resolve the situation. Your attention is what kids most want to get this attention, and sometimes children will misbehave. The best way to inspire good behavior in children is to pay attention when they behave well and take your attention away when they are misbehaving. This is completely counter-intuitive for us and can be a difficult habit to cultivate. But once you get used to it, it will become easier and more comfortable. A great way to do this is to play with your child when he is quiet in his corner and praise him when he obeys you the first time you speak.

Understand The Stage Of Development

This tip is easy to understand. Each child has a behavior; however, you cannot require three to act as the same as a child who is ten. That is, do not try to go to a three-hour lunch with your little boy hoping he will be quiet for the whole lunch. Do not want a two-year-old child not to put everything in his mouth. Each age has a phase, and there is no use to demand different behavior from a child.

Have Appropriate Expectations

Parents have high expectations. This is not wrong when expectations are possible. For example, do not expect a tired child to behave well, or a one-month-old baby to sleep through the night.

Create Structure and Routine

A child with a structured routine tends to behave better. They already know what to look forward to and are used to it. A child with a routine feels safe and thus lives more calmly. A child without a routine has a sense of insecurity that will disrupt much in the time to educate and encourage good behavior.

Uses Disciplinary Strategies

Rather than humiliating or beating children, there are positive disciplinary strategies that teach, set boundaries, and encourage good behavior in children. Some of these are: give options, put somewhere to think, talk, give affection, and a system of rewards (reward can be a simple compliment, it does not have to be gifts or food).

Understand That the Bad Behavior Worked So Far

If throwing tantrums and disobeying worked for him to get your attention so far, changing this behavior will take time. He will have to realize and understand that you will no longer pay attention to him when he behaves badly, but when he behaves well.

Instilling good behavior practices in young children is a must for any responsible parent, but sometimes it can also be quite complicated and laborious. However, beginning to instill this type of behavior as early as possible will help build a good foundation for the child's behavior and attitudes in the future.

Here are some more ideas to help parents with the task of encouraging good behavior in their children.

Models To Follow

Children tend to mirror the behaviors of parents and those with whom they coexist more closely. Therefore, be careful about your actions and language used when the child is around to avoid misunderstanding ideas and misconceptions about how you should behave towards others. This includes talking properly and conducting politely to both your partner and family and the child. Try to avoid loud, unstructured arguments when the child is around. We do not mean you can't disagree with your spouse, because the child must also be aware that these exist. But try to have the arguments always controlled and civil around children.

Be Firm

Parents should be affectionate, but still adamant about instilling discipline in their children. The child must know how to respect his parents, even when they do not have what they want. Understanding when to say "no" at the right times is an essential step in your education.

Establishing Limits

It is fundamental to establish limits, rules, and consequences for unwanted behavior. Increase limits on children to be able to distinguish right from wrong.

You started tracking your child's progress long before he left the warmth of your belly: in the tenth week, the heart began beating; on the 24th week, his hearing developed and listened to your voice; in the 30th week, he began to prepare for childbirth. Now that he or she is in your arms, you're still eager to keep up with all the signs of your little one's development and worries that he might be left behind. Nonsense! Excessive worry will not help at all, so take your foot off the accelerator and enjoy each phase. Your child will realize all the fundamental achievements of maturity. He will learn to walk, talk, potty, and when you least expect it, you will be riding a bicycle alone (and no training wheels!). He will do all only in his time. Consider what is expected for each age just for reference. The best thing to do is to set aside the checklist of the abilities your child needs to develop and play together a lot. There is no better way to connect with and build your child than through playtime. To help you even further realize the goals mentioned above or processes, I would like to say some tips here that stimulate a child's intellectual, motor, social, and emotional development:

Books

The parents' role is fundamental for children to learn to love reading and make books a pleasure, rather than an obligation. For 17%, the father was the one who played the role. From the third month of your child's life, you can use plastic books in the bath. From the sixth, when the baby can already carry objects to the mouth with his hands, leave cloth books in the cradle - in addition to being able to bite them, he will not be able to rip the pages! At all ages, talk about the cover, the pictures, the colors, and let the child turn the pages.

Memory

Memory is a form of storing knowledge and must be permeated by a context. Start by helping your child memorize words by showing a represented object. If you're walking on the street and crossing a bicycle, point and say, "Look, son, a bicycle." This is how he will build associations. From the first year, he will say a few words and try to repeat the names of what you show. But it is from the age of 2 that the ability to retain information increases.

Creating

Create characters and a dream of fantastic worlds. All of this is important in developing the creativity of little ones; it also contributes to problem-solving. To make the narrative more exciting, how about testing the improvisational ability of the two of you? Separate figures from objects, landscapes, colors, foods, and animals can be drawn or cut from magazines. By age 7, as the child is already literate, you can help him record your small booklets' adventures.

Always Ask

When you pick up your child from school, you always say, "How was your day?" And he says, "Cool." It was not exactly what you wanted to hear, right? To avoid generic responses, develop the questions so that the child needs to express what he thinks and justify his response.

Ask: "What did you enjoy most today?" And he will be forced to grow more elaborate reasoning, requiring him to work linguistic and logical skills. At three years old, he can already relate experiences he went through and say whether those were good or bad. At 4, you can ask for details, descriptions, and colleagues who were with him.

Clap, Clap, Tum, Tum

One of the best ways to develop motor coordination is to teach rhythm to your child. To do this, use your hands. From the seventh month, clap with him to the sounds of your favorite songs, interspersing slow songs with other accelerated songs to see the difference. You will see that your baby will be able to hit his little hands.

Everything Fits

From the age of 7 months, the baby begins to hold objects; in about a year and a half, he will start to put the pieces together. Besides being a good exercise for coordination, the child will learn which part will fit within the other. For your child to love and learn from this, he can play with pots and plastic mugs while you prepare lunch. They also offer small puzzles from the age of two and a half (about six pieces).

Step By Step

Climbing stairs is a great exercise to develop agility and coarse motor coordination and help strengthen muscles. At one year of age, the child can already perform the activity, but only by placing both feet on the same step, one at a time. He will gain strength and balance with growth until, by age 3, he will probably rise by placing one foot on each step alternately. Even at this stage, he must be accompanied by an adult to avoid accidents.

Bonding & Trust

Establishing relationships of trust is essential for the development of the child. The first people he does it with are the parents. For this, one factor is necessary: never lie. If he asks if the injection will hurt, be honest, and say it will, yes, but it will pass. Tell him he's going to get wet;

it's going to hurt, he's going to be cold, so he knows what to expect and learns to trust what you say.

Congratulate your child when he is good at something, encouraging him to continue. If scolding is necessary, pay close attention to how to do it. Saying "what you did was naughty" is quite different from saying, "you are naughty!" Do not let the child think that the criticized trait is part of his personality, so he will not incorporate it into his self-image.

CHAPTER 15:

Temperament and Behavior

Temperament is defined as the heritable and biologically based core that influences the style of approach and response of a person. The child's early temperament traits usually predict their adult temperament. The child's behavior is the outcome of their temperament and the progress of their emotional, cognitive, and physical development. It is influenced by their beliefs about themselves, about you, and the world in general. While it is inborn and inherent, there are specific ways to help your toddler manage it to their advantage.

Nine dimensions or traits related to temperament:

The activity level pertains to the amount of physical motion that your toddler demonstrates while engaged in some activities. It also includes their inactive periods.

- Is your child a restless spirit that cannot sit still for long and always wants to move around?

- Is your toddler the quiet, the little one enjoys playing alone or watching TV?

Rhythmicity refers to predictability or unpredictability of physical and biological functions which include hunger, bowel movement, and sleeping.

- Does your child thrive on routine and follow regular eating or sleeping patterns?

- DO they display unpredictable behavior and dislike routine?

Attention span and persistence are the skills to remain focused on the activity for a certain period.

- Does your toddler stick to complete a task?

- Are they easily frustrated and look for another activity?

Initial Response (Approach or Withdrawal) refers to the reaction to something new and unfamiliar. It describes their initial feelings to a stimulus like a new person, place, toy, and food. Their reaction is shown by their mood or facial expressions like smiling or motor activity, such as reaching for a toy or swallowing food. Negative responses include withdrawal, crying, fussing, pushing away, or spitting the food.

- Are they wary or reluctant around unfamiliar situations or strangers?

- Do they welcome new faces and adjust comfortably with new settings?

The intensity of the reaction is associated with the level of response to any event or situation. Toddlers respond differently to events around them. Some shriek with happiness or giggle joyfully, others throw fits, and many barely react to what is happening.

- Do you always experience trying to guess the reaction of your child over something?

- Does your child explicitly show their emotions?

Adaptability is the child's ability to adjust themself to change over time.

- Is your child capable of adjusting themself to sudden changes in plans or disruptions of their routine?

- Distractibility is the level of the child's willingness to be distracted. It relates to the effects of an outside stimulus on your child's behavior.

- Can your child focus on their activity despite the distraction that surrounds him?

- Are they unable to concentrate when people or other activities are going on in the environment?

Quality of mood is related to how your child sees the world in their own eyes and understanding. Some react with acceptance and pleasure while other children scowl with displeasure just "because" they feel like it.

- Do they display mood changes always?

- Do they generally have a happy disposition?

Sensory Threshold is linked to sensitivity to sensory stimulation. Children sensitive to stimulation require a careful and gradual introduction to new people, experiences, or objects.

- Is your child easily bothered by bright lights, loud sounds, or food textures?

- Are they totally undisturbed with such things and welcome them as such?

There are three main types of toddlers:

- Active or Feisty Toddlers—These children have a tremendous amount of energy, which they show even while inside their mothers' uterus, like lots of moving and kicking. As an infant, they move around, squirm, and crawl all over the place. As toddlers, they climb, run, jump, and even fidget a lot to release their energy. They become excited while doing things or anxious around strangers or new situations.

They are naturally energetic, joyful, and loves the fun. But when they are not happy, they will clearly and loudly say it. These toddlers are also quite obstinate and hard to fit in regular routines. To help them succeed:

> Acknowledge their unique temperament and understand their triggers.

> Teach them self-help skills to get going if their energy is low or how to calm down when their activity level is very high. Some simple and effective ways to calm down are counting from 1 to 10, taking deep breaths, doing jumping jacks to get rid of excess energy, and redirecting them to other activities.

> Set a daily routine that includes play and other activities that enhance their gross motor movements. Please provide them with opportunities to play and explore safely. It is necessary to childproof your home.

> Insist on nap time. An afternoon nap will refresh their body and mind, preventing mood swings and tantrums.

> Do not let them sit in front of a television or do passive activities. Break the boredom by taking them outside and play in the outdoors.

> Become a calming influence. Understand how your temperament affects their temperament and find ways to become a role model.

- Passive or Cautious Toddlers—These children prefer activities that don't require a lot of physical effort, move slower, and want to sit down more often. They are slow-to-warm-up when meeting new people and often withdraw when faced with an unfamiliar situation. They also need ample time to complete their tasks.

To help them succeed:

> If your child is less active, set guidelines or deadlines to prompt them to finish the given tasks.

> Invite them to play actively by using interesting sounds, bright toys, or gentle persuasion.

> Always accentuate the positive. Be lavish with praise and words of encouragement when they display efforts or achieve simple milestones.

- Flexible or Easy Toddlers—These children are very adaptable, generally calm, and happy. But sometimes, they are easily distracted and need a lot of reassurance and love from you.

To help them succeed:

> Be realistic and expect mood changes when something isn't smooth sailing. Don't be too hard on the child when they display unusual outburst.

> Please provide them with interactive activities and join him. Sometimes, it's easy to let them play their own devices because of their good-natured personality. It is necessary to introduce other options to enhance their skills.

> Read the signs and find out the reasons for subtle changes in the behavior and attitude toward something. Be observant and have a particular time for him.

CHAPTER 16:

Roles of Parents

The most potent desire or drive in a man is often his physiological need to fulfill the act of procreation.

Modern society and families have changed drastically from generations. The new attitude towards sex (right or wrong) has led to an increase in unplanned pregnancies.

Anyone can be a sperm-donor and be the biological father of a child, but it takes more to be a dad. It takes a lot more also to be a mom than carrying a child for nine months.

We often assume that parenting should come automatically and that we will be better parents than the parents who raised us. Relationships are like rose gardens when well-kept. They are beautiful. But if we leave our relationships un-kept, we will end up with dysfunctional relationships that bring us nothing but stress.

Roles that a Parent Must Focus On

There are six leading roles that a parent must focus on: Love, Guidance, Provision, Security, Friendship, and Development.

Each child is different, and some of them need more attention than others, especially strong-willed children, but we must fulfill our role as parents regardless of the difficulty. One thing all parents must learn is that having children is undoubtedly a life-changing event.

No matter how many children, each child is different and unique with a different set of challenges.

Love

Some parents believe that loving a child will come easy, and for the most part, it does. However, there are moments when love becomes strained, and tempers flare. Maybe the child is not on your schedule and not allowing you to sleep (which happens the first few months of life).

Strong-willed children may often test the boundaries of love. They may often leave you exhausted and even depressed with their antics.

When you become challenged in raising a strong-willed child, try and get help. Even when you are stressed-out from parenting, you still have a responsibility to love the child. If you start to feel the strain, seek help, and try to break it.

But when we talk about love in relationships, we are not just talking exclusively about some sense of mutual endearment or fondness.

Parenting a strong-willed child will require what is referred to as "tough love." As children learn about the world, they live in, and they will often do make choices they shouldn't. As parents, if we love our children, then we must encourage them to do what's right. Sometimes we have a misplaced sense of what love is in parenting, and we focus too much on endearment in times when we are required to show tough love.

When we focus on being liked or loved by our children rather than on encouraging them to do what's right for their good, then it's not them that we love but ourselves.

You must ask yourself, are you sacrificing their long-term fulfillment and happiness in life for your short-term sense of peace and endearment.

When your child takes a jar of jam from the supermarket aisle and smashes it on the floor because you refused to buy a toy for them, what do you do?

However, you choose to correct the behavior is down to you, but you must correct this behavior. Suppose we willingly allow them to develop a sense of self-entitlement and lack of respect for authority. In that case, we are not showing love, as we facilitate and encourage behavior that will prevent them from developing into well-rounded adults.

Some parents result in yelling to correct the bad behavior. But shouting does not help at any stage during development. When tempers flare, and words are spouted out, there is no telling the damage they can cause.

Although the child needs to understand that what they just did is wrong, it does not help get angry. As parents, especially with strong-willed children, we must be in control of our emotions at all times.

Many parents get upset with toddlers who simply don't know any better because they have not learned the difference between right and wrong. This lack of emotional control will only exacerbate the situation.

Love is the ability to look past mistakes and guide your kid regardless of the emotional toll of doing so.

Love is tender and gentle even when gum gets stuck in their hair, and things are a bit messy. They have to learn somehow, and giving a child the proper space to learn makes a world of difference.

When counseling parents, I often tell them, love is the most powerful weapon you have as a parent. I have seen, so many children's lives are transformed when the parent simply starts to foster a greater sense of love in the home. When you create an environment of love, parenting will become easier.

They obey not because they are scared, but because they love you and want to make you happy.

A practical example I can give you on this is how I taught my child to clean her room. The frustration of coming home and seeing the place looking like a bomb was set off. As I said, yelling doesn't always work with strong-willed children, so I tried a different approach.

I said to my then 5-year-old, "Your room is messy again. Should we clean it up together before we make your bedtime hot chocolate?"

Then I proceeded to help clear up and turned it into a fun game. Soon she enjoyed clearing up so much she would ask if I wanted to help her clean-up. A few months after that, she would clean up all by herself and then shout, "Mom... dad, my room is clean... Can I have my cocoa now?"

But it gets better after six months of her newfound sense of accomplishment tidying up her room, and she started to observe when things were untidy in the house and ask why we hadn't cleaned up, mimicking my voice as best as she could.

The moral of the story is I replaced frustration with love; I was able to see things more objectively and help correct the undesirable behavior. I have seen others get the same results by replacing yelling with patience and love.

Guidance

It is often said that the first five years are the most formative of a child's life. It is the parent's responsibility to teach them and build up the child emotionally. When they have done a good deed and correct them when they have done something not so nice or pleasant, praise the child.

Guidance is more than teaching extremes or polar ends of morality. A recommendation is about helping them develop a moral compass, direction, and the noble traits and qualities we want them to have in life without indoctrinating them and stealing their ability to come to their conclusions.

A child does not understand the word "no," Unfortunately, one particular mention is the most familiar word a child will hear growing up.

During a child's exploration, a parent may look over to discover little Jane is digging in the dirt of a flowerpot. Of course, the mess is easy to fix, and the enjoyment of the soft, squishy ground between the fingers is new. However, it is the mess, not the action, that causes a resentful "NO!" from the parent. It is not as if the parent doesn't want Jane to play in the dirt; it is the mess she is causing.

The child may not see the difference in playing with this sandbox inside the house to play outside. Yet, many parents may flare up and even spank the child as they lose emotional control. Understanding that your child does not understand the difference and taking the time to explain may be more beneficial than shouting at them in anger.

Many parent's sources of frustration stem from them repeating their lousy parenting habits and expecting different results. Yelling and spanking are not always effective and can serve only to re-enforce your child's strong will.

In situations like above, it would be wiser to remove the child from the sandbox outside and explain the difference. Redirection is one form of guidance. Although it is simple to remove the child and explain the difference between the sandbox and the flowerpot, there will be times when it is not so easy.

Security

One of the essential roles of a parent is to provide security. As our children are developing, it is our duty not only to guide them but also to protect them from harm. There are many dangers in the world they are growing up, particularly those brought about by the very choices our children may make.

But regardless of the source of danger, it is the parent's duty as a responsible adult to stand up for their child. If the child is bullied in school or feels pinned against various odds, it is the parent's job to fight for their child. These days, many parents leave the child to battle on their own with the mentality of the survival of the fittest. This mentality, however, may work in nature, but as humans, this concept is flawed. To build trust with a child, the parent must prove to the child that they will fight for them.

However, it is the parent's responsibility to provide the child with a safe environment free from verbal, emotional, and physical abuse. Even if that does mean taking away a new phone so that the texts stop, or the computer, so the hate mail ends.

Friendship

Inwardly most parents desire to be best friends with their kids. At one point in their lives, we may have been the center of their world, but kids will often become disinterested in their parents as time goes on.

This is why it is important where possible to foster friendship with our children at an early age. But the company with our children should not be used as an emotional crutch if we are unfulfilled in our own lives.

Becoming friends with our kids is about fostering a loving relationship, where the child knows we are their parent, but still feels they can talk to us, hang out with us or share with us without always having the obstacle of the type defined role of parenthood.

CHAPTER 17:

Steps to Becoming a Peaceful Parent

Becoming a peaceful parent is not always an easy task. Modern life demands can mean that parents are already under stress, deadlines, and pressures even before children are thrown into the mix. Some days, it can feel like our kids are testing the limits of our patience to the breaking point.

Depending on the situation, reacting may put a quick stop to misbehavior, but it rarely allows for teaching moments to occur. Reacting leads to yelling, ordering children to their rooms, in-the-moment punishments, and often overlooks or ignores teaching opportunities. It's also stressful for parents! Too much anger can make parenting unenjoyable and leave you feeling out of control.

Even the most practiced of parents will have moments when calm seems far away and anger flares. In the face of these moments, it's all too easy for positive parenting strategies to go out the window.

Patience Is Vital—Tips and Techniques to Stay Calm in Critical Situations.

Let's look at some mindful strategies for staying calm, finding patience, and responding rather than reacting:

Commit Yourself

This is not an instant-fix tip, but it does help. Making a formal commitment to yourself that you are not going to lose your temper won't stop it from happening ever again – but over time, this consciously made commitment can help you to be more aware of what's going on situationally and internally when you lose your temper. The parenting situations that bring them on, you can start to make more mindful choices in those frustrating moments. Don't give up. As you begin to notice your anger and become better at managing it, your parenting's effectiveness can increase. As that increases, your child's misbehavior will start to decrease. Decreased misbehavior means less stress, which leads to less anger. In other words, consistently being mindful of your frustration over time can lead to a happy snowball of more enjoyable parenting!

Could you Put it in Perspective?

It's not uncommon for overstressed parents to start asking questions like, 'Why are they doing this? Is it because I'm not a good parent? Am I failing somehow?' 'What if they NEVER learn? What if they end up living under a bridge?' Try to calm down and remember that button-pushing, boundary testing, and misbehavior are all normal. They are a healthy part of your child's attempts to experiment with and understand the world around her. Expect that these things will happen. Recognize that your job is not to eliminate such issues overnight, but to guide your children through the process of growth and discovery that comes with learning how to function safely and healthily in the human condition. Your child's behavior is outside the norm; seek specific guidance from your pediatrician.

Take a Deep Breath

Believe it or not, taking a moment to breathe is more than just pat advice. A few calming breaths can be done in under thirty seconds but do wonders to calm down. Deep breathing delivers oxygen to your blood and brain, helping you relax and think more clearly under stress. This exercise can also allow you to pause and collect yourself before you react to breathe with you.

Splash Water on Your Face

The face helps some people to change their internal landscape just enough to step away from the anger. However, only apply this strategy or any strategy that requires you to step away.

Add New Tools to Your Toolbox

Come up with a list of anger management techniques that have worked for you in the past, then go out and find some new ones to add to the list (hint: this is a great place to start!). When you feel anger coming on, pull one of these 'tools' from your anger management toolbox—being prepared with options when things can do wonders for one's ability to regain control.

Remember that Feelings are Contagious

If you are angry, anxious, or stressed, your children probably will be too. Kids are smart—even when parents control their reactions, little ones will likely pick up on the fact that mom or dad is upset. This can stress children out and lead to further misbehavior, adding fuel to the fire. Taking a moment to remember that our anger is making things worse can sometimes give us pause; we need to apply a calm-down strategy.

Take a Break

Sometimes taking a short break can give you the space you need to regain your calm. This strategy can even be turned into a teaching moment as you model a healthy coping technique for your child. Tell your children that you are upset, and you need to take a break to calm down. Then leave (providing it is safe to do so), take a quick walk, run through some breathing exercises, do some yoga poses—whatever helps you calm down best. When you return, you can ask your children why they thought you needed a break and jump into a teaching moment around coping with difficult emotions.

How to Stop Yelling at Your Child

A common but unfortunate side effect of anger is yelling. While yelling can sometimes put a stop to misbehavior at the moment, it's less effective in the long run for promoting discipline. It can also undermine parent-child relationships, create stress for everyone involved, and interfere with authentic communication attempts. That being said, it's probably not the end of the world if you yell at your kids one day. Beating yourself up over it is usually not helpful. Just as you want to teach your kids to learn from their mistakes and move on, if you yell at your child, learn from the experience, make amends, forgive yourself, and then move on so that positive parenting can take effect.

Discussing the yelling that is sometimes necessary for safety situations, such as warning your child to get out of the road in the face of an oncoming vehicle. The focus here is on yelling as the result of anger or other negative emotions.

Let's stock up that peaceful parent toolbox a little more by looking at some tips and tricks to stop yelling:

- **Ask your kids to explain their feelings**. It can be accessible in a heated moment to feel like your child is acting out just to make you angry. Understanding the real reasons why a child has misbehaved can help add a little perspective and cool the fuse of our anger.

  It's also suitable for kids who need to be heard and validated at least as much as adults do. Just listening to your child's feelings may be enough to reduce the misbehavior, which will, in turn, help your frustration levels.

- **Get a stress ball**. Many people swear by these small devices. Having a stress ball to squeeze can give you something else to focus on when you're about to lose your cool, and the physical use of your hands can help take the edge off of your stress. You can try keeping one in your bag and pulling it out in heated moments.

- **Don't take it personally**. Know that your child's misbehavior is not personal. Transgression is a normal part of the development and is expected as she learns to self-regulate her actions and emotions. Taking it personally will not only add to your stress at the moment, but it can also lead to resentment over time.

- **Disengage**. Until you can calm your anger, do nothing. If you've already started yelling, stop where you're at. The more often you stop yourself, the more quickly you'll notice that you're crying. Eventually, this strategy can help you avoid yelling altogether.

- **Don't force a teaching moment**. Positive teaching moments can't happen when you're yelling. Wait until you've calmed down before trying to teach your child.

- **Take preventative action**. If you know that having the plant knocked over sets you off, put it out of reach. If you know that your children's' fighting over a particular toy will lead to your yelling, put the toy away until they are ready to play without fighting. If you know that going home from the park will lead to yelling, if your children refuse to come home, make a plan to deal with their refusal more constructively. Identifying situations that lead to yelling can help you eliminate them when appropriate and plan personal coping strategies when not.

- **Set realistic expectations**. Frustration is more likely to occur when your kids fail to meet the behavioral expectations you've set for them. Setting expectations that are too advanced for their developmental level will only lead to 'failures' on their part and frustration for both of you. Give them —and yourself— plenty of opportunities to succeed by setting behavioral expectations that are in keeping with their developmental level.

CHAPTER 18:

Positive Parenting Principles

Educating and disciplining children implies, among other things, establishing clear rules and limits. This is not always easy, even more so these days, but if parents adopt positive educational practices early on, it is possible to prevent future difficulties and problems. Cláudia Madeira Pereira, a clinical and health psychologist with a doctorate in clinical psychology, points out some acceptable practices that will make this task easier:

Talk to Your Child

Even if you are exhausted after a day at work, take some time out of your day to talk to your child. At dinner or before going to bed, ask him how his day was, using phrases such as "Tell me what you did today," "Tell me about the good things that happened today," or "Did something bad happen."

He can resort to several solutions. First, allow him to speak and listen to him without judgment or criticism. If you prefer, look for positive aspects that you can highlight and praise. Also, tell him about "what" and "how" to better deal with similar situations in the future.

Pay Attention to Good Behavior

Sometimes children learn that bad behavior is the best way to get parental attention... This is especially true for children whose parents pay attention to them only when they misbehave, even if that attention is negative, scolding them and rebuking them.

Promote Your Child's Autonomy and Responsibility

Some tasks, such as dressing in the morning, can be difficult for children. Even though it would be quicker for you to dress your child, you would prefer to encourage their autonomy and responsibility. Help your child by giving short and simple instructions on how to do the tasks.

To do this, use expressions such as "Take off your pajamas," "Now put on your shirt," or "Finally, put on your pants." Finish with a compliment, using phrases like "All right, you did a good job!" Sometimes it will not be enough to tell your child what to do; you may need to show him "what" and "how" to do it.

Establish Clear Rules

Be clear with your child about a set of rules. First, explain the direction succinctly and concretely. Second, make sure your child understands the direction and knows what is expected of him. In order for your child to be able to respect the rules more efficiently, try to give clear and straightforward directions, empathically, and positively.

You say like "It's time to go to bed. Let's go to the room now, and then I'll read you a story," usually work. It is common for children to challenge the rules in the early day,s but stay firm and consistent. Your child realizes that the new law is to be followed.

Set Limits

Try to be patient, and stand firm. Tell your child that an individual behavior must stop, explain the reasons, and inform him of the consequences of not obeying. In that case, preferably use phrases like "If you keep doing, then..." Immediately and consistently implement the products whenever lousy behavior occurs.

But do not resort to punishment or physical punishment (such as beating), as they only aggravate children's behavioral problems. Prefer to take a hobby or an object appreciated by your child for some time.

Stop the Tantrums

Try to ignore the tantrums, not paying attention to the child at such times. If possible, step back and pay attention to it only when the tantrums stop so that your child realizes that they can only get their attention when they stop throwing tantrums. At that point, prepare yourself, because your child will put him to the test. At first, it is normal for tantrums to get worse. However, by systematically applying this method, the tantrums will eventually disappear. You must be aware of your child's good behavior and value these behaviors whenever they occur, for example, by giving a compliment, a kiss, or a hug. If you do, the child will feel more accompanied.

Learn to Control Your Negative Feelings

There are times when any mother or father feels the nerves at the edge of the skin. Then try to do something to help him or her. You can, for example, listen to some music or take a few minutes of meditation. When you feel calmer, go back to your child and start again, using conciliatory phrasing in a sweet tone, like "I felt I did not know what to do, but I do know what to do with it now."

Have (A Lot Of) Patience

When you raise your child's communication (verbal and non-verbal) empathic and festive, it will contribute to a healthier and happier relationship between both. Educating and disciplining your child will require a great deal of your time and patience. No wonder they say being a mom and dad is tough, but it will be well worth it at them because it is the most rewarding job you can have.

CHAPTER 19:

Parenting a Strong-Willed Child

S ome toddlers can be difficult, and the need to train them comes in. We should not just claim that they would understand when they are grown, no. It may be too difficult for you to stop it when they are grown. They are toddlers, they are not dumb, and they know the difference between right and wrong.

Common Struggles Toddlers May Have

To begin, we need to understand why toddlers could be difficult. For the first time, they realize that they are separate individuals from their parents and caregivers. The initial thought is that he/she is part of the parent, but when they reach the toddler stage, they realize that this isn't true. Furthermore, toddlers do not understand the logic of waiting and the logic behind having everything. They have no or little self-control, and in a nutshell, he/she may have a hard time balancing his/her needs with what you are providing as a parent or caregiver. Toddlers could be difficult; they could be funny too. Here are four everyday situations your child could be struggling with:

1. He says no when he means yes. These happen when you are offering him a favorite treat.

2. He has a meltdown anytime you fail to understand his words.

3. He doesn't want any substitute. The blue pajamas or nothing else, even though they may not be washed or even after offering him the purple one.

4. He acts out when frustrated. Gives up everything when angry.

What is listed above are only acts which toddlers put on to manage strong feelings; since they are new to almost everything, they lack reasonable control over what controls them and how they can control it. They are toddlers; they soon find out that they have vocal powers, and that is when the crying, shouting, and yelling increases. They may also want to make different noises to see how they sound and the reactions of adults around them to such noise. They impulsively go into an activity without much or any thinking. They react differently to different situations; in fact, you can even place a tag around them. You can most often start with some funny names like bubbly, daredevil, determined, stubborn, cautious, adventurous, etc. It may beat you to know that some challenging toddler behavior is developmentally correct; they may be defiant, bossy, sassy, or impulsive. Still, they are just byproduct of what the child needs-independence.

Challenging Behaviors and Their Practical Solutions

Interrupting

Nothing can be so exasperating than a child who breaks in every time you are chatting with a friend. Toddlers don't interrupt with words all the time but their actions. And that is because they always seek attention from their parents and may be jealous if a friend or an adult is getting all of it. In this aspect, it is your fault. You can do the following:

- Chose the right locale for your meetings. A place where your child can enjoy while you talk with the adult. A park having a sandbox is something nice.

- Get a baby sitter. This would help a lot and would allow you to use all focus or concentration during the meeting. It is knowing that your child is in safe hands.

- Teach your children polite behavior. An excellent way to teach them is by reading them some books like The Bad Good Manners Book, by Babette Cole's Aliki's Manners, and What Do you Say Dear? By Style Joslin. Any book on good manners, you can lay your hands on. Could you read it to them every day?

- Schedule your phone calls. You wouldn't want your child to disturb you while you are on the market, so make the necessary preparations.

Lying

First, why do children lie? They have an active imagination, and they are very forgetful. These cute angels may also have what we call angel syndrome. A child who thinks that his parents believe he can do no wrong would do wrong on purpose. When asked, a lie comes to mind. Toddlers do lie, and it is natural for them to do so. How can you stop this?

- Always encourage truth-telling. You should not be angry at your child when he or she tells you the truth; instead, you should be happy. Show your child that honesty pays off.

- You should not accuse your child of any reason. Your comments, remarks should help your child not put him down.

- Don't weigh your child down with too many expectations. He or she would not understand. They are children, toddlers, not adults. You shouldn't be expecting too much from them.

- Build your trust. Assure your child that you trust him or her and don't puncture that trust.

Running Away

A running away toddler could be very funny. Like really? Where do they think they are going? But you have to be careful when this happens outdoors, especially on the walkway. Why do they run? Just like any other attitude displayed by a toddler, running away comes from a new sense of independence and the fact that he has legs that can run. You can't stop this; you can only control it:

- Stay close to them, and it should be okay for you to look ahead when they are running.

- Show him where he can run and where he can't. Allow him to explore the safe areas

- Entertain your child.

Tattling

Some of the time, kids tattle because they have not developed the social or emotional skills required to solve skills all by themselves. Tattling has a positive effect, too, and it means that your child is showing you that he/she understands the rules and knows right from wrong. Before we go too far, what is tattling? It means merely telling somebody, especially somebody in authority, about something terrible or somebody else's wrongdoing. Do you get a report from your child about everything? "Mom, Michael is playing in that person's car, Dad, Sarah is keeping a crayon in her pocket, Mom, Brian is playing with a sharp object... etc." That's tattling. The following steps can be taken:

- Assess the situation: Before you conclude that your child is a whiny tattletale, take stock of the problem.

- Put the work back on his shoulder for tattling. When your child understands that tattling only gets him more responsibility, he tends to mind his own business.

Teasing

You may agree, or not, teasing is just what life brings. It happens when it happens, and even toddlers are not left out of it. It is excruciating when toddlers are teased, and you should understand that as a parent. What can you do when a toddler is bullied? This may not work well for toddlers as they would require a verbal response.

- Your child should not respond. This could be hard, but it is a trick that can repel those guilty of the teasing offense.

- You can coach your child to "agree" with what the teaser is saying. He/she would look dumb when a child says, "I agree I suck my thumb."

- Ask for help. Your child can ask for help from anyone or any adult around.

CHAPTER 20:

Managing Anger in Children

Mothers everywhere throughout the world have a difficult time dealing with their children. Regularly, they exclaim unnecessarily at children in their anger and loathe their activities from that point. Mothers try hard not to ruin their children's moods, but rather sometimes conditions outside anybody's ability to control show signs of mothers' improvement. They are unfit to endure the fiendishness and rebellion of their children. Indeed, even the best of mothers can lose their temper quickly.

The excitement of anger in you could be because of stress, budgetary issues, absence of adequate rest, appetite, or sickness. These variables repress you physically, and you show your failures as anger on your children.

Here are a couple of my proposals for you.

When you feel your anger is expanding alarmingly, move far from the scene. Practice some deep breathing and tallying exercises to cut down your tempers.

Return into your musings and tune in to what you said in your anger. This would doubtlessly not be your aim. Moreover, you might not want to set a case of a hollering mother to your children.

Practice how you will respond if your children make trouble. Practice out various circumstances and attempt to hold fast to these on certain occasions. This brings down the occurrence of anger.

Sometimes anger could be because of disappointment. You feel furious if children don't live and perform to your desires. You think to be a disappointment as a parent. Sometimes additionally, are the reason for your anger.

Put aside a specific day or time of the week for yourself. Leave your children with your better half or another person and enjoy yourself. This could go about like an enormous destructor, and you can return revived entirely and brimming with vitality.

Anger is an emotion just like any other, which means that some people experience more of it than others do. The same is right for children. Sometimes your child will only be mad at you for no apparent reason, which can be very frustrating. A long time of constant disconnection and alienation from your child because of their anger will soon get you as angry as them or even more so.

Understanding your child's angry behaviors is the beginning of controlling your own anger because anger between children and parents is highly interconnected. We will look at some of the angry behaviors that children engage in and why they get angry, including the psychology of angry children and anger in different development stages.

Causes of Anger

As a parent, you keep up with your child's development and help them to grow holistically. Because children usually have not developed the full range of communication and self-expression tools that adults use to get their needs met, they tend to resort to anger to express their needs a lot of the time. When your baby was a toddler, your mother instincts would help you to interpret different angry cries accurately. However, as your child starts developing a whole life of its own with friends, school, and hobbies, you might find yourself falling short.

Hurt

This is the most common and universal cause of anger in children. Hardly any child will remain calm after getting hurt. Unless a child has been taught to suppress their pain by the parent, they are usually pretty honest in their expression of hurt. Everyday, things that might hurt a child include being neglected, the feelings of rejection, losing a friend, or feeling like their parents prefer a sibling over them.

Sadness

Children care a lot about the people and things around them because they make up their entire universe. The people in this universe include their playmates, parents, and close family. Things like school, the family house, and toys make up part of the universe. A child will be the saddest when this universe is threatened. A playmate moving away means that they will have either to play alone or find a new friend, which can be a terrifying experience. Other changes like separation and divorce, moving houses or school, or death are also very distressing.

Fear

Just like adults, children worry about their wellbeing and that of others. For example, some children get angry when they see their parents or loved ones struggling with an illness. In fact, a child is more likely to get angry when there is an ill family member than when they are sick themselves. Children of parents in dangerous careers like firefighters, the police, and soldiers also fear for the parent's safety, especially when they realize just how dangerous the job might be. For example, a child witnessing their father in a risky situation can get very upset and angry even if their job is reflected on television. The child might then withdraw and avoid the parent to try to protect themself from any possible future pain.

Frustrations

Children need to learn everything that adults take for granted, including movement, communication, and fine motor skills. They also need to watch as their bodies grow as they get older. At the same time, they will be comparing themselves to their peers in the house, at school, and in the playground. When a child lags in reaching some development milestone, it is widespread for them to get frustrated. The frustration manifests as anger and tends to last quite a long time.

Guilt

Children don't usually have the finely tuned range of emotions that adults have. So, when a child is feeling guilty for some mistake that they made, the first instinct is usually to lash out. Sometimes children will even feel guilty about problems they did not cause, such as a death or their parents divorcing. When you teach your child to do something and are unable to do it or forgets about it, this guilt will probably manifest as anger. This is especially tricky because you'll probably be angry at yourself. The way you handle such a situation affects the parental bond you form with your child as well as their emotional development.

ADHD

Children that have Attention Deficit Hyperactivity Disorder tend to have serious challenges in doing simple activities that other kids their age do with ease. The constant embarrassment and frustrations of performing worse than other children on ordinary tasks make them more likely to lash out and withdraw. The situation is worsened even further by parental frustrations and lack of compassion for their situation.

Embarrassment

A child who feels silly or awkward in a social situation and a child who just performed severely in a baseball game is likely to react the same way—by getting angry. Some children get angry when they are embarrassed and might even cry or hit whatever is closest to them. The fear of being judged makes them lash out in anger to distract themselves from their disappointment with their own behavior.

Angry Behaviors

Children display their anger in different ways. Some of the ways that children express anger can be interpreted as normal child behaviors, which is why some parents overlook them and fail to look for the underlying cause of irritation. It's useful to recognize anger in your kid while still young, and they have not learned to mask the rage or hide it entirely from you. The sooner you find the underlying cause of angry behaviors, the easier it will be to solve the underlying problem. It's also essential that you deal with your child's anger issues appropriately.

Overreacting to an episode of anger might give your child the wrong idea about expressing anger. It's when your child forms a pattern of angry behaviors that you should be concerned. However, severe, isolated incidences are usually a pure expression of anger by a child who does not know how to express their anger. Take these moments as teachable moments and teach your child to express their anger correctly.

Children develop anger management issues when they suppress emotions like grief, fear, and hurt. The vulnerability that these feelings bring terrifies a kid and makes them defensive. This defensiveness makes children defiant, even cruel. Everything a child does to suppress exposure will always be intended to assert their independence. While they are locking you away to show you that they do not need you, it is just a disguised cry for help.

Withdrawal

Sometimes a child just wants to talk to their dolls or be alone, which is perfectly normal. Assuming a child is enjoying their own company, lonesomeness isn't a problem. It becomes a problem when your child stays alone, but does not seem to be enjoying it and is sad. Kids who feel like their problems aren't recognized or appreciated by their caregivers tend to express their anger by withdrawing. A child will express reluctance to family activities, spend a lot of time alone, and lock themselves in rooms like the bathroom or their bedroom alone. A child who does not have many friends and plays alone might be dealing with some serious anger issues and intervention.

Temper Tantrums

A two-year-old child with a temper tantrum where they kick and hits on everything in sight because you did not buy them or toy, they wanted at the mall is quite common. This is a widespread habit of children in the terrible twos. It is when your nine-year-old does something like that, you should be worried. Generally, you must see an improvement in your child's ability to handle disappointments when things don't go their way. It's just a part of the growth in their emotional and behavioral capabilities.

Irritability/Impatience

An impatient child wants to get what they want "right now!" and not a second later. They will make a fuss and become irritable at any time there is a delay. This goes for anything from a juice box coming out of the fridge to getting a toy delivered after buying it online. Irritability usually shows frustrations in other areas of life, such as reaching development milestones. The irritability will probably continue until they get to the same level as their peers unless you intercede and help them resolve the frustration.

Aggression

Aggression in children is usually a sign of anger at the most distressing levels. With violent behavior, the child is generally feeling pretty helpless and vulnerable. And along with violent behavior like kicking and biting, you'll start to see them engaging in destructive behaviors. This includes smashing toys, tearing books, and chucking away food (often at other people's heads). Destruction of property is usually the loudest cry for help and indicates that your child needs exceptional service, especially when the behavior is consistent and intentional.

Fighting and bullying

The occasional skirmish over a swing at the playground can merely be a sign of a strong-willed or dominant kid. As long as you teach them to be more aware of other kids' needs, there should be no trouble there. What you should look out for is a growing habit of getting into confrontations with other children. Especially worrisome is a child picking fights with older children. It's usually an indication that children want to prove themselves, often due to frustrations in attaining developmental milestones.

Insults and Bad Language

When you don't teach your child to handle their anger constructively, it will likely burst through the surface with explosive insults. When anger episode remains unresolved for a long time, the occasional insult gives way to foul language that usually comes in explosive outbursts. Children raised by angry parents often notice and adopt their parents' habits, such as insulting others and cussing. However, the insults and cussing are usually a veneer to cover up their fears and very often self-blame for the strife around the house. In the early teenage years, children will have started to model their parents' behaviors, including physical violence and drug use, due to a difficult home situation's frustrations.

Hurting Animals and Other Children

Children are usually very gentle with animals like pets. Any form of cruelty, like hurting an animal, shows that a child has some unexpressed anger that they are repressing. In many cases, seeking to hurt an innocent animal, as well as nastiness towards a younger sibling, indicates that a child may have been or felt abused. It's a way of paying back a physical assault in kind.

Reflexive Opposition

When children are angry with their parents, they are more likely to refuse to follow instructions out of spite. Children get hostile when they are angry at some unfairness that they cannot do anything about. The only way to even out the score becomes rebellion. The same goes for vengefulness. A child who is continuously seeking revenge against people who wrong them (peers or adults) is usually fighting back against the anger they feel for being misunderstood or a parent treating them with no compassion. This is very common for children who have grown up under a strict parent and received disciplinary action for every mistake they made.

Blaming Others for Mess-ups

A child who is always blaming others for mistakes is usually hiding their anger at having disappointed themselves. The fear of consequences for errors might also cause it.

How to Deal With an Angry Child

Parental anger management goes beyond improving your wellbeing as a parent. As crucial as parental wellbeing is, it does not make up for being clueless about how you're supposed to handle your angry child. Parental and child anger are intertwined. If your child is angry, they are likely to pass the anger on to you with their actions. And when you're angry, you'll probably do something to anger your child like screaming at them In this section; we will cover the practical strategies that you can apply in dealing with your angry child.

Delay

This is the most critical lesson in handling your anger. Delay your anger for as long as possible regardless of the mistake that your child made. For example, if you are picking them up from mall jail, delay the confrontation until you get in the car, then until you get home, and then after a time-out in their room. You get around to addressing the issue at hand, and you'll have calmed down enough to have a clear head for problem-solving.

Breathing Exercises

Take a few calming breaths before dealing with any child-related stress. This allows you to quiet down your anxiety and stay grounded. Only then can you manage trying moments with your kids gracefully and calmly.

Recreation

Sometimes all you need to keep your child happy is some happy moments. When you engage in entertainment such as sports with your child, the physical activity acts as a salve to anger and allows both of you to release the frustrations trapped deep within. The time you spend together in play strengthens your connection to your child and facilitates some healthy communication.

Teaching Self-expression

Children express a range of emotions like fear, worry, embarrassment, and sadness, among others, with anger. For a toddler who cannot speak, this may be acceptable. As your child grows and learns to talk, you should teach them how to express their needs, fears, and worries. Question your child about his or her feelings when they are upset so that you can become more adept at interpreting their frustrations. A good sense of self-expression will help your child talk about issues that bother them instead of getting angry.

Healthy Communication

Sometimes a child will get angry because they need to feel heard and seen, and they aren't getting that from the world. If your child is doing something, you should be the greatest fan. When you're a parent, communication with your child goes beyond words. Children communicate with their body language, their actions, and their performance in school. It is your place to decode everything your child is telling you and move to fulfill their needs.

Understanding/Relating

When you capture your child doing something naughty in the spur of the moment, your own adult interpretation of right and wrong tends to take over and override your ability to relate. For example, a two-year-old child would not have the smarts to know that flour isn't something to play with. It would be best if you always tried to look at a situation from your child's perspective before handing out your punishment.

Listening

Parents with naughty kids tend to have a lot more trouble with this particular strategy. You assume that your child did it even before you know the situation just because they have given you so much grief in the past. What this does is that it makes your child feel like you don't believe in them that you are not on their side. Who knows, maybe your daughter or son's impossible explanation will crack you up and bring some comic relief to a tense situation.

Forgive

Sometimes it helps to react with compassion in place of anger, especially when you have been interacting with your child through anger a lot. For example, when you need to teach an important life lesson that might help your child change their behavior, you can get a lot further over an ice cream than screaming at them across the room.

Be the Parent

The role of a parent entails providing, protecting, and guiding. It's the same even when you have caught your child in a mess-up. It would be greatest if you were more mature and more levelheaded so that you can solve the problem at hand. Sometimes your child is only acting out because they lack the knowledge to deal with their personal issues. You should offer guidance on how to do so or find a mentor if you are unqualified to deal with a problem. Finally, it would help if you were a role model for your child in everything that you do. If you don't know how to hold your anger or if your life isn't organized, your child will probably mirror that.

CHAPTER 21:

No More Yelling
(How to Teach Without Yelling)

W hy do we yell at our children? We love our children; we do not want any harm to come to them; we do not want to see them cry, and we never want to see them upset; yet, we yell.

Most parents yell at their children for one of a few reasons. The first reason is the most obvious; the parents yell at their children because they feel they have run out of options. They think that the discipline has not worked; talking to the child has not worked; that pleading and bribing the child has not worked. Therefore, they resort to yelling.

The second reason that the parents yell is that they do not know how to parent any other way. Most of the time, the parents that yell were yelled at when they were children. It is simply passed from one generation to the next, and the parent does not know how to break the cycle.

The third reason parents yell has nothing to do with the child, but it is simply because they have allowed themselves to become overwhelmed with life. They feel that they're not being heard, not only when it comes to their children but also in life. They may have taken more than they can handle, and, as a result, they end up feeling emotionally charged all of the time. Because these parents do not know how to deal with their emotions, they end up yelling at their kids, even when their child makes the slightest mistake.

What happens when we yell at our children? Studies have shown that yelling at our children has the same effect on them as spanking and that yelling has psychological consequences that can last long into the future.

When we yell at our children, we are changing the way that their brain works. Yelling is nothing more than another form of abuse, and it affects the child's mind in the same way as physical abuse does. Yelling can increase a child's risk of developing depression, mental disorders, and personality disorders; it can also increase the risk of suicide and decrease brain activity.

When a child is yelled at by the parent, they learn that they should be afraid of the parent instead of trusting them. This means that the child will be less likely to try and please the parent, which usually will cause the parent to become more upset and yell even more. Meaning that the children will have a hard time trusting others as they grow and will have a hard time feeling secure as adults. Yelling can also lead to anxiety issues as the child grows.

When a parent yells at a child, the child quickly learns that it is easier to tune the adult out than to listen to the constant yelling. This, of course, causes the adult to become even more upset because the child still is not doing what they requested, and it causes even a more significant divide between the parent and child.

As I stated earlier, there is never any reason for you to cause damage to your relationship with your child. There is nothing so severe that your child could do that it would be appropriate for you to generate the child not to trust you.

You have to remember that you are your child's safe place. You are the one person that they are supposed to be able to turn to, no matter who turns against them or what is going on in their lives. You are their entire world, and they want you to continue being so. Yelling at your child shows them that they are not even safe when they are with you, and it will not produce a well-balanced child as they grow older.

What are you as the parent supposed to do? You have to learn alternatives to yelling. You can do many things instead of yelling at your child, but before we get into those, I want to take a few minutes to talk about your life in general.

Most parents yell at their children because their own life is out of control. You have to get your life under control, and you have to do it NOW. Make sure that you take the steps that you need to take to reduce the stress in your life, get your budget under control, and make sure that you are getting done everything you need to get done daily.

Once you have your life figured out, it is time to start changing your behavior. Yes, it is time to focus on how you behave instead of how your child is behaving.

Taking deep breaths is a great way to calm yourself and stop yourself from yelling at your child. Close your eyes and inhale through your nose, hold the breath for a few seconds, and exhale through your mouth. Really think about what is going on. Is it really the child that you are upset with, or are you just upset in general?

Calmly address the behavior. Just because you cannot yell at your kids does not mean that you cannot address lousy behavior and get them to understand that it is unacceptable. For example, if you have a hard time getting your toddler to pick up their toys after they are done playing with them, calmly tell the toddler that if they do not pick up the toys, you are going to take them away. Give them a few minutes to pick up their toys, and if the toys are not put away, calmly bag up the toys and take them out. Allow the toddler to earn the toys back through good behavior.

See how simple that was? You taught your toddler a lesson, the boys got cleaned up, and you did not have to yell your head off and scare your toddler half to death.

We have been taught that punishment is a teaching tool when, in reality, it is merely a way to cause pain in one way or another. A teaching tool is a discipline, which is ultimately the opposite of punishment. Take a few moments to look at the situation and think about how you can teach your toddler what you want them to do and how you can ensure that they do it in the future. Then make sure that you follow through every single time.

Instead of yelling, use a firm but calm voice. Trust me, and nothing will tell your toddler that you mean business other than a quiet, firm agent. Keep your voice low so that your child has to pay attention to hear from you and make them work to listen to what you are saying. The calmer that you can stay, the more impact your words will make, and the more attention your child will pay to what you are saying.

Before you begin screaming at your child because they have misbehaved, take a few minutes to figure out why the toddler has misbehaved. This is something that I have tried to focus on throughout this book because, as adults, it is so easy for us to forget that toddlers usually have a reason for misbehaving. It has nothing to do with breaking the rules or upsetting you. Generally, when a toddler misbehaves, they need something, whether it be food, a nap, or time away from an individual situation.

Follow through instead of nagging and then yelling. If you tell your children to turn off the television and you come back five minutes later to a child still watching television, walk up, turn off the television, and redirect your child. So much yelling could be avoided if parents followed through and stopped what I call lazy parenting.

Lazy parenting is talking simply to hear their own voice, knowing that what they are requesting is not going to be done, threatening the child without following through, and then screaming in anger when the child does not do as asked. Don't practice lazy parenting.

If you find that your child cannot do the tasks you are requesting of him or her, you need to adjust your expectations instead of screaming your head off. For example, my youngest son suffers from ADHD, as well as a few other issues. This means that while I can tell to his sister—who is only 1 year older than him—to go clean her room and she is able to do it, I have to break the tasks down for him, telling him each step, one at a time as he completes the one before. I had to change my expectations because telling him to clean his room usually meant that he went to his place, sat on his bed, and looked around wholly overwhelmed with the task.

Remember that each child is different, and while one child may be able to do one task, it may be more challenging for the next child, and you might have to adjust your expectations, which is still much more straightforward than yelling at your child.

CHAPTER 22:

Calm and Confident Leader

S o much of disciplining toddlers lovingly and respectfully depends on this energy, that of a calm and confident leader. Toddlers look to their parents for successful cues on how they should proceed in the world, and modeling is the most effective way to show them what is expected of them.

In all of your interactions with your toddler moving forward, remember this. You can and should respectfully acknowledge their fears, frustrations, issues, and upsets, but you should do this as the calm and confident leader they need. In doing so, you set the alarm for both their success and yours.

Your Child is Afraid

Anxiety is one of the major problems most parents face during potty-training, which can be very crippling. The child may be suffering from general anxiety, reflecting on the potty-training process or suffering from potty-training anxiety. Either way, it is important to face this problem head-on, as you won't be able to get anything done if your child is afraid.

First, you should identify the type of anxiety your child suffers from. If the child suffers from general anxiety, you can visit a therapist for diagnosis and treatment. There is a condition known as a generalized anxiety disorder in which the kid worries about a variety of issues, which should not be a source of worry normally. Below is an excerpt from a Boston Children's Hospital publication describing the condition.

Fear can make the child refuse to sit on a potty or toilet. Some children even get scared of making a bowel movement in the potty while some may be afraid of the toilet flushing. Anxiety can also cause the child to wet themselves or defecate in places you don't expect.

If the child is afraid of sitting on the potty or pooping in the potty chair, you should start by encouraging the child to sit on the potty periodically with clothes on at first, then with clothes off later. You can get them accustomed to the potty by decorating it with stickers together and getting toys which, the child can only play with when he sits on the potty. Make sure the potty is comfortable enough for the child. To help with this, let the child join you in shopping for the potty before you start potty-training. You should then pick the one the child chooses.

The child has an accident while playing.

It is common for a child to wet or soil themselves while playing, usually due to excitement or distraction. First, you should make sure it isn't due to a medical issue such as incontinence or an overactive bladder.

Generally, children are not able to control their bladder until around the age of three or four. Even at that age, accidents are still common, especially during the night. The digestive tract has nerves which can be triggered by an emotional, exciting, or stressful event.

The child may get carried away playing and ignore the urge to ease themselves until it becomes uncontrollable or may simply wet themselves due to too much excitement or stimulation. To prevent this, you should help the child follow a consistent bathroom routine and make sure they ease themselves before going out to play.

Potty accidents when playing could also be caused by constipation or by the child holding it in deliberately. The child may choose to hold it in, either as a result of an emotional reaction or anxiety. However, accidents may then happen during play as the child gets too relaxed or too excited to control their bladder or bowel. When this happens, do not ignore the situation or yell at the child. Let the child calm down first and then proceed to clean the mess together. The child shouldn't return to playing until he has been cleaned up and the mess disposed of properly.

While the child is playing, you can also make them take short breaks to go to the bathroom. This will help in emptying his bladder and bowels and also to calm him down. You also can limit any adrenaline-inducing play for the meantime. Things such as throwing the child up or swinging them around can cause an adrenaline spike or a bit of fear, thereby making the child lose control of their bowels and bladder.

Though potty accidents can be frustrating, you should keep in mind that accidents while playing are normal during potty-training and result from a natural response to excitement or anxiety. Since the child is still developing, issues such as this may occur frequently, but the child should grow out of it with age. However, if this gets too severe or continues till over the age of five, it is advisable to visit a medical professional.

Your son/daughter doesn't want to go to the bathroom with you.

Your child may refuse to go to the bathroom with you or anyone else present. This isn't unusual. Children start to develop a sense of awareness at a period, and they start being conscious of their bodies. The child may refuse to go to the bathroom with you or anyone to show independence. You must, therefore, be prepared to handle this carefully as a parent.

Leaving the child unsupervised, in this case, will lead to lots of cleaning for you. They have to learn how to use the potty or toilet, wipe themselves and flush, and wash their hands. If they learn how to do these correctly, they'll have the freedom to use the bathroom on their own.

From another perspective, your child may be self-conscious or ashamed of his body. You should check for any sign of abuse, either physical or emotional. A child getting ashamed of his or her body suddenly may be a sign of abuse. Do visit a therapist if the child's behavior gets suspicious.

Do not make fun of any of his physical attributes. This can affect the child's self-esteem negatively. If the child is uncomfortable with you being with him or her in the bathroom, you can ask a family member of the same gender to accompany them.

The child may refuse your company in the bathroom also as a way of showing independence. This is okay, but you should make sure he or she has learned the process correctly. Let them recite the steps to take until you are satisfied. You can remind them of what he or she should do while they are inside to be safe. Pediatric psychologists have explained that it is vital for the child to create boundaries around their bodies as they start gaining independence and self-awareness.

Respecting your child's boundaries will go a long way in creating a sense of self-respect and improving the child's self-esteem. This will also teach the child to respect other people's boundaries as children learn through imitation. However, you should teach the child to be open with you and to feel free to talk about any issue.

The Child Poops Next to the Potty

You may have gotten your child to stop going in his or her underwear, but you may be faced with another problem—the child misses when he or she tries to poop in the potty or poops next to it instead. To stop this, you should first observe the child to determine why he does it. So you have to get the specific cause. From my experience as a parent, I'll list the primary reasons why a child "misses" or may poop next to the potty deliberately.

First, you may have trained your child to stop using diapers or going in their underwear, but the child may not be used to the potty yet. They know they shouldn't poop in their underwear, but may be scared of using the potty. They then choose to poop next to the potty instead. That is why it's essential to get your child familiar with the potty chair as soon as you start potty-training.

Please encourage them to sit on the potty at frequent intervals and make sure they are comfortable sitting on the potty. You can motivate with toys and children's books. Praise them if they eventually poop inside the potty. If accidents occur, clean up the mess and let them see you put it inside the potty. They'll finally learn that poop should always go in the potty.

Also, if the potty isn't easily accessible, accidents may happen. Children have a hard time correctly recognizing the urge to go beforehand, so they may be hard-pressed before he eventually decides to use the potty. However, if they can't get to the potty on time, they may no longer be able to hold it in, thereby causing them to poop close to the potty instead. You should make sure that the potty chair is placed where the child can reach it easily. After getting a suitable location, make sure the potty is placed there consistently.

As we've said many times, you should make sure your child's underwear and clothes are easily removable. This will help your child hop into the potty on time as precious time won't be wasted on trying to get his clothes off. If it's too late for the child to hold it in, he may poop just before he sits on the potty.

Don't get worked up if he poops next to the potty instead of in it. When this happens, calmly correct them and motivate them to do better next time. Let him or her know you; we appreciate their effort in trying to use the potty instead of going in his underwear. Be patient with the child. Potty-training doesn't last forever, and you'll be over it in no time.

The Child is Very Stubborn

A stubborn child can seem impossible to potty train, and you may run out of options quickly as the child continues being headstrong. The child may counter every instruction you give him with a strong "No" and only accepts things on his terms. How then do you potty train such a child? You might be tempted to yell, spank the child, or punish him some other way. Potty-training, which should be fun for the child, now becomes a power tussle each day.

You should save yourself the stress of potty-training a child that isn't ready. If you decide to wait until the child is ready, in the meantime, you can prepare the child through some methods. You can get fun potty-training books or videos made for children.

Even when the child is ready for potty-training, you may still encounter some resistance. First, you should get rid of all the diapers in the house. Let the child be aware of this and calmly tell him diapers are no longer an option. With no other choice, the child will eventually cooperate.

If the child firmly refuses to sit on the potty, do not try to force him physically. If you do this, he will eventually develop an aversion toward the potty. It would also be best if you didn't get into a screaming match with the child when he refuses to sit. It's your job as an adult to manage the situation calmly. Motivate them with words instead.

You can also create an illusion of choice for the child. For example, you can say, "Will you sit on the potty or on the toilet seat?" The child will be happy to get to choose themselves and will then select one of the options. Get the child used to the process gradually instead of trying everything at once. However, it would be best if you were firm with your instructions and demands. Repeat them until the child eventually uses the potty or sits on the toilet. Do not bribe the child or let them manipulate you; this will only make the situation worse.

My Child Wets the Bed

Nighttime continence takes time. Even if your child has been toilet-trained for weeks, months, or even years, accidents will happen. But don't fret. A useful technique that is highly recommended is the 'last-minute pee.' This means before going to bed, and your child should use the bathroom. As the name suggests, this should be at the very last minute before they are getting into bed. This is often all it takes to help a child stay dry at night. Also, make sure you have a waterproof sheet protecting their mattress and consider investing in some nighttime diapers if you have exhausted the other options.

My Child has Autism

Autism, or autism spectrum disorders (ASD) need not be a barrier to potty-training, provided you heed the advice given throughout this book. Bear in mind that you should only potty train when your child is ready. Even if your child is still in diapers longer than other kids, don't worry. It's not a race.

Potty-training will also take a little longer for ASD kids, so be patient. Use your knowledge of your child's quirks to help the potty-training process. For example, if the diaper-free sensation is quite unbearable for your child, consider cutting a hole in the bottom of it.

Use the power of routine to familiarize your child with the toilet process and do everything in the exact same order.

It's useful to use visual cues to really cement this routine—create a poster or flow-chart to demonstrate what happens when you use a potty. Include things like "Johnny needs to do a pee" right up until "Johnny washes his hands." Get a few copies and place one in the bathroom, which can be easily seen, and another in another highly visible part of the house. Talk about it often and refer to the poster. It can also help your child draw accompanying pictures—this very action will often help to cement notions about the potty in their brain.

Use environmental cues to comfort your child: ensure that the bathroom is calm, peaceful, and quiet. Use lighting to add to the sense of calm, and consider placing the potty somewhere private for your child.

The child follows the potty routine at home but not at the daycare.

You may be fully satisfied with your child's potty-training progress at home, but the child doesn't follow the daycare routine. It may even look as if the child has never been introduced to potty-training. The first thing you should do is to find out the actual cause. I'll help explain some of the possible causes with the appropriate solutions just below.

First, the issue may be due to the changing of environment. The child might be used to the potty or toilet at home, his books and toys, and your ever-present self. The daycare might be a whole new experience for the child, with strange faces, different facilities, and the many other kids present too. The child may also not be able to follow the usual bathroom routine at the normal time he does while at home. All these can be very confusing and destabilizing for the child.

To help the child overcome this, you can meet with the provider to help make some adjustments to the potty routine at the daycare for your child. If the daycare provider permits, you can bring along the child's home potty and toys to give them a familiar feeling. Also, inform the provider about your child's current level of progress. The child shouldn't be placed on a toilet seat if he has just started using the potty. The provider should stick with what the child is capable of.

Also, a shy child might not speak up if he has to use the bathroom, mostly if the daycare is filled with unfamiliar faces. The child may not want these strange caregivers to see them naked. To help with this, meet with the caregiver in charge of your child and introduce them. Let the child get comfortable with them and tell them they are free to call for the caregiver if they need anything. You can also implore the caregiver to pay extra attention to your child.

At the daycare, the child may be around children who haven't been potty trained yet. Surrounded by diapers, your child may be tempted or influenced to go in his or her underwear to be like the other children. To prevent regression, you can meet the caregiver to come up with a suitable solution together. The child can either be grouped with other potty-trained children, or you can make a copy of the child's bathroom routine at home, which would be given to the caregiver. The caregiver can then make sure the child follows this routine carefully.

You should also request reports from the daycare periodically to know about the child's progress. You should reward the child whenever they have a dry day and motivate them if accidents happen.

You've tried to potty train the child previously and failed. How do you start over again?

First, starting potty-training when the child isn't ready is one of the most common reasons for potty-training failure. A toddler who is not physically and mentally prepared for potty-training will have a hard time learning the process. This time around, you should make sure the child is fully prepared for potty-training. You can take a little time before you start potty-training again after the previous failure.

Also, switching to using diapers once you get tired of cleaning up is sure to fail at potty-training. Lack of consistency is part of the common reason parents fail at potty-training. When you get ready to start afresh, you must be prepared to spend a whole lot of time on the process. Choose a period when you'll be completely available. You should follow consistent bathroom routines and potty rituals this time around.

Another reason you may fail at potty-training is if you make the process as a strict and serious one. If you force the child to do your bidding each time or punish the child whenever accidents happen, the child will not gain the necessary confidence to develop bathroom independence. Potty-training should be a fun and rewarding experience for you and the child. Make sure to get toys, stickers, and training products suited for the child this time around.

You might need to switch from the previous methods you used or make them more fun. Be ready to learn together with the child this time around. It would be best if you also let the child be involved in the process. You can give them simple chores such as getting the soap or toilet paper, or any other simple task. Reward the child when he completes these tasks successfully.

Let the child know in advance that you are about to resume potty-training. Make the process sound exciting for the child to make them more enthusiastic. Also, as a parent, make up your mind to complete the process this time around.

The child holds it in and refuses to go to the toilet.

According to North Fulton Pediatrics, more than five percent of children refuse potty-training. To overcome this, you have to look for the root cause of the problem—why the child has refused to poop.

Refusing to poop might result from anxiety, or the child may be scared of sitting on the potty or the toilet. When you then stop using diapers at the start of potty-training, the child is now left with no choice but to hold it in as a result of fear. It has also been suggested that holding it in might be a reaction to a bad experience with pooping. For example, when the child has suffered from constipation or other bowel issues and has gone through a painful bowel movement, he may associate the succeeding bowel movements with that memory.

The child may just refuse to poop as a way of rejecting potty-training. The child may refuse your instructions and prefer to hold it in instead as an act of defiance. Stool withholding can also be caused by constipation itself. The child may continue to withhold stool if he finds bowel movement difficult. The more the child withholds, the worse it becomes as stool starts getting compacted in the child's colon. Watery stool eventually leaks out without the child being able to control it. The muscles that control bowel movements might also be affected.

Forcing the child to poop won't work in correcting this, but there are practical ways you can get the child to resume normal bowel habits. If the stool withholding is a result of anxiety, continuously reassure the child and make them comfortable. A child needs to be relaxed to have a smooth bowel movement. Some children are scared of pooping in the potty or toilet as they see the poop as a part of themselves. You should explain to such a kid that poop needs to go to the bathroom to stay healthy.

Let the child talk about his worries, and while you reassure them, help and face them too. For example, if the child is scared of the toilet, you can sit on the toilet in front of them to assure or encourage them to sit while you hold them.

If the child withholds stool as a way of avoiding potty-training, carefully explain why he needs to go and look for ways to make potty-training fun for the child. Do not place pressure on them to use the toilet. After that, stop talking about the issue. If the stool withholding is due to constipation, you can make some changes to the child's diet. Also, increase his fluid intake if necessary. A medical professional may also prescribe stool softeners or mild laxatives to get the child to release his bowels.

CHAPTER 23:

Common Parenting Mistakes When Training Toddlers

I t is introduced to some of the mistakes parents make when training their little children. If you find yourself susceptible to any of these mistakes, you should navigate them with better strategies founded on a basic principle shown in the latter part of this study guide.

Distorting the Routine

Toddlers work at their best capacities when the routine is predictable. Whether it is sleep, food, or alertness, you have to know your toddlers' daily activities and make them repetitive. Some parents don't know the circadian rhythm of their toddlers. This is the internal clock in the brain of a person. It measures the consistencies in the sleepiness and activeness of a person at regular intervals. As a parent, you should monitor the characters in the sleep- and wake-cycle of your toddler, as well as yours.

Using a Method of Coercion

One of the parental attitudes that experts sorely disapprove of is one in which the parent pressures or coerces toddlers into doing an action. It doesn't matter whether your toddler's activity is coerced into doing is wrong or not; pressuring your toddlers is a vice that has lifetime detriments on them. Coercion has terrible effects on your toddler's eating attitude.

Modest Method of Coercion Bribery

Smart parents find a way around things. This is detrimental to the toddler's behavior. They often apply a subtle coercion method by promising the toddler a reward of a favorite food after eating a disliked food. According to psychologist Dr. Leann Birch of the Pennsylvania State University, if the promised food is dessert, it makes the toddler value dessert more than more nutritious foods like vegetables and meats.

Serving Toddlers Big Food Items

According to the American Dietetic Association in Chicago, parents tend to serve children's food items that are not compatible with their stomachs. When the food is relatively significant to the child, they feel intimidated and frustrated to complete a considerable meal's seemingly massive task.

Succumbing to Your Toddler's Denial of New Foods

This should not be mistaken for coercion. It merely means some parents make the mistake of not trying the law of consistency when introducing new foods to their toddlers.

As Dr. Birch notes, it may require between 10 to 15 times of presentation before a toddler can finally adopt a new food. Dr. Jean Skinner, another reputable dietitian at the University of Tennessee, also posits that to fulfill the necessary criterion of your toddlers eating a variety of foods, you need to offer a variety of foods consistently.

According to Satter, a display of hysterical happiness when the toddler finally accepts to eat a new food may also make the child avoid the food eventually.

Intolerance to Messy Mealtimes

Excessiveness is when you expect a toddler to keep all the table manners you have acquired in the social world. Many parents think the taste is the only way food is enjoyed. While this is true for an adult, it isn't the case for a toddler. According to experts in Food and Nutrition Science, children use many sensory organs to enjoy food. They tend to enjoy the food more when they play with it and get themselves all messy.

Many parents who express sore displeasure to these messy eating manners have the tendency to distort the enjoyment toddlers have when eating. For children, forget about table manners and let them eat. The nutrition they consume takes more importance than whether they eat neatly or not. Having seen some of the mistakes that parents make when training toddlers, it is also beneficial to see some general consequences.

Rigidly Rebuking Your Toddler's Mistakes

Correcting mistakes that are made is necessary, but when the scrutiny becomes intense, you may be digging a very deep pitfall for your toddlers in the future. Parents who take an extreme disciplinary approach to their children's mistakes usually have the conception that this will make them better and perfect.

When the kid eventually grows into an adult and makes mistakes, their sense of personal worth takes a dent. They punish themselves by subjecting their-self to self-flagellating thoughts, which is a gateway to depression. They take a rigid approach to correct themselves. In extreme cases, they may resort to self-harm. Other significant areas where parents often make mistakes are eating habits and toilet manners.

CHAPTER 24:

Children Discipline - Parenting Tips

Taking a solid stand is anything but an awful thing for most guardians to learn. Children need discipline. It shows them what is proper conduct - and what isn't. Some of the time, training is vital to teaching children results. Keep it brief, short, and regard the youngster's sentiments. Being exacting doesn't mean manhandling a tyke or deprecating them. It implies leading the pack to show them the proper behavior in a legitimate, aware, and safe way.

For such a large number of guardians, a dread of squashing a youngster's soul, or overpowering them with an excessive amount of cutoff points, make them take a rearward sitting arrangement on the order train, just to be looked with bratty, wild, and impolite children for a considerable length of time to come.

Children do not just need limits; they need them. It makes them feel safe, and indeed, even cherished. They haven't correctly figured out how to control their inclinations and wants yet, and look to you, the parent, as a manual for demonstrating to them what conduct is all right and what isn't. The order is more than an apparatus for creating respectful children - it's a device to creating balanced and genuinely sound children.

Picking the correct type of order might be one of the hardest things a parent needs to do. Each youngster is extraordinary, and keeping in mind that breaks may work superbly with one another may require a light tap on the behind occasionally to express what is on your account. Follow these essential hints from youngster advancement master T. Berry Brazelton, M.D.

Regard a Child's Stage of Development

Knowing why your little child keeps on playing in the can even after you've disclosed to them no multiple times may enable you to all the more likely arrangement with your disappointments and make sense of if your tyke is, in reality, being disobedient, or merely investigating their existence in a typical and healthy way.

Fit the Discipline to the Child's State of Development

Babies can frequently be occupied absent much flourish, while more seasoned children may require a break or other type of control to get them to stop what they're doing.

Make sense of what works best for each phase of a tyke's development for better outcomes.

Pick Discipline That Fits the Child

All you needed to do was shake your head at my girl in objection, and she'd started sobbing uncontrollably and stop what she was doing. Not so with my child.

He once stressed that his conduct would offend you, so he needs a more vigorous style to train him directly from off-base.

Try not to utilize a similar form of control for each youngster. The chances are it'll work for a few and nobody else.

Be a Good Role Model

When your tyke sees you lose your temper when you don't get your specific manner, think about what, they'll do likewise. Tell your children the best way to deal with dissatisfaction and disappointment by being a good role model.

Continuously Show Children Love and Tenderness

At the point when the Discipline Is Over. Regardless of whether it's time alone in their room or tap on the hand, dependably embrace your kid and strengthen the way that you adore them, notwithstanding when they resist. It's comforting to realize that you're still #1 in your parent's eyes - notwithstanding when you mess up.

While there are some substantial burdens to unforgiving physical discipline (forceful conduct, dread, slight), a few guardians have discovered that taking a stable remain (in a delicate and adoring way), can regularly yield superior outcomes over talking, over-clarifying and breaks ever will. In any case, when do you realize when you've turned out to be excessively exacting and unforgiving? Watch for these signs:

- A kid who is overly pleasant and calm since they're hesitant to commit an error.

- A youngster who is excessively delicate to even the littlest measure of analysis.

- A pitiful tyke.

- A youngster who demonstrates manifestations of moderate to severe pressure.

- A kid who is relapsing in conduct (potty preparing, freedom, problematic rest, and so forth).

In case you saw any of these signs, it might be an ideal opportunity to ease up a bit and reexamine the perfect approach to train and rebuff your youngster's lousy conduct.

Parenting Toddlers

In case you are a parent of babies, you realize how depleting life can be on an ordinary premise. There are some fundamental parenting methodologies that you can use to help influence life to be progressively reasonable when you have toddlers or youthful youngsters.

It is essential to realize how to parent your children admirably with the goal that both you and your young youngsters are more joyful and more advantageous. Rather than being overpowered by the duties and difficulties that are always being displayed, parents need to comprehend that "picking your parenting fights admirably" is generally fantastic guidance. Simplicity upon your desires and requests and figure out how to appreciate your children's extraordinary time.

Preparing

Since you realize that you need to watch out for your toddler (or the puppy may finish up with another shaded coat because of a new use of indelible marker), it very well may be hard to complete your work, for example, maintaining the house in control, cooking sound dinners. The sky is the limit from there. To keep the remainder of the house running smoothly, preparing is essential.

One approach to have solid suppers and tidbits prepared in a short time is to cut up your soil products when you return home from the market. Additionally, by making a twofold part of suppers, you can put half of the feast in the more refreshing for later use without the problem of setting it up once more.

By vacuuming, doing clothing, and other family unit errands when your toddler goes down for his rest every day, the house can likewise be kept in good condition. If you telecommute, this is also an excellent time to get up to speed with those telephone calls that require a calm family unit to finish them.

Control

Once in a while, the most challenging part about having a toddler is the consistent requirement for an order. These are the years when your sweet child figures out how to be confident out of the blue, pushing all limits with the feared word, "No!" Your toddler needs delicate, however firm, so he knows precisely where the breaking points are and that there are results each time that he/she ventures over the line. By being reliable, your toddler will discover that there is opportunity inside those limits and will step by step to quit pushing against them as regularly.

At long last, since toddlers will, in general, be debilitating, it is imperative to require investment out yourself when circumstances become difficult. It is all right to leave your screaming toddler in one room while you chill out to get it together before coming back to apply discipline.

Support self-dependence with your toddlers; however, much as could be expected. You will get a break, and they will appreciate having the option to encounter extra autonomy.

CHAPTER 25:

Parenting Tips for Teaching a Toddler

Toddlers can be testing and can similarly be a great deal of fun once you know how they think. Finding some crucial devices and systems to help through toddler times is all you have to appreciate this brief span. Keep in mind a little while later, and they will be on to the following stage with various difficulties for you.

There are many parenting tips for showing your toddler. The rundown is perpetual. Anyway, there are a couple of fundamental rules that can be extremely useful.

These are my five top child-rearing tips for showing your toddler. With these benchmark factors, instructing your toddler will be more straightforward.

Ensure your toddler has enough rest. We as a full capacity much better when we have had enough rest. Consider how you feel when you are overtired. It is difficult to focus; you think horrendous and attempt as you may; you can't work appropriately in some cases. Toddlers are adapting so much consistently.

Ensure you have enough rest. This is self-illustrative. You may need to reevaluate your family's rest propensities, and schedules in addition to it might take a short time to persuade it to be healthy. Anyway, the prizes will be justified, despite all the trouble.

As a parent, how you feel supporting how you think and believe and, eventually, how you treat your toddler.

Have reasonable desires for both yourself and your toddler. This implies that they know about the developmental ability of your toddler. Once in a while, we can expect excessively quite a bit of them, and they aren't prepared for it yet. Now and then, we likewise expect only overly much from ourselves as parents as well. Be delicate on yourself and recall being a parent is a learning knowledge as well. This is an occupation you will learn for a mind-blowing remainder.

Take care of yourself as an individual, not just as a parent. It is anything but difficult to become involved with merely being a parent. For some, out of the blue, their toddler is the focal point of everything they do. Remember that you are an individual in your very own right. By taking care of yourself and investing significant time from your toddler consistently, you will feel invigorated. You'll even value them more. It is somewhat similar to taking an occasion from your activity. When you return, you are progressively revived, roused, and appreciate it more. Significantly, you model self-consideration to your toddler. This additionally reflects self-regard. If you don't regard yourself, you can't expect any other individual to. Be a decent good example for your little child and help them develop into self-respecting, confident grown-ups.

Be a unified front with your accomplice. If you back one another up, it shows your toddler that they can't play you off one another and undermine what every one of your states. If you don't concur at the time, bolster one another and talk about it a while later. Toddlers are brilliant and can figure out how to be manipulative in all respects right off the bat. Recall that they realize you superior to anything you do and realize how to push your catches to get what they need.

These are the pattern parenting tips for showing your toddler. When you execute different procedures for teaching your toddler to expand on these, they will be bound to be successful because these nuts and bolts are set up.

7 Tips To Unleash The Child's Creative Potential

In this section, the tips are based on the recommendations of renowned French psychologist and psychologist Michèle Freud. These tips help to unleash the creative potential of every child.

1. Support Total Freedom

Creativity is expressed when it is not repressed. Give the child complete freedom to express himself/herself. Let the child pursue interests instead of forcing him/her to sit down and finish tasks that do not cater to their needs.

One of the most critical mistakes is limiting the child's interest. Many parents mean well when they try hard to mold their child into their own concept of who he/she should be. For example, parents often smother their child's creativity when they force them to memorize flags and country capitals. Sure, it may seem impressive for a 3-year-old to know all the flags and affluence, even all the train stops in a faraway foreign country. However, if the child isn't really interested, all that hard work will be a colossal waste. Worse, the child's potential can be seriously hampered by the adverse environment fostered by a forced activity. Developing a child's creativity is allowing the pursuit and expression of anything that interests the child. Allow the child to use anything within his/her disposal to pursue these interests. Provide paints, brushes, easels, sports equipment, musical instruments, blocks, rings, gardening tools, etc.

Let the child pursue his/her own interests, even if it changes frequently. For example, a child may be interested in dinosaurs. Provide materials that cater to this interest. Provide toys and books. Let the child watch child-friendly shows that discuss dinosaurs. Take him/her to a trip to the museum. If the child shifts interest to bugs, let the child pursue that as well. Do not force the child to keep working with dinosaurs. Replace available materials with ones that support this new interest.

Some parents are concerned if their child changes interests. They try to curb this by getting the child to focus only on one or two areas that they prefer. Research showed that people most likely to become Nobel Prize winners engage in multiple creative arts. Just look at Leonardo da Vinci. He was most known as a famous painter. However, he was also an inventor. He also dabbled in medicine, with his perfect illustrations of the human body parts he observed when he dissected cadavers. Einstein is a great mathematician and scientist. He was also a fluent violinist. Einstein learned the violin then stopped for many years before taking it up again to become a fluent violinist.

2. Encourage Personal Expression

A child must have an active role in choosing what activity to pursue. Parents only work by introducing options. The child ultimately decides.

For example, parents can show the child how to play with a xylophone, drums, keyboards, guitar, and violin. Choices shouldn't stop there. They should also offer other objects such as a ball, building blocks, construction playsets, music to dance to or sing along with, paints, dolls, etc. The more choices the child has, the greater the opportunities for expression and exploration of creative potential. Again, parents are just to help and direct the available child options. Parents should not impose what they want for their children. Creativity should be an initiative of the child.

3. Do not Judge The Quality of Results. Appreciate the Child Whatever the Results

Creativity is all about creating. It is not about reproducing what is already existing. With these concepts in mind, parents and teachers should not judge a child's results based on others' work. The child's painting should be appreciated as it is and not compared to how another child used better colors and techniques.

Teachers and parents should also remember that a child's creative expression is precisely that—an indication of how he/she sees the world or experience the activity. It is not about having a child to play Mozart exceptionally well but more about the child expressing himself/herself through music. What is more important is the experience and what the child learned through the experience, not an actual output to be graded, critiqued, and compared with others' work.

4. Recognize and Support Emotional Sensitivity

Children naturally fear anything new, as adults feel the same, too. Adults can help children feel more confident by explaining what to expect with an activity. Fear is significantly reduced when a person or a child knows what to expect.

With children, simple explanations may not always work. Take advantage of a child's imagination to help work out fears.

Tell a fantasy story about a hero/heroine who conquered his/her fear.

Teach the child to verbalize fear. This also helps deal with emotions. Verbalizing can start by letting the child describe what he/she feels. Teach the child to give a name to that feeling. This way, the unseen surface starts to take on a form through that name. The child can then handle it because it has an image he/she has created for that feeling. Something known is more comfortable to hold than something faceless, nameless, and entirely unknown.

5. Support the Development of The Senses

Teaching and educating a child is more than just chanting letters and numbers, memorizing tables, and recognizing colors and shapes. Education should also be a means for a child to unleash creative potential. For this to happen, a child has to have a variety of sensory experiences. These experiences cater to their development level. This period of discovery can be taken advantage of to help children develop and fine-tune their skills and discover and enhance their creative potential.

For example, toddlers are at a stage wherein they are just starting to discover what they can do. Learning to walk and run is an exciting time for them.

Finding out that they can manipulate objects in their environment gives them a sense of awe and ride in their newly discovered capabilities.

By giving them a safe environment to move around, children become more confident to discover more about the environment and about themselves.

By giving them access to objects that can help them hone their skills and express their creativity, children can find and unleash their potential.

For example, a toddler starts to learn that he/she can use his/her hands to paint with the bright, attractive paints. Give them access to toxic-free colors and provide an area where they are free to paint. This activity accomplishes two critical things.

One, painting activity is fun and allows a child to practice and develop motor skills. Dipping their hands in paint and gliding them over a canvas or paper is one way to practice visual-motor skills.

The bright paints stimulate their visual sense, helping them discover the differences in colors. The paint's texture teaches them that there are different textures in the world; some are wet and cold like the paints. Some are hard like a brush.

Some things are gooey. The smell can also be another sensory experience. The child becomes more exposed to different smells. This helps their brains start to distinguish the different scents.

6. Provide Freedom for Creativity

Safety is a primary consideration. However, do not overdo it. According to Michèle Freud, it is not ideal to confine children in too-safe spaces with items designed especially for them. This kind of environment produces a monotony.

Remember, again, that children are at a point in their lives where everything is new and ready to be discovered. At this stage, the child has to be exposed to various objects to discover, learn, and be creative. Monotony kills the child's initiative to discover and create. Even adults get bored with the same things every day.

Go for variety. Children at a stage where everything new and exciting. Keep feeding their excitement and give them a variety of activities and interests to pursue. Once they grasp things they can do and start to discover that they can do creativity, they will naturally come out. Soon, children will return to some of their toys and find new ways to use or play with them.

7. More on "Real" Toys Than "Educational Games"

Educational games have become a go-to for many parents. They think that these are the best toys they can give their children in order to raise them smart and creative.

According to Michèle Freud, educational toys are not exactly what parents expect them to be. In fact, these educational toys can hamper creative potential. These toys were designed to be used in specific ways only. That leaves very little room for individuality. Once the child has discovered how the education toy works, there's nothing else to do with it. There is no room for creativity. There are no opportunities to discover new ways to use the objects.

One example is a book with buttons. A child presses these buttons and sounds, such as animal sounds, are heard. These are good books for younger children because they are engaging. Parents can read books and retain the child's interest in these sounds. However, once the story has been read more than a few times, the child can get bored. The once-exciting sounds no longer hold their interest. When this time comes, the book no longer has any other use for the child. Unless, of course, years later, when the child starts to learn to read. By that time, this book may not even be appropriate for the child's age and level.

An example is a set of building blocks. It's a set that a child can see many potential ways to play with. A child can stack these largest to smallest or reverse to practice balance and size dimensions. The child can use it to build, such as a pyramid or a cube or some other project. The blocks can be used for learning geometry, for instance.

Toys like these are better than the popular educational toys in the market. These do not dictate how it can be played. Instead, it's the child who gets to think of ways, creative ways to work with them.

CHAPTER 26:

Tips to Help Your Toddler Grow Up Happy

I s it challenging to be a mom? Fresh parents aren't carrying a book. It's our responsibility to do the best care job we can do. And this is a huge responsibility. A child was born with a clear mind and a clear conscience. The people guide them around them. Self-esteem depends on how the parents and primary caregivers treat themselves, their siblings, and them. That is so significant! Here are some tips for helping your child grow well, happy, and secure:

- Be aware that treating your child with respect and understanding is the most critical thing you can do for him/her. They study all the time. We should give them limits (which they need), without their self-respect being taken away.

- When they have something to say, listen to them.

- Inspire them to learn something new, or to get a job finished.

- Include those decisions in family decisions that affect them. In terms of rights, they are equal to us. They are all tiny humans.

- Teach them how to tell the truth of what happens to them. Teach the kids how to connect, and everyone gets an opportunity to express themselves.

- Again, note that a child's self-esteem level affects all their emotions, feelings, acts, and consequences for the rest of their life. Be tender with your affection, and be kind.

Having a parent is one of the best roles a human may have. Having acceptable parenting practices is essential to help your child grow up into a positive and self-reliant adult. Feeling good about yourself is necessary to be a happier person and a prosperous one in life. Your child has typical struggles and critiques to go through. To help them understand their imperfections, you have to consider positive parenting strategies and appreciate the qualities that make them unique. Here are some matters you can say to encourage them to grow up.

You are Destined to Be Unique

Naturally, some people take a look at what other people lack. This causes jealousy and envy, which isn't right. Rather than focusing on comparing your kids, just be thankful for whom they are. Think of them as unique people who have their way of making themselves stand out. Cheer and appreciate their distinctive talents.

Know Your Assets

Let them see it after you've realized just how good your kids are. A good way is to sit with them, get a pen and paper, and write down their properties. Help them know what kind of person they are, what they can do what is unique about them. Highlight their strengths, their ambitions, their successes, and their visions. Knowing where they stand out is the starting point for confidence in them. A sense of direction can boost their overall perspective on life.

Take Good Care of Yourself

There's nothing wrong with having yourself pampered. You can get to places by possessing a happy spirit, a balanced body, and a content soul. Invite them to do just that. Prepare veggies for dinner, buy them supplements, and create a regular family workout regimen. Teach them how to handle disincentives, failures, and confusion.

Even if trials come their way, make sure there's always hope as long as they keep an eye on themselves and don't let them crush these trials.

Accept Yourself

If you don't see it yourself, you can't make other people see your worth. Let them know they shouldn't be affected by what other people say about them. If they realize who they are and embrace themselves, they will benefit from any decision they make. Tell them what makes them happy and stick to that.

Below are A Few Tips to Help You Achieve That Goal

- Play with your child and use their name when you address them. That will make them feel unique and affectionate.

- It is encouraging when a good job is done, motivating when it's needed, and praising them for making an effort.

- When speaking with your child, always be sincere. If you just say the words and don't really pay attention, they'll know you don't mean it, and it'll lose its effectiveness.

- Reward good behavior, and discipline the child when necessary, naturally within reason.

- If something fails, let them know it's okay. They just need to make a little better preparation and try again. There's nothing wrong with occasionally failing as long as you've exhausted your best and strive to succeed in the future for betterment.

- When they talk to you, please pay attention, and engage in conversation by asking them questions. This helps develop their communication abilities and shows them how to engage in contact with others.

- Even if you disagree with something they do or believe in, let them know you value their opinions and justify why you disagree with them.

- Teaching self-confidence in your child is a vital part of their life, and they need to grow into a muscular, healthy adult. They should respect themselves and others and be proud of who they are but, at the same time, be respectful and sympathetic to others.

- Nevertheless, self-esteem should not be mistaken as vain or egotistic. There is a significant difference between raising optimistic children and brat, self-centered men. To instill the little one's self-esteem means we show them how to feel confident and content with who they are.

CHAPTER 27:

Consequences from Improper Training of your Toddlers

P arents must acknowledge that they are the ultimate reference materials for their children. To this end, the parenting method adopted in the children's training has long-term and short-term effects on them. In this chapter, you'll be shown some of the general consequences that follow your toddlers' improper parenting. According to the 2011 report by the UK's Department of Education, it is understood that the conduct of children who had improper parental guidance been twice as worse as the average child. This was traced to inappropriate parenting involving physical punishment, verbal abuse, coercion, lack of interaction, and inadequate supervision.

Greater Vulnerability to Psychological Disorders

In a child development journal, it is understood that children who are directly or indirectly exposed to physical or verbal abuse at their early age have a higher risk of having psychological disorders. In this study, there was no prevalence when psychological diseases are placed in comparison. However, these psychological disorders were all traced to factors in the early stage of children's development. It was found that the relationships with siblings in the family they come from, or relationships with their parents had been damaged. According to the Child Abuse & Neglect Journal, studies show that children who have been victims of abuse display post-traumatic stress disorder for a substantial period of their lifetime.

Defiance to Laws

Because of a research article published in the International Journal of Child, Youth and Family Studies, it is found that children who suffered parental negligence in their early days were more susceptible to being charged for juvenile delinquency. In this study, researchers were directed to investigate the connection between parental oversight and juvenile delinquency. Although, some of the intellectual gaps identified in that study have been filled in other studies.

One of these studies is the research published in Behavioral Sciences & the Law Journal. In that study, it was found that mothers who had once been charged with juvenile delinquency commonly give birth to or nurture children with antisocial attitudes and tendencies to defy laws. According to the study, this was traced to parental abuse and negligence. In such cases, the problems of defiance to laws may be generational.

Depression

In the 'Annual Reviews' the publication titled, "Parenting and Its Effects on Children: On Reading and Misreading Behavior Genetics," Professor Eleanor E. Maccoby of Stanford University explains that one of the causal factors of depression in children is parental adverse reactions towards their children. This line of thinking was also contained in a National Institute of Health journal submission by Danielle In the article, H. Dallaire, "Relation of Positive and Negative Parenting to Children's Depressive Symptoms." With these distinctive, credible reports reaching similar conclusions, it is hard to doubt that it is indeed proper that factors such as overall support, verbal condemnation, physical punishment, and even depression of the parents are causal to the depression of a child.

Failure to Thrive

One of the implications of failure to thrive in toddlers is the retardation of mental growth, physical growth, and the possibility of malnutrition. According to research submitted to the American Journal of Orthopsychiatry, it was learned that failure to thrive in toddlers is ultimately linked to parental negligence. Children who are victims of "failure to thrive" are found to have lacked good nutrition that is essential for healthy growth. This reduces their standard growth rate. A publication in the journal Pediatrics also traced the failure to thrive syndrome in toddlers to medical child abuse. It is found that parents who impose unnecessary medical treatments on their children make them vulnerable to the syndrome. In cases where your toddlers find it difficult to thrive, you need to check the medical procedures you have been exposing them to and the measure of care you show them.

Aggression

According to Rick Nauert's Psych Central article, "Negative Parenting Style Contributes to Child Aggression," the various research conducted by different specialists at the University of Minnesota all had similar conclusions; toddlers who were aggressive and quick to anger all had poor interactions with their mothers. The conclusion was that one of the effects of bad parenting on toddlers is an aggression on the children's part. The mothers studied treated their children aggressively, were verbally hurtful, and harmful towards their children. The more negative parenting, the greater the child's aggression to colleagues. This created a certain level of hostility between mothers and toddlers. Though, more research is now invested into knowing whether the relationship of the toddlers' fathers with their mothers influence on the bad conduct of the mothers towards their children is.

Poor Academic Performance

One of the consequences of parental neglect is the gross reduction in the toddlers' academic performance. This view is credited to a study conducted and published in the Child Abuse and Neglect Journal.

The study concludes that when parents have minimal interactions with their children, it impairs the children's' learning ability compared to their peers. The children also lack social relationships. Further research shows that neglect is no less disastrous than physical abuse in terms of the toddlers' academic performance.

According to another study in the journal Demography, children whose parents frequently relocate or migrate also tend to poor performance in school. The truth is constant relocation is usually a factor that is above the power of the parents. Nonetheless, it may have detrimental consequences on the child's educational growth.

In terms of children's mathematical performance, research has shown that the parents' mathematical interests can determine whether they are good at it. According to Melissa E. Libertus, an Associate Professor at the University of Pittsburgh said the connection is either environmental or hereditary. In this light, parents that are easily provoked at their child's academic performance in mathematics should know it might have genetic or ecological causes. Having seen some of the behavioral, cognitive and social consequences of improper parenting, it is time you were introduced to a grand principle for training your toddlers.

CHAPTER 28:

Managing Choice and Freedom

In my experience as a teacher, I found that many students came into the classroom, knowing exactly what they wanted to work on. If there was a science experiment going on in the corner, many students would come in and check on that first. Others would head straight to the reading corner. Some students loved to see what the latest materials were on the practical life shelves in the preschool classroom. Nearly all of them loved beginning sewing lessons. Throughout the day, children move from one activity to the next in a series of decisions they make largely on their own. Students are invited to presentations with the teacher who carefully guides and orchestrates the activity in the classroom.

Choice and freedom in the classroom can be overwhelming for some students, hindering their productivity and ability to progress. This can happen for both neurotypical and children with ASD. What can we do to support choice and freedom at home and at school?

In this chapter, we'll discuss the importance of freedom and choice in Montessori and learn why this can be challenging for ASD students. Then, I'll offer some strategies for increasing your child's ability to manage freedom and choice.

Freedom and Choice in the Montessori Method

In our lives as adults, we make decisions frequently. It's an essential survival skill. But, even many adults struggle with choices. For example, prioritizing a task list incorrectly can mean you need to stay up late to finish a project due at work the next day. Or, a struggle to choose what to purchase at the grocery store can reveal that we haven't prepared ahead of time with a meal plan or even taken a quick inventory of the pantry. These seemingly mundane skills all boil down to choices we make that can enhance or add stress to our lives.

The Montessori method aims to prepare students to handle complex decision-making from the very beginning of their schooling. Beginning with choice in activities (as long as certain routines and rules such as cleaning up are being followed), students are slowly given more responsibility. In the elementary years, Montessori students are encouraged to organize and execute field trips to nearby attractions or community institutions. By middle school, they might plan a trip that lasts a few days and involves several travel hours. The ultimate goal? Confident adults who are skilled at managing decisions in their lives, from buying groceries to making career choices.

How does freedom manifest itself exactly? Every Montessori classroom is unique. Yet, they all have the thread of freedom in common that's a function of the classroom setup and teachers' guidance. Shelves of materials, books, and command cards are arranged according to the subject area. After receiving a presentation, children are free to work with the material as they please, as long as another child isn't using it. Starting in elementary grades, lists, work plans, or student-teacher meetings are sometimes used to help track progress.

This ability to handle freedom responsibly doesn't come automatically. Rules and routines are taught in the classroom so that students know the classroom expectations. Using a rug or table for work, cleaning up each material after using it, and placing it correctly when done is basic. Students must also use a quiet voice in the classroom, avoid disturbing others, and wait their turn to use materials that others are using. Only some materials and activities can be used or done in pairs or groups.

The Prepared Environment

Why did Montessori include this element in her classroom design? In addition to believing that freedom and choice are important life skills to learn how to handle, she also knew that allowing space in the classroom also goes hand in hand with following the child. You can't follow the child if they are entirely restricted. Montessori carefully orchestrated the freedom and choices that children would have in the classroom.

She did this by building a prepared environment, the classroom, for the children she was working with. Distractions were kept to a minimum, with no loud, glitzy posters or excessive noise. Instead, the children's attention was drawn towards the learning materials, which were the most exciting.

Create Structure With a Chart

When a child arrives as a newcomer to a Montessori program, it's not uncommon to limit choices. Having the child use items from an individual shelf or providing additional guidance and support when picking materials is quite familiar. For children with ASD, this approach is a good start, but working out a routine and representing that visually is often the most helpful. For pre-literate or non-verbal children, images, or pictures of the materials used can be printed to create the schedule. These sorts of supports can be beneficial for adapting to this new way of doing things.

Also, some children may benefit from additional structure. For example, Lois Ormonde noted that she and her student often used a silent timer to encourage him to complete tasks. I also noticed the difference between two students on the ASD spectrum during my time teaching in the lower elementary classroom. While one student struggled to finish tasks, another finished them without any external intervention at all. However, the first student was highly motivated by creating a checklist of the work he wanted to complete and then crossing off each activity as he finished it.

Likely, be a different, unique solution for each child with autism. All children are individual, and what motivates them, makes them tick, and makes learning enjoyable.

Slowly Offer Choice

Over time, you can gradually offer the child some choice in the activities. First, you might provide that the child changes the order of the routine. Or, you may consider offering two new materials and have the child choose which one to try that day. In this way, the child slowly takes more control over their learning.

Why offer the choice if things are going well with structure and support? The externally imposed system requires constant reliance on an adult or outside force to regulate what's going on. To achieve true independence, children must be able to make decisions and make use of freedoms. By starting in a safe, controlled environment and slowly shifting the responsibility of choices to the child, greater independence is achieved.

Observe

Make sure you keep observing the child, ensure that needs are being met. For example, you may discover that a weekly schedule should also be posted somewhere in the room for the child to see in addition to a daily schedule. Or, perhaps you'll learn that the child is very motivated in some academic areas and can be allowed more excellent choice within specific subject areas. Most importantly, the child should be viewed as the leading indicator of what's working well or not so well. Changing several items in a routine at once could be stressful for one child, but could mean improvements for another. With careful observation, you can help guide a shift to greater independence and freedom.

Allow Observing

A critical element of a Montessori classroom is the opportunity that the children have to observe one another. Children are free to watch another child working, as long as they are respectful and don't interfere. Montessori believed that this was a vital motivating factor, especially for the younger students in the mixed-age classroom. Many students with autism, as well as neurotypical children, benefit greatly from observing. In addition to Montessori's insights on keeping in the school, a wealth of autism experts and organizations agree that allowing students to watch before being asked to try something can be very helpful. Lois Ormonde shared, "What worked for my student was I would model what he should do. Then, he would practice until he could do it." The organization, Montessori Education for Autism, also agrees, arguing that some students with autism may engage in "third party participation," observing other students use a material many times. Even if the child never decides to use the material on their own, they can benefit from this interaction.

While limits on observing should be imposed when children interrupt or distract others. Children with autism can become unobtrusive observers and gain much from the ability to stand-by and watch others when participating is too tricky.

Over time, with guidance, most children can gain greater independence and make more and more choices in the classroom or their education. By empowering children to make decisions with regards to their knowledge, their agency can be increased.

Conclusion

P arenting can be extremely challenging. However, by taking the steps that you have learned in this book, you can make it a lot easier. You no longer must question every decision that you make when it comes to raising your children. You don't have to feel as if you are failing any longer.

I hope this book was able to guide you through discipline strategies for toddlers. Rather than yelling or spanking, it would be best if you now had the tools you need to raise your toddler more lovingly. The discipline strategies discussed in this book should help you focus on disciplining your child, so they make positive decisions—whether you are looking over their shoulder or not.

Furthermore, this book should have helped you gain insight into the inner workings of your toddler's mind. Your toddler is still growing on the outside, and parents must remember that so is their brain. Toddlers cannot always follow the rules the first time or control their impulses or emotions. By employing the right discipline strategies and being consistent, caretakers can lead their children to a way of making decisions that encourage self-control.

The next step is to take what you have learned and use it to raise your toddler. As you set proper rules and follow through on the consequences you have set for your toddler, and you will notice a turnaround in their behavior. Likewise, by understanding their mindset and how your toddler thinks, you can appreciate their strange actions— which aren't that strange! Remember that you can always speak to your pediatrician if you have concerns, especially if your toddler is going through a difficult time or acting out in an exceptionally violent manner. There is always an answer when it comes to toddler discipline.

Every parent should remember that toddlers are just learning to explore the world. By encouraging healthy guidelines and allowing your toddler to study without giving them control of the house, you can promote healthy development and teach lifelong lessons that will lead your toddler to success. The guidelines provided in this book will strengthen your relationship, encouraging healthy communication, and allow your toddler to thrive socially and emotionally. You now have the tools in your box to be the parent your tot needs. You can start implementing all the strategies in the various situations when they arise, so you know you are raising a happy, healthy tot with confidence, responsibility, respect, and curiosity intact.

Remember the golden steps to listen, repeat, offer a solution, and correct the behavior over the long term rather than hoping one lesson will do. Your toddler is fantastic and deserves respect in everything he does, even if there are times when you need to use kind-ignoring to reset the brain into a calmer one that listens to you as much as you listen to your toddler.

You have the power to shape your child or hurt your tot. Reading through the information and strategies, you must be the one to implement what you learned positively, even using reverse psychology to keep your child interested and learning. Whether you are looking to teach moral values, respect, good ways, or confidence, the tools are within these pages for you to continue referring to as needed.

Enjoy this time in your toddler's life, where anything and everything can be exciting, fun, and entertaining. As your child grows, they will calm down, stop getting into everything, but will still need your love and affection. Love and respect are the two things you should never withhold, even in the throes of upset.

Good luck on your journey with your pretty toddler.

Part 2

TODDLER DISCIPLINE

Effective Guilt-Free Strategies for Toddler's
Tantrums. Learn Positive and Kind Ways to Create
Discipline in and Out of Home to Help Your Child
Grow Happy and Confident.

Introduction

Are you experiencing a tantrum atmosphere from your kids? What should you do? The teeth-jarring, ear-shattering, supersonic scream seems to pierce through the air when toddlers began their rampage of a never-ending temper tantrum. You would rather wish to join a zoo or a circus if it was a real option to get away from those little hooligans.

Raising toddlers is not an easy task. Raising your children is going to be the most challenging job you have ever had. Yet, it is also going to be the most rewarding and will give you more memorable experiences and memories than you could ever imagine. You live for your children in many ways; most parents do. We are very proud when it comes to our children, and these are excellent factors to have as parents.

Before you jump into disciplining and correcting your child for their misbehaviour, it is essential to see a more in-depth experience of what is going on in their minds. While you cannot let your child do whatever they want, you must also show empathy for their thought processes and all their emotions for the first time. It will make a deeper connection between you and your child. It will also build the type of relationship that helps you discipline while remaining supportive and understanding.

Along this journey, you will experience your good moments and your bad moments. Things may be going smoothly at one point, and then be completely turned on its head the next. One issue that parents can struggle with is toddler discipline. It is any parent, not just new parents. One form of toddler discipline may work on one toddler but will be completely ineffective on another.

You must understand that your toddler is still in the initial phases of developing their sense of self and will want to do everything for themselves. They might want to do things that they aren't fully capable of doing yet. It, in turn, might be a source of frustration. It, when combined with the fact that they aren't fully able to communicate verbally, means that they will start venting out their frustrations by throwing tantrums and by indulging in unruly behaviour.

It would be best if you always remembered while dealing with a toddler that it might not be their intention to misbehave. The way they behave is essentially their response to a situation. They are responding in the best way their underdeveloped maturity allows them to. So, you must be quite empathetic and understanding whenever you're dealing with your toddler. You must be aware of all that your toddler is going through along with their developmental growth. By becoming aware of these factors, it becomes easier to respond to them while disciplining them.

All children love attention, and a toddler's desire for attention is unlike any other. Being ignored is something your toddler cannot stand. Regardless of whether the attention he gets is positive or negative, he craves it. Most of the unacceptable behaviour displayed by toddlers is usually their cry for attention. They like being showered with constant attention. When this supply of attention is limited because of any reason, they engage in such behaviour that shifts the focus back.

There is no cookie-cutter approach to discipline a child, but choosing to balance love and firmness is the first step to raise beautiful children. Parenting toddlers is not easy. Still, this challenging phase is a lovely opportunity for you and your child to create memories, learn together, discover the world through his innocent eyes, and develop a strong connection. Remember that in life, the most important things are usually tricky and challenging to do and achieve. But behind the constant pressure to do the right thing is the silver lining, the goal to raise a resilient, responsible, and well-rounded child that can handle himself and the world as he grows older.

CHAPTER 1:

What is Discipline?

D isciplining toddlers pose significant challenges for parents. Toddlers are notorious for continually testing the boundaries set by their moms or dads. The fact that toddlers cannot communicate their feelings or thoughts becomes a real challenge for parents who want their kids to behave well or obey their instructions to prevent them from harm.

It is the parents' job to teach your child the difference between acceptable and unacceptable behaviour. Getting your child to behave the way you would like them to act is not as hard as you think. Learning takes time, and several weeks will go by when working on good behaviour before you see a change. It will be challenging, but try not to get frustrated if you don't see results right away.

What is Discipline?

Discipline is technically a method or a set of strategies used to prevent, resolve, or correct behavioural problems. The term originated from the Latin word "discipline," which means training and instruction. Its root word is "d'isere" or "to learn."

Primary Objectives of Discipline

1. Instill sound morals

2. Develop desirable behaviours

3. Modify unacceptable behaviours

4. Protect the child's emotional and mental health

5. Keep and enhance a close relationship with him

Parents use it to teach their kids about rules, guidelines, principles, expectations, and consequences. Toddlers do not have the essential skills to handle social situations or act appropriately. Parents need to guide and help their children learn desirable behaviour that will make them feel good and accepted. Discipline is not a one-time practice, but a continuing effort to develop and entrench good social habits to children.

Discipline Versus Punishment

Distinguishing the difference between discipline and punishment is critical for parents and caregivers. It is vital to remember that discipline is about teaching the child of appropriate and acceptable manners or behaviours. Punishment is about enforcing disciplinary consequences that may include spanking, verbal admonishment, and other punitive acts that hurt the child physically or emotionally.

The methods of disciplining the child vary due to cultural differences, beliefs, educational attainment of parents, customs, and values. In

Western countries, the debate over corporal punishment continues, while embracing other nations turn to "positive parenting" techniques.

Over time, history displays variation in discipline methods:

- **Medieval Times**. Children during these periods were subject to corporal punishment at home and throughout society. The primary reason why parents resort to harsh discipline was to ensure that their kids would have a place in heaven.

- **Colonial Times**. The Puritans in the United States during these times practised harsh punishments, which include beating children, even for minor infractions. Young children were allowed to play freely, but older children expected to be accountable and learn adult chores.

- **Pre-Civil and Post-Civil War Times**. During this slavery era in the United States, the prevalence of corporal punishment became common among African American families. The traditional styles of parenting were affected by the violent suppression of West African cultural practices. Parents are forced to teach children to display desirable behaviour when facing white people and expect dehumanizing actions that include sexual, emotional, and physical violence. Even after the Proclamation of Emancipation, which ended slavery, many Afro-American parents still used corporal punishment out of fear that if they did not, this would put their family at risk of discrimination and violence.

- **The Twentieth Century**. In the early part of the 20th century, the child-rearing experts advocated adopting proper habits in disciplining kids and abandoning the romantic view of childhood. The Infant Care, a 1914 U.S. Children's Bureau pamphlet, admonished parents who played with their babies and urged them to follow a strict schedule.

Unfortunately, up to this day, some people consider punishment and discipline synonymous. According to the Thesaurus, control is geared on self-control and regulation, while punishment is more about abuse or sentence.

But in reality, discipline is positive guidance that trains and teaches the child to develop abilities to manage his emotions and learn to make smart decisions that are acceptable to society. Whereas, punishment is about regulating or controlling the child's behaviour by injecting fear and imposing physical or emotional consequences that include spanking, hitting, name-calling, prohibiting privileges, shaming, and withholding affection. Discipline encourages the thinking brain to learn and adopt a new practice. Punishment inflicts pain or suffering for the action hoping to modify future behaviour.

Discipline teaches a child to behave according to the rules and focus on future behaviour. Punishment invokes fear of consequence to the emotional mind.

While punishment makes the child behave when you are present, it may result in the formation of behaviour that is manipulative, challenging, or defiant. Also, it can discourage him from attempting to try new things because of fear to bring disappointment, pain, or shame to the family.

To be effective, discipline must be:

- Administered by an adult who has an affective bond with the child (parents, teacher, or caregiver)

- Perceived by the child as reasonable and fair

- Consistent and appropriate for the behaviour that requires a change

- Self-enhancing or leading to becoming self-disciplined

- Temperamentally and developmentally appropriate

The primary goal of discipline is to guide the child to fit into the real world effectively and happily. It serves as the foundation of the development of self-discipline. It is not about forcing him to obey the rules, instead of teaching him what is right and what is not. Parents should make sure that while they are enforcing discipline, children should know that they love, trust, and support them. Trust is vital for adequate control. A harsh punishment that uses verbal abuse, name-calling, humiliation, or shouting will make it difficult for children to trust and respect the parents.

There is no shortcut for disciplining the child. Raising your children to become emotionally mature requires time and a significant amount of energy to teach acceptable behaviours and limits. It is a pleasure to see your child shows assertiveness without being aggressive, knows how to postpone self-gratification, tolerates discomfort when it is necessary and considerate of others' feelings or needs. All these are the outcomes of the firm and loving discipline.

An effective discipline sustains mutual respect between the parent and the child. The interventions should enforce consistently and reasonably that ensure his protection from danger and help him develop a sense of control, responsibility, self-discipline, and a healthy conscience. Any inconsistency will confuse the child, regardless of his developmental stage. It will also lessen your effectiveness as a role model or enforcer of discipline.

Some factors that affect the consistency of discipline are cultural differences between parents and disagreements on child-rearing strategies. Often, to resolve the disputes, parents seek the help of the pediatricians who can suggest practical ways to discipline the child using the principles that are supported by academic literature and research.

Discipline for Early Toddlers (1-2 years old)

At 12-18 months old, the toddler is not yet capable of controlling his response because of the undeveloped frontal lobe of the brains. This part is responsible for some aspects of emotions, along with other functions. During this stage, toddlers experience extreme emotions, crying, or acting out when tired, scared, hungry, want something, sick, overwhelmed, and need a diaper change.

Toddlers usually are experimenting and exercising their wills to gain control. It is necessary to exercise parental tolerance and enforce disciplinary interventions only when necessary to prevent destructive behaviour, limit aggression, or keep them safe.

A firm "No," a brief explanation of why it is not allowed, like "No, hot!" or removing your child from the situation, typically works. It is also important to supervise the activities of the child to make sure that the behaviour will not recur and, at the same time, show that you are not withdrawing your love and support. Young toddlers are susceptible to fear of abandonment. Often, you are at a loss of what he wants, so you need to skilful and observant to figure out what he wants.

Discipline for Late Toddlers (2-3 years old)

Your two-year-old child begins to understand and use language to express his emotions and wants. However, do not expect him to think logically, follow complicated directions, or predict his actions. He can follow simple instructions, but somehow forgets what he is doing. During this stage, he also learns to give orders, demands, and show aggression. It is usual for toddlers to be short-tempered because of low frustration threshold and little impulse control. A 3-year-old toddler can communicate his wishes and needs clearly, but his logical thinking skill remains underdeveloped. He often gives in and follows his impulses, but can remember simple rules. It is the period where he enjoys hearing the same stories and songs over and over again, loves routines, and learns by repeating sounds. During this period, the struggle to be independent, assertive, and master some skills continues. When the child meets some limits, he becomes frustrated that usually leads to temper outbursts or tantrums. Parents should realize that the acts do not necessarily mean willful defiance, disobedience, or anger and understand the real reason for the behaviour.

It is necessary to continue setting routines and limits and have a realistic expectation of what they can do. Do not expect your toddler to regulate or control his behaviour by giving directions or verbal prohibitions alone. It is vital to supervise and redirect him into another activity to prevent temper flare-ups. By knowing the pattern of the child's reactions, you can avoid tantrums and other misbehaviour. Parents need to be consistent during this time when instilling discipline. If you say NO, mean it and avoid changing your response when the child starts to throw a tantrum or whine. The objective of disciplining your child is not to punish, but to improve the child and help them act like they are supposed to. Since child discipline, at times, is indeed one of the least fanciful aspects of parenting, the challenge that comes with it might make you want to think that it is impossible to discipline your child without punishing them. The truth is, resorting to punishment is not an excellent way to teach a lesson to your kids. You might interview some parents, and you want to confirm what pattern of discipline they use. You might hear them say: "I use them interchangeably." But the right question is, are those words synonyms? Obviously no!

But why is it that the objectives of disciplining are never to punish? When a parent punishes a child, the child would undoubtedly be physically affected. Moreover, in most cases, the brain is involved. All parents would desire a healthy mind for their kids.

Additionally, punishment is fear-based. And constant fear is not healthy for the brain. But sadly, many parents hope that threatening as part of a sentence will instill fear, and that., in turn, will discard that undesired behaviour and pick up a desired one.

Little wonder that they didn't realize that they are unknowingly messing up their kid's brain. It is capable of mental disorder, stress hormone elevation, emotion dysregulation, and externalizing behaviour. In some cases, they become bullies or victims. In sharp contrast to punishment, discipline improves a child's well-being. It allows a child to focus on the right lesson; they avoid being vindictive, distrustful, and spiteful.

CHAPTER 2:

Types of Discipline

C hildren are fantastic. They have a natural curiosity, innocence, and energy which allows them to see the world in unique ways. Toddlers are at the very beginning of a beautiful journey; to them, the world is full of new and exciting experiences. Unfortunately, toddlers and even young children aren't aware of the dangers which exist in the world around them, so it's your responsibility as a parent to guide them and keep them safe.

Discipline means creating a set of rules and guidelines to help your child grow into a healthy and considerate adult. More importantly, the domain will ensure that your child does not run into the road, randomly hit strangers, or even throw food around in a restaurant. Good discipline will allow you to go out to various places with your toddler and enjoy the experience.

Unfortunately, it is simply not possible to draw up a standard set of rules which will miraculously provide you with the perfectly behaved child. Every toddler is different. The influences and pressures placed on them will vary according to the pressure on you and your approach to each issue. The guidelines you must create and enforce will continuously be changing!

Good discipline is established by reacting positively to any situation and explaining why a specific type of behaviour is necessary. It is also beneficial for your toddler to understand that there are consequences for not behaving correctly. Likewise, results must be relative to the issue, and you must carry through with it when your toddler has continued to misbehave. If you can't enforce the consequence, your child won't have any incentive to behave respectfully. Even when it's difficult to see your child upset, you must be aware that you're thinking of their future, which is more significant than anything else.

Types of Discipline

It should now be evident that there are several different approaches to disciplining your child. There isn't one specific type which has been proven "better," and many parents will find that they have a preferred method but use a little of each approach:

Positive Parenting

It is one of the better-known approaches and is being proven to have positive effects. Oregon State University started a research project in 1984 with 206 boys, which they felt were at risk of juvenile delinquency; the children met with the researchers every year until their 33rd birthday. The research has shown that positive parenting can improve behaviour and interactions between generations.

As its name suggests, this approach to parenting and discipline relies on being favourable to your child as much as you can. As a parent, you'll seek to remain calm, regardless of the situation. In return, traditional punishments, such as removing love or toys, stay as the idea is that your child will respond to you because of the bond you have with them and because they want to.

Reward and Punishment

This approach to discipline involves creating the rules you expect your child to abide by the following. If they don't behave according to these rules, you remove an item from them for a set amount of time; this will usually be their favourite toy. If you adopt this approach, you'll need to be consistent—once you have said you'll remove the item, you must do so. However, this can often lead to another issue. A toddler may begin to realize that this is a result of their behaviour, yet this won't stop them from being upset, and you'll then need to decide whether to comfort them or not.

Research suggests that this is the fundamental flaw with this type of parenting because most parents will not wish to remove a toy as it feels wrong. Unfortunately, if you say you're going to do something and then don't, you will have just taught your toddler that they can push it further the next time. Equally, if you remove the item and then comfort your upset child, you will be effectively rewarding their bad behaviour with comfort, which can encourage them to repeat the bad behaviour.

Reward and punishment are often referred to as "tough love." It is because it can be tough on the parent and your child.

Behaviour Modification

There is a technique that involves ignoring naughty or disrespectful behaviour. In contrast, praise and rewards are offered when your child does something right. If ignoring complaints or behaviour does not stop the action, the punishment would need to be awarded.

This approach focuses on consequences but will often overlap with the reward and punishment approach.

Emotional Discipline

Children are subject to the same range of emotional responses as adults. In many situations, they will be unsure of their feelings and how they should influence their approach. This type of discipline encourages your child to open up about their feelings. The belief is that understanding their emotions will allow them to learn how to deal with them and react positively in any situation. Research suggests that there is merit in this approach. Children capable of dealing with emotions will generally be calmer like adults and adapt to various situations.

Commanding

It is an old-fashioned approach to parenting and is based on the premise that children should be seen and heard. Adopting this approach means that you expect your children to do as they are told. If not, then you'll immediately dish out punishment with no specific reward for good behaviour. Punishment can range from loss of toys to physical spanking.

This approach works more along the lines of fear than love. It isn't seen as an appropriate or effective long-term method, and many children who have been brought up this way will reach their teenage years and rebel against the strict rules. The result is a child who does all the things that you have taught them not to. Besides, in many cases, the relationship between parent and child is, at best strained; more likely, it's simply non-existent.

Merits of Positive Parenting

Discipline is how you guide your toddler into becoming a well-rounded child and, subsequently, a positive adult. It's generally accepted that this is the best method for teaching your toddler into adulthood whilst retaining a strong bond between you and them.

There are several merits associated with this approach:

Recognizing feelings

Your toddler is surprisingly aware of what is happening around them. If they see from a young age that you are sad when they don't follow your guidelines, they will resist doing these things. It is because they will want to keep you happy, which is a natural desire in children.

By starting this at toddler age, you will enable your child to understand how their actions affect others and consider this before they act.

Emotions

Just as your toddler will learn your feelings and how to consider others before they act, they will also react to a positive parenting approach by feeling good about themselves. It is inevitable. A toddler will see that you're happy when they respond in a certain way, which will generate additional positive attention for them. They will quickly realize that they like the feeling. In turn, you can encourage them to feel good when they achieve something.

In contrast, if you adopt a punishment-based system, you will generally find that your child doesn't decide or speak up because they don't want to incur the consequences of a wrong decision. It will stunt their emotional growth.

Personality Development

It's highly likely that you enjoy being praised. After all, everyone likes to be recognized, and so what to do as praise inspires you to try again and achieve even greater things. The same is true when you apply a positive parenting approach to your toddler. Although young, they will quickly recognize the benefits and satisfaction of reaching for something and achieving it. Although your child is just a toddler, this can be one of the best times to start this approach. After all, they will have just started walking and are ready to try a host of new things!

Integration

Whilst you don't need to raise a child that follows the herd, you do want your child to be aware of how their actions affect others. It will allow them to develop the best approach to any issue whilst keeping most people happy. Only by adopting this approach in the adult world will they be able to achieve great success.

CHAPTER 3:

Why Every Parent Should Choose to Parent Positively

Positive parenting has been around for hundreds of years. It is seen in the action's parents take to help their kids set positive goals. It is seen in the support we give our children and even as we try to relate to them. These are all tremendous positive principles of parenting. The essential changes between then and now is that children were often told what to do and how to do it by their parents, but never really given a reason why. They just knew to do what they were told, or they may be punished or spanked. That is the beauty of positive parenting; it teaches kids the "why" behind the actions they are told to perform. Parents back then controlled their kids more than they dedicated themselves to training them to see fit.

It's Never Too Late to Start Positive Parenting

Positive parenting not only impacts your child's life in affirmative ways, but it changes the life of the parent as well. When conducted properly, this method of parenting builds a solid foundation to heighten self-esteem and positively driven emotions between both the parent(s) and the child. It has been proven by various health professionals, family counsellors, and psychiatrists that the relationship between the parents raising kids grows positively as well when implementing these practices. There is less stress when one parent does not have to worry about using heavy-hand or harmful techniques.

Trust is heightened, and issues that arise are seen more as opportunities than negative obstacles.

Children Are People Too

There are many simple tricks that, if we were merely able to change our mindset, will work wonders when it comes to discipline. Much of what you'll learn throughout the chapters in this book are simple things that will make you wonder why you hadn't thought and utilized them before now. Many benefits come along with being a positive parent. I will tell you that there, not an easy way out that it takes hard work and dedication to practice and utilize this style of parenting properly. But I assure you, there is a range of both short and long-term benefits that you and your children will positively grow from these!

Benefits of Positive Parenting

Positive parenting, by no means, lacks discipline. While as a parent, you still need to correct wrong behaviour, there are different things you can do to do this without yelling, hitting, etc. successfully. It is where learning about positive parenting can quickly become one of the best parenting decisions you'll ever make!

Secure Attachment

They should secure attachment is the foundation for healthy development in all children. It allows the healthy building of resilience for how your child is to act during their time as an adult. It also helps in superb brain development. To understand this, we must get scientific for a brief moment. The human brain doesn't mature until we are in our twenties. Our first 3-6 years of life on this planet are crucial for the further development of our centre of command.

Ability to Understand Feelings

Positive parenting thrives on the fact that you can share feelings between you and your kids openly. For example, if your child decides to run across a parking lot without looking at their surroundings first, and calmly explain to them how that action makes you nervous and how upset you would be if they were injured in any way. They will follow your directions because they don't want you to be sad if they get hurt. This type of behaviour from a parenting standpoint builds empathy between you and your child that will last a lifetime. It will also teach your child to think about the feelings of others before acting.

Decrease of Power Struggles

Disciplining your kids in harsh manners can cause them to feel shameful and poorly about themselves. They bury all that shame of their lousy behaviour within themselves instead of merely correcting it, which fuels them to act out in ways parents don't see fit continuously. If you continue down this path with your child, they will see you as an obstacle, which will result in power struggles. It's crucial to set up boundaries but do so with empathy and fairness in mind. If you maliciously treat your kids, they will grow up thinking it's okay to treat others that way too.

Healthy Emotional Development

When children grow up feeling good about themselves, they will mature into someone that has good self-esteem. They know they are easily capable of success with hard work and can truly feel good about positive accomplishments. Using harsh punishments can plant a sense of fear and shame that will later grow into them, making bad decisions or surpassing, making crucial decisions at all.

Uncover Motivations

It is known that all of us are motivated by different things. Children are human too, so this applies to them as well. As a parent, you only limit yourself when you use harsh punishments. If anything, you think more creatively through the means of positive parenting. When you learn how to isolate the things your child values, you can then use that to your advantage.

Building Strong Relationships

Positive parenting can allow plenty of room for positive relationships between family members to flourish since they are based on accomplishments and good memories. Parents must learn how boundaries are to be set through loving guidance. It builds a circle of respect for everyone in the family. When done correctly, parents will no longer have to discipline children but offer advice when they need it.

Development of Character

It is through the means of lively parenting sprouts children who are motivated by the desire for excellence in their lives. They wish to behave well to truly reach their goals, not because they fear being punished if they don't do as such. It says that when they grow up, they can watch their results and themselves as it seeks opportunities to do well in all the things they do.

CHAPTER 4:

The Positive Discipline to Instill in Your Child

It is vital to reinforce the objectives of Positive Discipline, remembering that it is about teaching essential life and social skills in manners that are encouraging and respectful to both the learners (children) and mentors (parents, teachers, caregivers, childcare providers). It is based on the concept that discipline must be taught to children with kindness and firmness, neither permissive nor punitive.

To make Positive Discipline more effective, it is necessary for parents, teachers, and other adult influences to create a nurturing environment that meets all the basic needs of the child, such as food, shelter, and clothing, extending to non-physical needs such as love, encouragement, and acceptance.

- Parental love is about the unconditional love that is acted out by providing care and gentle guidance, giving time and attention to children, and resolving any social conflict.

- Acceptance makes children feel that no matter what they do, whether wrong or right, they are loved.

- Encouragement is showing support in concrete ways that help children figure out how to avoid or correct mistakes, including finding their strengths to pursue passions and life goals.

In a nutshell, parents are the primary support of children who ensure their positive growth and development.

Positive Discipline at Home

Discipline begins at home. As early as possible, kids are taught to be responsible for their actions and distinguish right from wrong. Positive Discipline at home uses healthy and positive interactions to prevent inappropriate acts or behavioural problems before they begin and become habits. It teaches kids the correct behaviour and be respectful through appreciation, encouragement, consequences, and other non-violent strategies. The outcomes are:

- Children do better when there is routine, consistency, and lots of positive encouragement.

- A positive relationship with parents dramatically reduces the occurrence of challenging behaviour.

- A non-punitive discipline that provides significant long-term benefits compared to punishment.

- Children respond positively to parents or caregivers whom they trust. It is essential to use the strategies consistently by all caregivers.

Creating a Safe Environment

Childproof your home and supervise his movements to see that he is safe while exploring his immediate surroundings.

Establishing a Routine

Routines help children perform or behave appropriately because they know the expectations of their parents. A specific way to guarantee optimum care, safety, and enjoyment will help your child feel secure, more in control, and less anxious, hence developing strong self-discipline.

Planning Ahead

If you have to run errands and need to take your child with you, it is necessary to talk to him and let him know your expectations of his behaviours. It will prepare him and try his best to behave well. However, for little children who do not fully comprehend yet what you are trying to say, better have toys, crayons, books, and other activity tools with you when you go out to keep him occupied while shopping, waiting for the doctor's appointment, or travelling.

Having Clear Expectations

Discuss your expectation with your child. If you set 5 expectations like- Be Kind, Be Respectful, Be Responsible, Be Helpful, and Be Safe, do not forget to tell them. Have a conversation with him about the acts and deeds that demonstrate your expectations. Make sure that you also display those acceptable behaviours because your child is always watching your examples.

Offering Choices

Choices that are suitable for his age will help him gain a sense of independence and self-control. By offering options, you empower him to become more decisive and stand up for what he believes is right for him. It also applies to the consequences of misbehaviour or disobeying your rules. Make him choose between two safe, logical values that aim to give him a lesson and a warning not to repeat the mistake. Always follow through and enforce the consequence to make him see that you are serious about Discipline.

Building a Positive Relationship

Spending quality time with your child reinforces your relationship, helping him develop a strong sense of belonging, significance, and connection. Allow him to choose the activity or topic. It also lessens the occurrence of misbehaviour because he does not want to disappoint you.

Redirecting the Negative Behaviour

Maybe your child is bored, or for whatever reason, he starts acting out. It is essential to provide a suitable alternative that will stop him from misbehaving and enjoy himself. Always see to it that your child is well-rested, well-fed, and engaged in stimulating and fun activity. Redirecting his sudden malicious behaviour to another activity that interests him will generate appropriate action.

Calm Down Before You Address Misbehaviour

Do not try to discipline your child when you are angry, frustrated, or experiencing physical or mental fatigue because you will lose your objectivity. Calm yourself first and take a time out to steady your nerves. It will help you think clearly and handle the situation somewhat yet firmly.

Being Firm and Kind at the Same Time

It is the positive Discipline in its best form. You respond to each situation or misbehaviour with kindness and respect to your child, but firm enough to impose the consequences. It is also essential to let your child explain and justify his acts, but no matter how convincing his reason, make him understand that rules are rules.

Remind him that you set limits for a purpose- to keep him safe and prevent mistakes that may hurt him or others. If he chooses to defy any of them, he needs to face the consequences of his actions.

Catch Him Being Good

Do not let good deeds go unnoticed. Whenever you observe your child behaving properly, appreciate his efforts, so he is aware that he is doing well.

Distinguishing Factors Between Normal Behaviour and Misbehaviour

What keep you thinking that your child is displaying misbehaviour or expected behaviour? It is necessary to have truthful expectations about your kid's behaviour, considering the stage of his development. Every step has distinct challenges that trigger actions, which you can mistakenly view as intentional misbehaviour. By understanding these stages, you will know the difference. Here are some examples of typical or developmentally appropriate behaviour:

Example No. 1:

- Developmentally Appropriate or Normal Behaviour: Tantrums

- Developmental Tasks: The child is beginning to handle his frustrations and throws tantrums when upset and does not understand why he needs to do something. A classic example is when he does not want to brush his teeth or go to bed early.

Example No. 2:

- Developmentally Appropriate or Normal Behaviour: Energetic and Active

- Developmental Tasks: The need to explore and discover. One manifestation is the difficulty of sitting quietly for a long time, like during church attendance or storytelling period.

Example No. 3:

- Developmentally Appropriate or Normal Behaviour: Independent

  • Developmental Tasks: He wants to do things on his own like feeding himself, choosing clothes to wear, or picking the toys he wants to play.

Example No. 4:

- Developmentally Appropriate or Normal Behaviour: Being talkative

  • Developmental Tasks: He becomes curious about everything around him, so he asks many questions. His vocabulary is also growing, so he is excited to use the words he learns.

When your child is misbehaving:

  • Hault whatever you are doing and give your full attention to your child.

  • Remain calm and speak with your normal voice tone.

  • If out in a public area, remove him from the situation that triggers his emotional outburst.

  • Get down to his eye level.

  • Make him understand what you feel before reminding your child about your expectations from him. "I know that you still want to play, but it is time to go home."

  • Discuss the expected behaviour and asks him what he needs to do about it.

• State the consequence for the misbehaviour.

• Follow through with the result.

• Acknowledge when you see your child correcting his behaviour.

• Reconnect and restore your relationship through affection, hugs, or plays.

Dealing with a little child can be tiring and challenging, so do not forget to take care of yourself. It is a must to find time for yourself and find support when necessary.

• Eat a healthy diet and exercise regularly.

• Spend time in nature or have a "me" time to relax.

• Engage in activities that make you feel good and happy. Do them regularly.

• Keep in touch with family and friends.

• Say no to extra responsibilities.

CHAPTER 5:

Disciplining Children—
How to Be a Better Parent

One of the best difficulties of child-rearing is teaching children. Between the periods of toddlerhood (around two) and approximately ten, children are wipes. They learn and assimilate everything around them. They copy their good examples and endeavour to emulate conduct, they have their quarrels and spats and emergencies, and they're just steadily going to the conviction that the world does not rotate around them.

Furthermore, your activity as a parent is to support them, direct them, value them, and discipline children when they need it. It's never simple disciplining children, yet you ought to recollect that the motivation behind disciplining children is to teach, and uphold limits, to adjust conduct. It's not to rebuff, it's not to menace, and it's not to lash out in dissatisfaction (however, every parent will get disappointed with their children sooner or later). You will probably give the social limits and anticipated conduct into your tyke, regardless of the amount they appear to the article.

It Starts With Rules

Your children request steadiness throughout everyday life. If you've at any point asked why they'll happily watch a similar video for a long time after day, that is a piece of it. Making things unsurprising to their brief timeframe skylines is what they're doing, and they anticipate that you should be unsurprising. Consistency originates from defining rules and limits. Grown-ups realize that they can't do all that they need; children are as yet learning this exercise (frequently over and over, and with no natural elegance to it, to be gruff). It's your activity in disciplining children to ensure that rules are established, that limits are set, and that disrupting the norms is expensive. Children are as yet finding out about activities and outcomes; if you've at any point snapped your teeth at children's TV, that lectures toward the end with the nuance of a jackhammer, which is the explanation behind it. Your children must be given house rules, they should have those rules disclosed to them, the outcomes must be appeared for breaking them, and they should have the connection between disrupting the norm and the discipline clarified.

To make house rules, pursue these tips:

1. It would help if you had a rundown that is short enough that your children will recall them. Three to four rules are useful for babies to first graders; around ten is sensible for a long time seven and up. The states ought to be SIMPLE, similar to "No hitting" and "No running in the house."

2. Those rules should be disclosed to everybody on the double. Ask for inquiries, and answer them. Clarify what the rules mean, and afterwards, have your children tell them back to you as a perception check.

3. These rules should be posted in an area where everybody can see them, even little children. Yet, they should know where the rules' writ is.

Rewards as Well As Rules

Disciplining children is more than making rules to pursue; they need affirmation and reinforcement when they comply with the laws. With no positive reinforcement, rules without anyone else will rapidly be viewed as subjective and uncalled. You'll have an emergency staring you in the face. Children work amazingly well about compensating them for practices. Make those prizes express and gain the ground towards the reward visual and self-evident. Take a stab at setting up an outline with the names of your children on the left-hand side, and the rules that you need them to comply with over the top; each time your kid complies with a standard (like "heads to sleep without a complain"), put a star on the graph, and reveal to them for what reason they're getting it. Express gratitude toward them, since that will give a prompt reinforcement. At the point when the whole outline gets filled, they get something uncommon.

What can be 'something exceptional'? It can be about anything understandable, yet they needn't be detailed. About anything can do—here's a rundown of demonstrated prizes.

- I am getting to pick what the family has for sweet for that night.

- ome PC amusement or TV time.

- A play day with Mommy and Daddy.

- You are going out—to a child's family café, a motion picture, or the recreation centre.

- Pulling a money box toy out (you stock up a container with some toys from the Dollar Store early for this)

- Another book or being perused an old most loved one.

- A visit from their companions, or a sleepover.

- I am getting to pick what amusement the family plays on family diversion night.

It is only a glimpse of something more substantial regarding remunerating exemplary conduct. The reward is as significant as the rules in disciplining children.

At the point when your kid disrupts the guidelines (they will—it's a piece of testing limits for them, and is a piece of an effective learning process), it's your activity disciplining children as a parent to disclose to them what rule they broke, have them recognize that they defied the norm, and distribute discipline. You ultimately should be quick and firm on this; disciplining children ought to be ready, with the goal that it strengthens activities and outcomes. It may not, as your children dissent, be reasonable. However, it should be quick and have a constrained court of claims. (One thing children will attempt to get the two guardians to give different rules is gaming the framework).

When you're disciplining children, and clarify what rule was broken, sit at their dimension. Look. Have them recognize the standard and that they broke it. At that point, convey discipline.

Traditional disciplines for disciplining children can fluctuate from having a toy removed for a period to breaks. When the regulation is made, you have to rehash the standard that was broken, have them recognize the rule.

Afterward, you have to embrace them and reveal to them that regardless of you cherish them. At that point, let them recount to their side of the story. The point here is that you, as the parent, are the person who sets the rules and dispenses equity; however, that no infraction of a standard will at any point cost them your affection, which is their most profound dread.

Prevent Your Toddler from Hitting Other Children

When babies are predictable about anything, it is that they are eccentric. The odds are high that your little heavenly attendant will eventually get baffled and hit somebody yet or another. It could be one of their companions. In any case, the causes and arrangements are the equivalents. Presented below are a couple of tips prevent your little child from hitting.

Tip Number 1: Do not enable the situation to transform into a joke or a diversion. Your kid likely ended up baffled since they believed they couldn't get the point they were attempting to make. They are just barely building up their communication skills.

Regardless of whether the situation seems interesting to you, don't giggle or overlook it. Hitting can rapidly transform into a genuine issue. It would help if you told the youngster, without reservation, that hitting isn't alright and not permitted. Try not to change the situation into something the kid will need to rehash to make you snicker once more. Children love consideration regardless of how they get it.

Tip Number 2: Never, ever, ever hit them back or permit another person to raise it. A few people endeavour to give the situation a chance to resolve itself by giving the children "a chance to fight it out." It does not work to stop the conduct over the long haul. Restoring the hit is fulfilling and fortifying the terrible behaviour.

Tip Number 3: Set up different ways for your tyke to impart. Children are generally hit as methods for communication and not out of outrage. They are merely attempting to constrain the world into what they need it to be. If your kid has begun hitting, invest energy-demanding those are finding different approaches to convey and request what they genuinely require. The hit was a strategy to get consideration from the other party. Demonstrate the different tyke approaches to get that consideration without hitting. It can be as straightforward as urging them to offer the other kid a toy instead of running them. Doing this can fortify that there are better approaches to get the outcomes they need.

Tip Number 4: Always investigate the whole situation. It might be that your tyke conveys fine and dandy without hitting as long as they are all around rested or not over-animated. If you focus on setting the hitting scenes, you stand a superior possibility of keeping them from happening in any case.

Tip Number 5: Be alert for potential hitting situations. When your tyke will come in a worldwide hit when with a specific gathering, you can make a routine about watching them all the more near endeavour to find out what caused the youngster's dissatisfaction. You would then be able to prevent the hitting situation from creating in any case. You can even advance in to stop the hit in mid-procedure if you are ready enough.

Tip Number 6: Sometimes, you need to expel them from the situation. When the issue has heightened to the point where the tyke is not calling it quits and empowering better communication isn't working, you may need to expel them from the situation. It is an excellent use for the standard "break" discipline technique.

Tip Number 7: Insist that your tyke apologizes for hitting. It isn't the kind of consideration they were searching for and, for the most part, functions admirably to demoralize rehashing the action.

You are never going to have the option to keep your kid from regularly hitting anybody. It is something that children do. You can, anyway, set up a situation where the youngster learns and make an effort not to rehash the conduct.

CHAPTER 6:

Things to Consider When Disciplining Toddlers

Many parents attest to the reality that disciplining a toddler is like facing constant uphill battles. These little bundles of delight can turn to too stubborn kids who test the patience limits of caregivers and adults around them.

It is also the phase of childhood where they begin to assert their independence. One of their first words is "No," affirming the toddlers' love to do things in their way. They enjoy running away to escape. Typical toddlers are full of energy. They run, jump, play, explore, and discover everything that interests them. They love to use the sense of touch, exploring things with their feelings. Because toddlers are easily stimulated by what they see or hear, their impulsive nature can make them clumsy and touch things. Parents need to teach their children safe ways to touch or handle things and not touch hot objects. Although raising a toddler entails a lot of hard work, seeing your child grows and develops his skills is fascinating. However, because of the developmental changes that rapidly happen during the toddler stage, it is necessary to use a disciplinary approach to foster the child's independence while teaching him socially appropriate behaviour and other positive traits. There is an assumption that parenting techniques apply to all too often, and the kids will react or respond in a similar pattern. But every child has his own set of traits. They are in his DNA, which he inherited from his parents. Some toddlers are shy or even-tempered, while others are outgoing and have aggressive natures.

By understanding the child's unique personality and natural behaviour, you can help him adjust to the real world. It is necessary to work with his character and not against it, considering the following factors you need to consider when disciplining your toddler. Giving proper care and nourishment, providing positive and healthy activities, and instilling positive discipline is vital to his physical, mental, emotional, social, and behavioural growth.

Temperament and Behaviour

Temperament is defined as the heritable and biologically based core that influences the style of approach and response of a person. The child's early temperament traits usually predict his adult temperament. The child's behaviour is the outcome of his temperament and the progress of his emotional, cognitive, and physical development. It is influenced by his beliefs about himself, about you, and the world in general. While it is inborn and inherent, there are specific ways to help your toddler manage it to his advantage. Nine dimensions or traits related to temperament:

1. The activity level pertains to the amount of physical motion that your toddler demonstrates while engaged in some activities. It also includes his inactive periods.

   • Is your child a restless spirit who cannot sit still for so long or want to move around?

   • Is your toddler the quiet, little one who enjoys playing alone or watching TV?

2. Rhythmicity means the predictability or unpredictability of physical and biological functions, including hunger, bowel movement, and sleeping.

   • Does your child thrive on routine and follow regular eating or sleeping patterns?

   • Does he display unpredictable behaviour and dislike practice?

3. Attention span and persistence are the skills to remain focused on the activity for a certain period.

- Does your toddler stick to complete a task?

- Is he easily frustrated and look for another activity?

4. Initial Response (Approach or Withdrawal) refers to the reaction to something new and unfamiliar. It describes his initial feelings to a stimulus like a new person, place, toy, and food. His response is shown by his mood or facial expressions like smiling or motor activity, such as reaching for a toy or swallowing food. Negative reactions include withdrawal, crying, fussing, pushing away, or spitting the food.

- Is he wary or reluctant around unfamiliar situations or strangers?

- Does he welcome new faces and adjust comfortably with new settings?

5. The intensity of the reaction is associated with the level of response to any event or situation. Toddlers respond differently to events around them.

Some shrieks with happiness or giggle joyfully, others throw fits, and many barely react to what is happening.

- Do you always experience trying to guess the reaction of your child over something?

- Does your child explicitly show his emotions?

6. Adaptability is the child's ability to adjust himself to change over time.

- Is your child capable of adjusting himself to sudden changes in plans or disruptions of his routine?

- Does he find it difficult to cope with changes and resist it as much as he can?

7. Distractibility is the level of the child's willingness to be distracted. It relates to the effects of an outside stimulus on your child's behaviour.

- Can your child focus on his activity despite the distraction that surrounds him?

- Is he unable to concentrate when people or other activities are going on in the environment?

8. Quality of mood is related to how your child sees the world in his own eyes and understanding. Some react with acceptance and pleasure while other children scowl with displeasure just "because" they feel like it.

- Does he display mood changes always?

- Does he generally have a happy disposition?

9. Sensory Threshold is linked to sensitivity to sensory stimulation. Children sensitive to stimulation require a careful and gradual introduction to new people, experiences, or objects.

- Is your child easily bothered by bright lights, loud sounds, or food textures?

- Is he undisturbed with such things and welcome them as such?

Active or Feisty Toddlers

These children have a tremendous amount of energy, which they show even while inside their mothers' uterus, like lots of moving and kicking. As an infant, they move around, squirm, and crawl all over the place. As toddlers, they climb, run, jump, and even fidget a lot to release their energy. They become excited while doing things or anxious around strangers or new situations.

They are naturally energetic, joyful, and loves fun. But when they are not happy, they will clearly and loudly say it. These toddlers are also quite obstinate and hard to fit in regular routines.

To help him succeed:

- Acknowledge his unique temperament and understand his triggers.

- Teach him self-help skills to get going if his energy is low or calm down when his activity level is very high. Some simple and effective ways to calm down are counting from 1 to 10, taking deep breaths, jumping jacks to get rid of excess energy, and redirecting him to other activities.

- Set a daily routine that includes play and other activities that enhance his gross motor movements. Provide him with opportunities to play and explore safely. It is necessary to childproof your home.

- Insist on nap time. An afternoon nap will refresh his body and mind, preventing mood swings and tantrums.

- Do not let him sit in front of a television or do passive activities. Break the boredom by taking him outside and play in the outdoors.

- Become a calming influence. Understand how your temperament affects his temperament and find ways to become a role model.

- Passive or Cautious Toddlers—These children prefer activities that do not require a lot of physical effort, move slower, and want to sit down more often. They are slow-to-warm-up when meeting new people and often withdraw when faced with an unfamiliar situation. They also need ample time to complete their tasks.

To help him succeed:

- If your child is less active, set guidelines or deadlines to prompt him to finish the given tasks.

- Invite him to play actively by using interesting noises, bright toys, or gentle persuasion.

- Always accentuate the positive. Give praise and words of encouragement when they display efforts or achieve simple milestones.

- Flexible or Easy Toddlers—These children are very adaptable, generally calm, and happy. But sometimes, they are easily distracted and need a lot of reassurance and love from you.

To help him succeed:

- Be realistic and expect mood changes when something is not smooth-sailing. Do not be too hard on the child when he displays unusual outburst.

- Provide him with interactive activities and join him. Sometimes, it is easy to let him play his own devices because of his good-natured personality. It is necessary to introduce other options to enhance his skills.

- Read the signs and find out the reasons for subtle changes in the behaviour and attitude toward something. Be observant and have a special time for him.

CHAPTER 7:

Successful Ways to Discipline Toddlers

When you have youngsters, it is advantageous just as unpleasant, and you should figure out how to train toddlers when you can. It will guarantee that they gain since the beginning what they may or may not be able to. Toddlers are a challenge every day as they find out about the world and the confinement points and limits they can push. Your child-rearing aptitudes will be tried; however, you will see incredible outcomes with excellent tyke discipline strategies.

It would help if you secured that you get familiar with the straightforward method of exact order; your little child is at a period of honesty. You should instruct them that their activities will have results not exclusively to themselves yet, additionally to other people. For particular order to work, you should empower your little child and never rebuff, or control. Your baby will form into a minding kid with the proper measure of order, and your home will be a cherishing tranquil one. You will require a flexible arrangement of guidelines and ability, you need to train toddlers, and if you are clear about this. It will make it simpler.

The control intends to instruct, train, and teach, which is exceptionally valid; your baby should be shown these things at an in all respects at an early age. Attention and results should be educated. Even though, you will love giving your little child's thoughtfulness. They have to realize when it can and when it isn't. Your youngster discipline techniques should be firm, however, sufficiently straightforward for your small child to get it. You should force outcomes, yet ones that your minor child will get it. Toddlers react to limits, and even though they will push them, they improve to having structure and limitations.

Rewarding your little child for ethical conduct is a fantastic method to train them; they will, before long, discover that they possibly get the reward when they are great. Realizing when to utilize a discipline can be a test for you. Focus on beneficial things your little child is doing and not the terrible things. However, this is more difficult than expected. Typical results help you with discipline toddlers; they will help them learn they have fouled up without you venturing in.

It would help if you located a happy medium between your little child understanding what they have fouled up and forcing an excessively harsh discipline. Even though you should recognize terrible conduct, you should endeavour to disregard it. Toddlers will respond better if they are compensated for their bad behaviour

Your tyke discipline strategies should be a great idea to do this. At the same time, there will be circumstances when your little child accomplishes something wrong if you discipline toddlers appropriately; at that point, they will before long start to demonstrate advance. Before long, your baby will comprehend that their shrewd direct isn't accomplishing anything; they aren't getting consideration from you by any stretch of the imagination. Youngsters are incredibly sharp, and it doesn't take them long to comprehend the ideal approach to earn rewards from you.

CHAPTER 8:

Three Keys to Calm and Effective Discipline

One of the hardest things about early parenting (or perhaps any parenting), especially when it comes to tantrums, is discipline. It's impossible to write a book about avoiding tantrums without addressing discipline alongside the communication topics we have already covered.

Hopefully, you will find it helpful that I have researched far and wide on this tricky concept and have a few conclusions. The following images have worked for many of the families I have coached and for us.

Here are the three keys to successful discipline when it involves your child:

1. Discipline is best used as a teaching tool, not a punishment

For that reason, discipline is most successful when the child's negative actions are logical, natural consequences. If we teach our children that they shouldn't misbehave because if they do, scary or painful punishments may happen, we automatically pit them against us in their developmental journey. We are also not mirroring real life. In real life, if we forget to pay rent, a car doesn't hit us. We get a fine and eventually kicked out of the apartment. Consequences for our children need to be logical and as close to natural as possible.

Instead of punishing our toddlers, we need to enlist them as coworkers in their development. To do this, we can use discipline to help them learn the difference between appropriate and inappropriate behaviour.

For example, let's say your toddler willfully throws a block at your dog's head after you have explained (for the thousandth time) that that is not allowed (can you tell I'm writing from experience?). If you throw him in his room alone for a 'time out,' it doesn't have a direct link to his behaviour. It teaches him that sometimes he will be locked away, or love and companionship will be withdrawn if his behaviour doesn't fit your liking. Since connection and friendship are the mainstays for children, this causes his foundation of love to be shaken.

In time, the damage that this causes to the relational attachment bonds in his heart will cause him to believe lies about who he is. Either he will make his whole life about doing the "right" thing, afraid that he will cause people to withdraw love and connection makes a wrong move, or he will conclude that regardless of what he does, the attachment will be removed from him for inexplicable and unpredictable reasons. This could cause him to become rebellious and reckless in his disregard for the rules.

So, in the block throwing, it makes more sense for the consequence to be that the block is taken away for some time. Now, the way that this happens matters.

As the parent in this situation, if I yank the block away and say, "No! Now you can't play with that anymore," there is no link being made that gives my child an idea of avoiding this situation in the future.

I'll have a better chance of teaching him how to navigate and reason his way through if I take his hands in mine, get down on his level, and make eye contact. I might say something like, "It's against the rules to throw the dog's block. The rules are here to keep everyone safe. That can hurt her (insert the sign language sign for 'hurt' here). She feels scared when you do that (insert sign for 'scared' here). Please tell her you are sorry (insert sign for 'sorry' here)." Then I might ask him to show her how he can pet her gently. That is a way for him to make amends for the action. The last thing I might do would be to say something like, "since you broke the rule and you threw the block at her, you won't get to play with the blocks again for a while." He might be upset at this point, but I might say something like, "You seem frustrated (insert sign for 'frustrated' here). It's hard to lose the toy you are playing. That's just what happens, though, if we throw the block at the dog and break the rules. So maybe next time you might choose not to throw the block at her, and you will be able to keep playing with the union."

Now, smaller babies will often do things like this by accident, in which case it isn't a cause for discipline, but guidance. If a baby cannot understand consequences (typically under the age of 14-16 months), redirection is your best friend. It's still a good thing in those cases to explain the rules and why we don't throw the block at the dog. However, it's typically not helpful to discipline unless the child is consciously doing malicious behaviour. Redirection is more appropriate if the offence is committed without understanding.

2. Discipline and guidance must be consistent – it's all about the long game!

Babies and toddlers learn by repetition. Thus, it requires a significant amount of patience and consistency on the parents or caregivers when helping tiny humans develop. In the scenario above, this behaviour is likely going to occur more than once. Most toddlers test the limits and boundaries over time set for them to decide how to behave in the long run.

If my child and I had that particular interaction from the previous example one time, and then the next time he does the same thing, and I don't respond in the same way, he will be confused. He may think that somehow he influenced or had some control over how I handled the situation. If I let him continue to hurt the dog,

I reinforce the ideas that:

1. It's ok to break the dog,

2. The rules sometimes don't apply,

3. He doesn't always have consequences to his rule-breaking actions.

So, will he be likely to repeat this behaviour more often? Probably. Will he also become more aggressive in trying to break other rules? Very likely.

Now, as parents and caregivers, we all have rough days. We have those days where we can't exert energy for yet one more "talk" with the little one about rules or what is allowed. Or maybe even the consequences are a detriment to us (i.e., the toddler throws the toy that keeps them busy while we balance the checkbook, and we don't want to take it away because we need that time to focus. Am I the only one?).

So don't shame yourself if you are having one of those moments. Maybe redirect to a safer set of toys that can't hurt anyone while you get your work done. However, know that your overall track record of consistency is what regulates your child's understanding of what rules of conduct are and what is right vs. wrong. Overall, you want them to see that corresponding consequences will happen, for the most part, when those rules are violated. It's about what your child learns over time that will stick with him or her.

3. Get on the Same Team

Let's go back to the previous concept of working side-by-side with one another instead of head-to-head against each other. Keeping with the idea of discipline as a teaching tool rather than punishment, it's essential as parents should be to empower and work with our children. If, at any point, we are head to head working AGAINST them, we are not only less likely to get the desired behaviour we are looking for, but we are more likely to make our parenting much harder. It is because children who do not see an advocate in their parent will continue; they will fight back harder as they grow older and more vital.

One of the best tools I have found to maintain a working relationship with my toddler through his most challenging behavioural situations, is to offer to help him when he is having a hard time doing what I ask him to do.

For instance, let's say that I tell my toddler it is time to clean up. To help that transition, I usually give him a couple of minutes' notice and say something like, "just to let you know, we will need to clean up in about two minutes, so go ahead and pick one more thing to do." Then after two minutes is up, I would say it's time to clean up now and ask him to start putting his toys in the bin. If he starts to walk (or run!) out of the room instead, I would stop him and decide how to handle it.

Instead of punishing or disciplining him right then, knowing he is a toddler who is still learning, I might say something like, "I can see you are having a hard time listening to me and cleaning up your toys. I'll help you." At that point, he is much more likely to help. So I would take his hand, and we would clean up together.

If he is still resistant, then I would use some redirection tactic. I might engage him in putting away the yellow blocks while I put away the blue ones. If the child is younger than 3, it is appropriate for the adult to clean up as the child. I might also play a game with it – we might pretend that the toy box is the goal, and we get points for every stuffed animal we toss in. This is a crucial moment to be coworkers in doing the right behaviours. In this instance, punishment doesn't make sense because it doesn't reinforce the proper action, which is to listen to the parent and do what they are asked to do. But it does support a negative stigma and feeling that will now be attached to that particular request the parent makes. If I use a scary or painful punishment in this situation, the next time I ask my child to clean up, he is most likely to remember it has been a negative situation and not very likely to change his behaviour motivated by fear.

Whatever discipline as teaching technique you use, be consistent and believe in what you are doing. Believe in the long game! Suppose you consistently act on your disciplinary convictions. In that case, you will be more likely to remain calm since you already know how you want to respond to those teaching opportunities. This will be better all around for you and for your child's development.

CHAPTER 9:

Communication is Vital

Communication is vital, and the one you have with your baby is no different. The period from ages 1 through 4 is essential to your toddler's emerging language and social skills. During this stage of development, parent-child communication is all about significant interaction, modelling communicative behaviours, and fostering confidence, safety, and self-development.

One thing to remember about communicating with your toddler is that it is a dynamic, two-way interaction. One reaches out, the other response. As you and your toddler learn to interact in increasingly responsive and effective ways, he will develop an increased sense of safety, confidence, empathy, and self-determination.

Let's consider some of the critical components of effective communication.

Effective Communication: Talking

The way that a parent speaks communicates much more than mere words. When you engage verbally with your toddler, you are modelling how a conversation works, including necessary skills such as listening, empathy, and turn-taking. As toddlers observe you talking to themselves and others, what they learn about human interaction contributes to communicating effectively and exists in a social context.

But setting a good example isn't the only thing to keep in mind. Parents speak to their toddlers also impact how effective the communication is (does the toddler understand in an actionable way?) and the toddler's developing emotional and social understanding.

Talking to your toddler in ways that are too aggressive or too passive, can negatively affect their emotional and social development and detract from the potential benefits of teaching moments and healthy discipline. Instead, parents should speak firmly but kindly as they seek to communicate with their toddlers.

With these essential points in mind, let's consider some crucial tips for talking about how your toddler can understand:

Tip 1: Use eye contact. When talking with your toddler, don't expect them to listen or know if you're talking at them. Set aside any distractions, make eye contact, and let yourself connect fully with your little one.

Eye contact will help your toddler pay attention to what you're saying and stay engaged. It will also help bolster their sense of personhood by clarifying that you are interested in them.

Tip 2: Speak to them by name. Using your toddler's name while talking with them is another way to keep them focused on the conversation and give them a sense of importance as a co-communicator. It's especially useful to use names when validating or trying to let them know that you approve or disapprove. For example, 'Wow Jonny, that sounds so frustrating,' or 'I love how you shared with your sister, Alex,' or 'We don't throw food, David—please stop.'

Tip 3: Don't yell. Once you start crying, the chances are that your toddler's behaviour will become worse, either right then and there, or manifested the next day or week. Yelling sets a poor example for your toddler and is likely to cause them stress that could become damaging. You may also frighten them, further adding to their anxiety and fueling further misbehaviour as they try to cope. Instead, speak in a calm but firm voice. If needed, take a moment to breathe and calm down before speaking.

Tip 4: Be assertive but not aggressive. Sometimes kids misinterpret our responses and may not realize that we are serious about a limit or think we are engaging in play. Be clear about the purpose of your communications by using an assertive tone and body language when appropriate. However, do not mistake assertiveness for aggression. Assertiveness effectively communicates ideas and expectations; aggressiveness expresses anger, fear, and dislike.

Tip 5: Smile. Babies and toddlers are incredibly responsive to facial expressions. As you no doubt discovered during the first year, sometimes a well-directed smile is all that it takes to brighten up a discontented baby. The same holds for toddlers. Offering smiles during a conversation, let your toddler know that you enjoy talking with them and that the conversation is meant to be fun.

Tip 6: Minimize the use of 'no.' While some limits will undoubtedly focus on what your toddler should do, many will be focused on what they should not do. Hearing 'no' over and over again throughout the day can be exhausting for your little one. Try to talk to him in favourable terms that model reasoning. For example, instead of saying 'No Michal! Don't throw your food,' you might try 'Hmmm, throwing our food makes the floor sticky. Let's try saving it for later instead.'

Tip 7: Don't talk too much. When speaking, could you keep it simple? Toddlers have short attention spans, and talking too much will likely cause your toddler to lose interest. One day, 2-year-old Jimmy threw his toy car straight at the window in his bedroom. His mom responded by saying, 'Now Jimmy; you can't throw your toy car at the window because if you end up breaking the window, we're going to have to buy a new one, and that costs a lot of money, and besides, throwing things is dangerous—what if you hurt someone? How do you think it would feel? Do you think it's nice to…' at this point, Jimmy has stopped tracking.

His mother uses too many words, discussing people who aren't even present and speaking in terms that a 2-year-old can't follow or relate to with this. Instead, she might say something like, 'Jimmy, don't throw your toys in the house. Throwing is for outside.' At two years of age, short, direct explanations of not more than 2-3 sentences are the most likely to understand.

Tip 8: Use good manners. Using 'please' and 'thank you' will model good ways for your toddler and help her see that kids and adults alike deserve respect in conversation.

Tip 9: Ask questions. Asking open-ended questions is a great way to show interest in your toddler and encourage their participation in the conversation. When trying to promote interaction, avoid problems that can be answered with a short yes/no. Instead of asking, 'Did you go to the park with Grandma?' question, 'What did you do at the park?'

Tip 10: Don't limit the conversation to directions. Finally, don't just use talk to give your little one directions or feedback. Their language skills are growing a mile a minute at this age, and they are learning that language can be used for all kinds of purposes. Support this growth and create positive interaction patterns by asking them about their day, their opinions, asking them to tell stories, solve problems out loud, etc. Responses will be limited at first, but need not be any less enjoyable.

Effective Communication: Listening

Listening goes hand in hand with talking. It isn't easy to do one effectively without the other. Being a good listener will encourage your toddler to talk and help them develop good communication skills. Remember, effective communication with your toddler is dynamic and interactive, modelling both talking and listening abilities.

Listening serves several communicative purposes, including gathering information, opening the door for empathy, building relationships, giving respect, and gaining perspective. Listening will help you to understand what is going on in your little one's mind and heart, letting you relate to them better as you help them solve problems.

Tip 1: Ask for details. When your toddler tells you about what happened at church or that her baby doll feels sad, show that you are listening by asking for more information. What happened first? Second? Third? Why is the baby doll low? How will you make her happy? Such questions elicit a new language and help your toddler practice critical cognitive functions such as recall, mental modelling, and problem-solving.

Tip 2: Pay attention. In today's world, multitasking has become a way of life, even when it's unnecessary. To show your toddler that you're listening and engaged, set aside devices such as phones or tablets, and give them your full attention.

Tip 3: Use active listening. It refers to listening that is purposeful and fully engaged. During active listening, you are entirely focused on what is being said. Body language cues, including eye contact, mirroring facial expressions, and an attentive posture, all contribute to active listening. When you listen actively, your toddler will be more likely to feel that what they have to say is essential, and they will be encouraged to speak more.

Tip 4: Be physically interactive. High fives, hugs, and gestures are great ways to show that you are listening and interested in what your toddler is saying. Getting bodies involved will also make the conversation more engaging and meaningful.

Tip 5: Give unconditional love. Toddlers seriously lack impulse control and often don't know how to express themselves in socially appropriate ways. They may speak out of anger and even say things like 'I hate you' or 'You're ugly.' Remember, don't take it personally! No matter how your toddler speaks to you or what the content of their message is, make sure that they always know that you love them, no matter what.

Unconditional love creates a safe space where toddlers can speak freely and make mistakes without fear of losing your love or affection. This freedom will do wonders for their language skills, confidence, and trust in you as a parent.

CHAPTER 10:

Family Ground Rules

U sually, there are far too many rules in some families when all required are some general steps that facilitate what we hope and expect from all members of the human race. There is no need to be challenging or creative in making something about governing every element of your children's lives. Agree on basic rules for your family and get them made d own and shown where both parents can refer to them. Teach your kid how to do the correct thing, instead of dwelling on his errors. There usually are just these few basic rules in the Montessori-inspired home (an ideal growing environment for your child):

• Treat others with respect.

• If you are using anything, put it right back when you are done.

• When something breaks or spills out, clean it.

• Tell the truth and do not be afraid to confess when you make mistakes. You will keep the family ground rules plain in mind. Explain these positively, not as restrictions. Rather than saying: "don't go there!" Your kid will be asked what laws he will follow. Teach him how to implement them as if you were educating everyday life skills at any lesson.

Model a specific behavioural pattern you try to promote in your child. Try consciously to draw your child to do something appropriate and reinforce and appreciate even the tiny steps in that direction he is taking. Please do not wait until a new skill has been mastered-encourage him all along the way. You may do many ways other than chastising, intimidating, or discipline while your child violates a ground law. You can give him options by suggesting a more suitable choice. You can remind him of the rules and regulations and ask him to stop politely but firmly. If the situation is not emotionally charged (such that, if you are not personally aggravated), the primary lesson about managing such cases can be re-read. Be consistent. If you find you cannot get yourself to reinforce a rule repeatedly, that should not be a ground-rule. There are a few good rules that are much better than dozens, which are often ignored. Cut the word "no" eventually; each child will say stubbornly: "No, I don't want to!" This is a struggle for power that begins in the infancy years and often goes on during early adolescence. Numerous people call the "terrible twos" the toddler stage, but they do not have to be — not with two-year-olds or older children. Power struggles occur in situations where adults and children are determined to take their path. No party is willing to go back down. Below, each one feels threatened and frustrated. The parents think their children are challenging their authority directly. Children in situations like this usually feel powerless and try to assert their independence in their parental figure and establish more of a power balance. Effective practice needs an initial upfront investment. However, in the end, your initial investments would get significant behavioural payoffs. Below are ways to get you going when it comes to learning how to motivate your child to obtain long-term results successfully:

Fulfil Your Child's Attention Needs

Children need treatment, pure and raw. When we do not hold this "feedback box" full of constructive publicity, kids may be searching for whatever feedback they might find – also negative. They will push our knobs with destructive emotions because even negative attention in the attention bucket is a "deposit."

However, it doesn't necessarily mean you have to be on the side of your child 24/7—just having taken a few minutes a day with your child to spend one-on-one, nuisance-free, and doing something they would like to do, will reap enormous benefits in their behaviour. Please take 15 minutes with each child once or twice a day, and play a game they have selected or read their favourite novel. Let the handset turn to voicemail. Do not answer the email. Just let dishes remain in the lavatory. When you fill the attention baskets for your kids firmly and constructively, your children will become more collaborative and less inclined to attract attention in a threatening manner.

Life is busy for everybody, so having extra time in the day can at first be overwhelming, but think of that as an investment in your friendship with your kids, so enhancing their behaviour. In the first place, trying to give them what they need to avoid impoverished behaviour patterns can have an important part when it comes to realizing how to raise your child.

Set the Goal and Hold On To It

Given the hectic schedule that plagues households nowadays, staying compliant with everyday routines can be challenging. Yet, the fact is that while kids have stability, they succeed and learn their limits. If goals are expressed explicitly in advance, the children have a context through which to function.

Parents have not to go crazy with hundreds of laws, but concentrate on your most essential children. Be particular about the basic rules and the consequences if someone violates the rules—make sure that everyone in the house realizes the results before time and that the discipline is linked with the misbehaviour. When he fails to conform to technology's time limits, he loses his technology rights for the following day or week (depending on age). However, it is not relevant to making her clean the basement because she did not do her homework. Therefore, it is not a suitable consequence. So be truthful above all. Respond with the agreed-upon outcome any time children break the rules.

CHAPTER 11:

Setting Limits and Boundaries

O ne of the roles of oldsters is to coach their kids to accept limits and live within those limits. On the opposite hand, if the kid pushes against the limit too hard and too often, it's going to be that the limitation must change. Parents should ask themselves if the kid is prepared for more responsibility. If they, as parents, are ready for various limits. On the opposite hand, you cannot be with all of them the time, watching every move they create. They are going to high school, youth group, out with friends, etc. If they need to "date," they go to try to it. Would we want this happening secretly or where we all know what is going on? We've recently decided that, rather than a blanket "no dating" rule, we'll change this limit to permit dating if the kid shows the emotional maturity to be ready to handle it. How will we all know the child can take it? Because they're going to be doing things healthily—not sneaking or lying, and lecture us may be a great start. Setting limits may be a great point, and folks need to try to you only need to learn when to regulate those limits. If they're too strict or relaxed, you ought to know to line a limit and establish boundaries even when your child is born newly; you will not watch him stick a fork into the electrical socket. You would not want him to be antisocial and disrespectful.

Setting Limiting isn't Being an Authoritarian

Again, shouting at or hitting a toddler is counterproductive, and dangerous behaviour shows a scarcity of respect for the kid. It may cause other problems, although it'd be challenging to understand when authority ends and when authoritarianism begins.

To help, remember: authoritarian is one who exercises power using as a reference only his point of view (which is usually seen because the only correct), the physical force or energy that confers his position or the position he occupies, never taking under consideration what the opposite wishes or thinks.

He also rarely acts for the great of the opposite, which counts most of all is his benefit. Thus, an authoritarian father doesn't let the kid enter the space because thereon day he's during a bad mood. Still, in another well with life, he not only allows or maybe requires the boy's presence.

On the opposite hand, the father, who has authority, hears and respects his child but may sometimes need to act harder, sometimes even imposingly. Still, the goal is always going to be the kid's well-being, protect him from danger, or guide him towards citizenship.

We want to point out here that if we act with security and firmness of purpose, but with affection, we will achieve our academic goals without authoritarianism and less, without even hitting our youngsters.

In other words, giving limits doesn't clash—neither is it the other, as many might imagine - with showing love, care, attention, and security.

Setting Limits With Love

Like I explained earlier, testing limits may be a good thing for teenagers - it is a normal and healthy thing to happen. The issues start when either parent does not feel comfortable setting limits, or when children don't learn to bargain for changes within limits and act out instead both of those things aren't easy to try to, and it takes some work and patience. Here are a few ideas about the way to set limits effectively and persist with them.

1. Find Out Where Your Line Is

Our job as parents is to stay with our youngsters safe. During a physical and mental way, you do not want your teenager to be in situations where they're physically in danger: as an example, around a bunch of youngsters that are drinking, drugging, and driving. You would also like to protect their minds against specific sorts of music, movies, and things they're viewing on the web.

It's essential to line limits along these lines. When kids are young, that's not too hard as they grow old, it becomes much trickier; after all, you're trying to coach them to form sound decisions on their own so that they will become healthy adults.

2. Consequences and Rewards

The consequences are how of maintaining limits; tips are how of giving your kid hope. The products also are how of responding when your child tests limits to forcefully. For us, this has recently happened with one among our youngsters she has been sneaking around our limits, and she or he got caught.

We immediately confiscated her telephone every week, which may be a natural consequence because the telephone helped her form bad decisions; therefore, the lack of it would help her develop better ones. As a gift, we'd let her lollygag around with a child that we'd generally say no to—if she proves herself to be liable for following our rules.

3. Allow the Kid to Precise His Feelings Freely

Give the kid a chance to express his feelings about the bounds you set free; though, those feelings are negative. Respond by repeating their opinions in your own words—"I know you are feeling overlooked when mommy has got to spend such a lot time with the baby."

4. Rules and Limits Should Vary With Age

Regulations and boundaries you set for your child should be appropriate for her period for the health/safety of the kid and adults, or for other reasons above all, clearly, explain both the rule and, therefore, the rationale for having it.

5. Avoid Fixing Too Many Restrictions and Limits

Experts say it's much better to possess a couple of rules that you only consistently enforce than to have many laws that you enforce just one occasion during a while; therefore, avoid setting too many rules.

Setting Limits at Your Toddler's Level

There are many factors to consider once you set limits; you would like to specialize in where your child is relative than where you feel that he should be. Here are some things to stay in mind:

- He acts out of bounds not because he's purposely bent drive you crazy but to determine his independence; therefore, be a benevolent dictator; once you set rules, remember to offer him his share of power.

- She is no longer a baby, but she isn't yet a full-fledged child at an equivalent time. Expect her to throw her two-year-old tantrums once you set down the law.

- His memory is concise, which can mean that he doesn't remember once you say, "I've told you almost a day for a month to not paint on the wall."

- She wants everything now. Try negotiating, substituting, and delaying gratification in small doses. "I know you would like to travel to the park as soon as I put these dishes away, we're off" or, "Oh, I see you would like that candy. How about having a cracker and helping me get your stroller to travel outside?"

- He doesn't have a clear sense of right and wrong. His mother and father still are his conscience; the farther he's from you physically, the more likely he's to forget everything you told him about what's right and evil.

- She seems to be learning words so quickly that you might imagine she understands everything but become the guest lecturer from Harvard, giving complicated explanations for each rule, and you will lose her. Don't say, "you must wash your hands because they're filled with bacteria, and you'll get a communicable disease that might be hard to cure with the strongest antibiotics," when "let's wash our hands" will do the trick.

- He often doesn't understand the difference between real and pretends he may eat play-dough cookies as if they were cookie batter.

- Some battles you cannot avoid, some you'll, she is physically ready to get around, and almost everything removes the delicate crystal bowls and locks up dangerous liquids unless you want to be a guard all day.

So, these are simple rules on the way to set limits for your toddlers. They're still young and innocent, and it's up to you to guide them. Don't force limits because it will kill their creativity; allow them to explore, make mistakes, and learn along the way.

CHAPTER 12:

Things to Consider in Establishing Boundaries for Your Toddler

Make a Plan

Y ou must be strategic and come up with plans about how you want to handle your toddler. As a parent, you must assume an active role instead of a passive role in parenting. Well, the good news is that, as an adult, your prefrontal cortex is relatively developed, unlike your little one. You are capable of strategizing and reasoning. Now, it is time to put these traits to fair use. By paying little attention to your child's behaviour, you will develop various triggers or circumstances that cause your little one to fall apart. It might probably be a transitional activity like shifting from playtime to mealtime, or even a specific action like bedtime. Spend some time and think about all these triggers. Once you are aware of his motivations, it becomes easier to deal with them. You can quickly come up with certain limits well ahead and use them when the situation arises. It also helps you to understand your limitations and the kind of behaviour you expect from your child.

Mindful Of Your Language

Whenever you give directions to your child or are setting limits, you must never use weak language. You must be firm and avoid using ambiguous words.

Try to avoid using sentences like, "I don't think you should do that." Instead, you can say something like, "You must not do that!" or "You will be in trouble if you do that." Even if they say the same meaning, the way you get it matters a lot, especially while dealing with a toddler. If you want to become mindful of your language, here's a simple exercise you can try. The next time you are conversing with your toddler, record it on video. When you have time, watch this video, and make a note of the language you use. If you notice any verbal habits you wish to break, then you can start working on them. Using wishy-washy language is a strict no-no. Using weak language will enable your child to think that he can test your limits. You must re-establish authority and make him understand that you are the pack leader, and he must follow you. Keep in mind that you are dealing with a toddler and not an adult, so the way you talk to him must be different from the way you converse with other adults.

Non-Verbal Communication

Non-verbal communication is as important as verbal communication. Most of the communication that takes place is usually through our body language and facial expressions. Therefore, it is quintessential that you start paying attention to these things whenever you communicate with your child. Non-verbal cues must never be ignored. If the face says something else, you will only end up confusing your child. For instance, if you use a pleasant tone while talking about any mistake a child makes, it will only confuse him. Never use a severe manner when you are praising your child.

There are proper time and place for the different styles you use. Maintain a neutral facial expression and don't allow extreme anger to show on your face. After all, you are not trying to scare your toddler away now, are you? Don't use threatening body language and make yourself open. If you maintain a neutral facial expression, crouch down, and place yourself near your child, you can effectively convey that you mean business. From a child's perspective, your presence is often vast and intimidating. So, get down to his level while explaining any limits or boundaries to him.

Your Tone Matters

Another aspect of non-verbal communication you must pay heed to is the tone you use. Always make sure that your style is warm and welcoming, but firm. When you use a sharp type, you will end up scaring your young child or even over stimulating him. When this happens, his flight or fight will be triggered, and his ability to understand you will dwindle drastically. Another trigger you must be aware of is yelling at your child. Never yell at your child while trying to discipline him. You can calmly explain any rules you wish to set without scaring him away. It is quite challenging to get a scared child to listen to you. He might comply momentarily but will get back to doing what he was doing once again. While setting boundaries, you must have long-term goals in mind and not just momentary compliance. If you don't want him to repeat any dismal behaviour, you must effectively convey it to him. Don't startle and scare your child.

Immediate Compliance

Adults often have a tough time accepting a "no." So, expecting a child to comply with whatever you say without putting up a fight is not realistic. You must have a truthful view of your expectations while dealing with toddlers. Whenever you set a limit, establish a limit where it is a limit for you. Once you do this, then make sure that there is a little space left for feelings. It is highly unrealistic to expect a child to reply with an "okay sure" when you say "no" to him. If you talk to him in a calm and reassuring tone, the chances of him understanding and respecting your "no" without putting up a fight will increase. If you don't want to give him another cookie, say, "I said no more cookies. I know you want it, but you've had enough." By acknowledging that he wanted something, and by denying it, you are helping him process his emotions. The only way to deal with and work through challenging emotions is by handling disappointment.

Have some faith in your little one and his ability to process his feelings. Keep yourself in check whenever you are dealing with your child's big feelings.

Reasonable Expectations

You must set certain expectations related to your child's behaviour. As he grows, the way he behaves will change, so must your expectations. You cannot expect a one-year-old to behave the way a six-year-old does. For instance, a two-year-old might have a tough time-sharing his things with others without putting up a fight, whereas a five-year-old might find this quite sassy. A four-year-old might always ask you, "why?" whereas it is normal for a three-year-old to keep saying "no." Understand that as your child ages, he is developing—not just physically but also mentally and emotionally. It is a lot to take in for him, and you must be happy that he is as pleasant as he often is. Dealing with change is overwhelming, and you must manage your expectations while dealing with your toddler. You must hold it all together and be his support system. Don't get frustrated with him if he doesn't behave the way you expect him to.

Decisiveness

You must always be decisive while setting limits and boundaries for your child. The slightest hint of indecisiveness will give your child the confidence to take you for granted. Even if you do change your mind about a decision, you must be decisive. It is not just about setting a rule, but you must be decisive while following that rule. Let us assume that you tell your child, "You can watch TV for a while longer," on Monday because you are busy with some work, and then on Tuesday, you tell him, "You cannot watch TV today," because you are tired and want to sleep.

You cannot change a rule according to your convenience. Being a parent is seldom about convenience. Being consistent and decisive about practice is almost as important as a rule itself. Children respond well to consistency. If you keep changing the rules, you will only end up confusing him.

Using Humour

Humour is a useful tool that can diffuse tension and help convey your message quickly. Using humour is a great parenting tool. You can start animating an inanimate object like a toothbrush or a rubber ducky and use a silly voice to convey your message. For instance, saying something like, "You better get dressed before I count to five," in a funny British accent will get your news across without scaring your child.

Good behaviour must come from within, you can teach it, but you cannot force him to behave like you want him to. If he starts doing something only because he fears punishment or knows he will be rewarded, you are not teaching him good behaviour. Fear of punishment and rewards might work for the time being. Still, you aren't teaching him the importance of good behaviour by doing this.

CHAPTER 13:

Getting to Know Your Toddler

Toddlers often have already developed a personality of their own. However, most parents try to override their child's personality and creativity because they feel it does not run well with their household runs. As a parent, you think you know what is best, and most of the time, you do. However, you have to understand that toddlers are becoming little people. They have their ideas, and they are starting to think for themselves.

You must remember, your child and their feelings are valid. They are not little robots for you to order around and treat like they are supposed to be zombies. Children need support from their parents to become their person, and it starts when they are a toddler.

Of course, you want to make sure they are respectful, and a child with an attitude will need more discipline than a sweet and already obedient child; however, you do not want to disregard your toddler's mood if they have one. This is because one day, they can become a persuasive leader and very passionate. Put them on the right track to become a good leader. Do not try to squash their can-do attitude.

Listen to Them

Your child may not be the most articulate yet, but they still want you to listen to them when they talk. Children have the craziest ideas, and listening to those ideas can give you valuable insight into how their minds work. If your child is talking about something that you find impossible, don't say that. Listen to what they are saying. Let them know that it has not happened yet and that they should work on making it happen. Build them up, and don't tear them down. Even if you don't understand a word they are saying, listen to the passion in their voice. Children are the most passionate people on the planet. They have not yet hit society where power is seen as being crazy, so it is silenced. Don't stunt their love.

Believe in Them

Children are very impressionable. You could have a very outspoken and ambitious toddler that turns into a slacker as they get older. This is because someone along the way told them that they were not good enough, or that what they wanted couldn't be done. Most of the time, sadly, this is their parents. From the time they are toddlers, you should believe in them. Let them climb that rock, but be there to catch them. Let them try to read and help them. Be there to raise them and help them reach their potential. Even if you are skeptical, tell your child it is possible.

Your child will develop their personality more in their toddler years, than all their years together after that.

For parents who wish their tiny baby to stay innocent forever, life does not happen to work in their favor. Our babies rapidly morph into mini versions of us, which means an entirely different phase is in store for naïve parents. Once the walking and talking begins, there is no turning back the clock. The role of parenting becomes a whole new level of challenge, which means your life or home will never be quite the same again. Your little you are going through the physical changes and why it is crucial to toddler-proof your home and life.

The toddler stage is quite a unique one during human development in the fact that toddlers are no longer consider babies by they are not considered to be preschoolers yet either.

Many crucial developmental components occur during this time frame, which is why, as parents, we should always be encouraging growth and watching for signs that our young child may be falling behind developmentally. Of course, all children learn and grow at different paces.

Gross Motor Development

Gross motor skills are physical capabilities that utilize large bodily movements that require the entire body. When your child is a toddler, they stop toddling and look so incredibly awkward when they walk. They begin to walk and can do so more smoothly. They can run and at much faster rates, as well as hop and jump. They can actively participate in throwing and catching a ball and push themselves around by themselves or while upon a riding toy.

Fine Motor Development

Slight motor movements are vastly different than gross motor skills because they require the ability to utilize precise movements to perform adequately. During the toddler stage, children can begin to create things they imagine with their own hands. They can build towers out of toy blocks, mold clay into recognizable shapes, and are more than capable of scribbling on paper with crayons or pens. They quite enjoy toys that allow them to insert specific forms into one another. This is also when parents will notice which hand their child prefers to use over the other, as they begin to become either right-handed or left-handed.

CHAPTER 14:

Toddler Milestones (One Year Old)

The terms 'milestones' or 'norms' describe the recognized patterns of development that occur as babies and gain new skills. A vast amount is going on during the first two to three years of your child's life; for example, between birth and the age of two, their brain doubles in size. It is normal to compare your child's development with other children and be cautious if doing this. While there is an average age at which milestones occur, the time range during which each skill is mastered can be around six months. For example, while 12 months is the average age that a child can walk holding one hand, this can happen as early as six months for some children while others won't achieve it until 18 months old. This is all considered normal. Development and learning happen in fits and starts, resulting in rapid growth and consolidation periods. Again, this is perfectly normal.

Your toddler grows and develops in the five key ways, which are described below:

1. **Physical.** This explains how he uses his body and includes large movements such as walking, running, and climbing. These are his gross motor skills. Fine motor skills cover more specific activities such as writing, pointing, and using a spoon.

2. **Cognitive or intellectual.** This includes reasoning, understanding, and knowledge.

3. **Language.** This covers verbal communication such as receptive speech (what he understands), expressive speech (the

words he uses), articulation (how words are pronounced), and non-verbal communication.

4. Emotional. This includes the growth of feelings about himself and others and how he manages his emotions.

5. Social. This covers how he relates to others.

There is also an order or sequence to this development.

Development progresses downwards. Babies control their neck muscles first and then their arms, back and finally the legs and feet.

Development progresses from the inner body to the outer body. Children co-ordinate their arm movements before they gain control of their subtle finger movements.

Remember, all children are unique and will develop at their own pace. However, if you have concerns about your child's development, always trust your instinct and talk with your doctor.

Understanding the range of skills that your child is beginning to develop can help you think about and plan activities that support each stage of development. Described below are some examples of the different milestones your child will pass through. Your toddler will be well past many of the first ones. He has come a long way already. Remember that 'normal' development for toddlers is considered within six months, either side of these pages.

Physical Development

Six weeks—hold his head up

Three months—lift both his head and chest off the bed when lying on his tummy and hold a rattle in one hand

Six months—roll over and sit up with support

Nine months—can sit unsupported and can pick up small items using finger and thumb

12 months—walk with one handheld and turn the pages of a book

18 months—climb onto an adult chair and squat to pick up a toy

Two years—run, walk upstairs, kick, draw circles and lines and drink from a cup

2.5 years—jump off a step, stand on tip-toe, hold a pencil with a tripod grasp and build a tower of seven or more blocks

Three years—walk backward, ride a tricycle, kick a ball with force and accuracy, start to copy letters and cut paper with scissors

Intellectual Development

One month—recognize their primary carers and smile at them

Three months—interested in toys and starting to understand cause and effect

Six months—immediately turn at the sound of their mother's voice

Nine months—watch a toy being hidden and then look for it, recognize familiar pictures

12 months—point and look to where others look

18 months—refer to themselves by name

Two years—begin to understand the consequences of their actions, e.g., when something falls and breaks, show empathy, follow simple instructions

2.5 years—know their full name, continually ask 'why,' 'what,' 'who'?

Three years—match primary colours, sort objects into categories, understand concepts of 'one' and 'lots,' like to do things unaided.

Language Development

One month—make non-crying noises such as cooing

Three months—cry when expressing a need and become conversational by cooing and gurgling

Six months—understand the meaning of words such as bye-bye and dada

Nine months—follow simple instructions such as 'kiss teddy,' understand and obey the word 'no.'

12 months—speak two to six recognizable words and understand many more

Eighteen months—use up to 40 comments; the term used most commonly is 'no'!

Two years—speak over 200 words and often talk to themselves, understand over 1000 terms, keen to share songs, conversations, etc

2.5 years—talk audibly and intelligently to themselves while playing

Three years—use personal pronouns and plurals correctly, remember and repeat songs and nursery rhymes

Emotional Development

One month—gaze attentively at the carer and begin to show a particular temperament – placid or excitable

Three months—respond with evident pleasure to cuddles

Six months—are warier of strangers and show distress when their mother leaves

Nine months—need the presence of a known carer and often require a comfort object e.g., favourite teddy

12 months—tend to have fluctuating moods and are affectionate with familiar people

18 months—alternate between clinginess and independence

Two years—often feel frustrated and express this through tantrums (half of all two-year-olds have tantrums daily), starting to say how they feel

2.5 years—still emotionally dependent on adults

Three years—show affection for younger siblings, develop fears such as the dark, understand things from another person's perspective

Social Development

One month—smile in response to any adult

Three months—show enjoyment in routines such as bath time and smile at familiar people and strangers

Six months—offer toys to others and finger feed themselves

Nine months—play alone for long periods

12 months—enjoy socializing at meal times and help with care routines such as washing

18 months—play alone but enjoy being near a familiar child or sibling, can follow stories and rhymes

Two years—dress with minimal help and enjoy trying out new experiences with knowledgeable adults, like to help others so long as this doesn't conflict with what they want to do

2.5 years—will play more with other children, but may not share their toys

Three years—make friends, willing to share toys, enjoy helping adults.

CHAPTER 15:

Toddler Developmental Milestones (One Year Old)

N ow when you look back to the time you gave birth to that innocent, helpless baby and compare it to the present day, you find that many changes have taken place in your little one; well, meanwhile, the significant changes have barely started. As much as it is the end of the beginning, this is also another beginning. It is the first of all the milestones your child will reach; it is the first significant birthday your kid will be having.

This is where your child leaves baby or infanthood to become a toddler. At this point, your toddler begins to grow and develop in many aspects; your toddler starts to toddler-versions of human characteristics. I'll be giving insights on what you should be expecting in the subsequent twelve months in the following section.

12 Months

- They can utilize their feet to push themselves along on ride-on toys.

- They show interest in balls and playing with them.

15 Months

- They can walk without your help, but with the assistance of walking with their feet spread apart and their arms to contribute to proper balance.

- They can get themselves up from sitting to standing positions by utilizing their hands to push themselves up and sit down.

- They can bend down to pick things up themselves.

- In time, this action will turn into being able to squat. To help your toddler develop this motor skill when they start to bend over an object, show them how to bend their knees.

- Practise makes perfect, of course, line up some toys and have them pick them up. This will also help in the mental development of when clean-up time is as well.

18 Months

- They can drink from a cup without assistance.

- They can draw/scribble/write on paper using a variety of utensils.

- They are capable of climbing onto low furniture.

- Toddlers will inevitably attempt to climb whatever they think they can get on, blatantly because of the mere fact it is there.

- Climbing is a vital physical development. So do not prohibit them from climbing, but rather create safe opportunities for them to do so. Throw sofa cushions on the floor and create a padded playground for them to enjoy.

- Ensure that heavy furniture and other objects in your household, such as bookcases and televisions, are properly anchored down so that your child will not knock them over on themselves.

- They can build a tower out of block-like toys.

- They can now pick up small objects since they have practised the pincer grip.

- They can push wheeled toys in front of them.

- Once your child becomes more confident in their walking abilities, they will desire to push and pull around toys and other objects. Ensure that during this stage, you offer them push or pull toys to play.

Motor Skills Now

As the name toddler implies (toddler means a child that toddles, with toddling meaning to limp). However, walking at this stage is not guaranteed, as this is when the whole "toddling" thing begins, kids can at least stand on their feet without help. Before now, they would have gone through the crawling stage, and by their eighteenth month, the unsteady walking should have begun. With the arms not to go unmentioned, there is also an upgrade in the arm-strength, which increases their ability to apply force when needed. Sitting without help is another feature of the improved gross motor skills.

This aspect refers to the coordination of the eyes with the hands and fingers. This is said to happen earlier than the gross motor skills, so before the twelfth month, your kid should have begun holding small objects, turning book pages, and the likes, other advanced ones get to come in gradually.

However, if these things can happen a little earlier or later, this should not be a cause for alarm; the time differs from kid to kid, but if you observe that it let your paediatrician know. The paediatrician will better pass this information, so you need to make inquiries before this time (if the doctor hasn't discussed it yet).

Communication and language skills. This includes improvement in speaking skills and the use of sign language. Kids who, with all the effort they put in trying to speak, were only blabbers will now show some noticeable improvements in their speeches, where words like dada, mama, no, and some other elementary words, have formed out of the previous gibberish. Here, kids also learn to use and understand simple sign languages, which most commonly comes first being head-nodding, then there could be other signs like touching of genitals to show that they are pressed, making thirst gestures, and so on. Apart from expressing themselves, they also understand these gestures and words. They already fully understand the nodding motions and can differentiate a "yes" nod from a "no" nod.

Cognitive skills. Although it might not be sharp yet, a little mental processing-ability should be noticed. They now understand that some things, even if not seen, are still in existence. Therefore, they can search for items that are not directly seen, probably under one or two covers or behind an obstacle.

Physical growth. At one-year-old, kids go through a noticeable change and development in their bodies; they grow huge compared to when they were given birth. So be prepared for a wardrobe change; they are going to outgrow the old ones.

Parents should also try and tend to their explorational needs because, at this stage, kids begin to explore their environment and the world they're just coming to understand. Try creating an exploration-aiding climate. Also, as always, healthcare is essential, be sure to take them to paediatricians regularly for thorough check-ups, and vaccination should be taken seriously. All the baby-proof security measures should still be intact for safety reasons; they are still babies, you know.

CHAPTER 16:

Toddler Developmental Milestones (Two Years Old)

S o, now that the first year is gone, your toddler is on course of becoming a big kid, and there are significant developments in every aspect of their lives. There is an improvement in the products that have occurred at age one.

2 Years

- They can push buttons and turn knobs.

- Most can walk down the stairs by holding onto the railing and placing them onto a step.

- They can quickly run in one direction and stop when they need to.

- They can walk backwards.

- They are capable of running.

- Each child is different, but some toddlers may go from crawling to sprint at rapid rates. Some children take risks faster than others.

- Encourage your toddler to play tag on softer areas, such as sand or grass.

- Chase your child around, encouraging them to run from you then have them chase you around.

- They are capable of getting themselves off the floor without using their hands.

- They can take off articles of clothing.

2 ½ Years

- They can undress.

- They are learning ways to pick out clothes and dress appropriately.

- They can throw a large ball in the direction they intend.

- They can walk upstairs.

- They can kick a large ball, even though it usually does not go in the direction they intend to.

- They can feed themselves with the utilization of a spoon.

- They can drink from a regular cup.

- They can run smoothly (and with speed).

Communication: Speaking becomes clearer; two-year-olds can say a three-word long sentence, an upgrade to their one-year younger self, don't be surprised when you see your two-year-old singing the songs you sing to them.

Movement: Walking becomes steadier, with a significant balance in the heels and toes usage. Kids at two already begin to run, of course, when you pass the walking stage, why not go for running, right? Straight to the next level. They also do a lot of climbing, from furniture to playground equipment, as long as it looks climbable (to them), they can climb up and down. Pulling toys along while walking is also common among kids around this age; since they are now more prominent in size and are steady on their feet, they now have the power to pull things along while they move (depends on weight).

Hands and Fingers: Spontaneous scribbling, another feature in kids at this age, building towers of three or more blocks is also present. An upgrade to that of "year one."

Cognition: Cognition is improved to the point that imagination now comes into play. They can directly engage in make-believe (imaginative) games; they begin to recognize and discern differences in shapes and colours.

Of course, there is continuous growth and development in different parts of the body. As they grow to become independent and begin to feel that natural urge for independence. If not given, can be a cause for power struggles, tantrums, and the likes; they tend to want to feed themselves, dressing themselves (although with clothes that are easy for them to handle), they can even get to be picky about what to eat, and this comes from the fact that they want to imitate older kids or adults, and soothe themselves with the feeling of doing things by themselves. This age also comes with the sense of fear. At the same time, younger kids might not have this issue. Fear can begin to set in at around the age of two; kids can have different and random reasons for anxiety, a monster under the bed, fear of spiders, fear of the dark are just a few of many fear factors for kids, its left in the hands of the parents to help them handle these fears (refer to part two, "monsters under the bed"). This also is a perfect time to introduce toilet training (of course, without pushing). Good luck with the "terrible twos."

CHAPTER 17:

Toddler Developmental Milestones (Three Years Old)

Welcome to the "three-agers." Although not as rapid as in the previous years, growth continues, there is still a continuous improvement in the foundation laid in the first year, traits are significantly more vital. Children can begin cooperative play (play involving other kids) instead of a solo game where every kid plays alone, even if they are beside each other. This is the bridge between toddler-age and preschool-age; this is more or less the age where toddlers officially become preschoolers because they already begin to understand better how different things work. Movement ability gets to its peak around this age; steady walking is no more a piece of news; they can now even go up and down the stairs without help, walk, run, jump, the complete package is present. Three-year-olds will ask you more questions; they need your help to satisfy their curiosity as they begin to explore the world around them. Exploration expands as they grow. At this age, the rate is very high; parents should help enhance their creativity by providing an exploration and expression aiding environment (refer to part two, "hobbies and creativity").

3 Years

- They can feed themselves using both a spoon and a fork.

- They have begun the potty-training process.

- Looks down at diapers, and grabs and pulls them off when soiled.

- Crosses their legs or squats when they need to go.

- They are capable of throwing and catching a ball if they utilize two hands.

- They can kick a ball with more force.

- They can jump.

- They can walk both up and down the stairs without the parent's help.

- They can begin to play with ride-on toys like bicycles.

Parents should make it an obligation to make sure that kids have been taught to express their discomfort or displeasure with words rather than throwing tantrums. Kids of this age are also said to understand emotions; they show feelings and sympathy, don't be surprised when you see your three-year-old giving hugs when they see other kids or friends (yes, they now have friends). Also, kids around this time should have shown their preferred hand.

If your kid hasn't yet been potty-trained, now is more of the perfect time to get it into them; there should be no case of unreadiness; kids at this age are mostly ready to be toilet-trained. For example, you don't expect them to lace their shoes or put on their belts (dress or trousers), but they can at least put on their socks. There can also be a lot of limit-testing; they sometimes want to know what happens as a result of their action, they also tend to test limits if it sparks any reaction from, so when this happens, parents should play smart and don't give them what they want, try the ignorance method and don't get the impression that the kids can always get your attention with limit testing. Don't forget that your kid is transiting from a baby to a big kid, a little bit of strictness is required to make them know what is wrong from what is right, as this builds their adult-personality.

CHAPTER 18:

Temper Tantrums

Temper tantrums are representative of infants, though some kids hold them on for several years if they find that they are a way to get whatever they want. Children often throw a hissy fit when they are very stressed, starving irritably, physically exhausted, or sound ill. As your child becomes more "knowing," outbursts may be her way of pushing the boundaries of seeing how you will respond. Kids still choose to cry and whine at the worst possible moments. You may drive your car, go grocery shopping, eat at a steakhouse or a friend's place and she does just when you would least suspect your child to make a scene. We incline to want to get her to stop doing something right away. We are ashamed, and our degree of tension is high. That is because parents often turn to intimidation and prohibitions. Instead, we need to recognize that the tantrum signifies something, so the only way that helps is to get to the underside of it and attempt to meet the child's needs.

Types of Tantrums

There is a significant difference between temper tantrums and one hurled by an angry, frustrated kid who tests the limits. The first type of tantrum necessitates little more than a parent who determines the cause, remains calm and upbeat, and helps with food, rest, or comfort. While it may be awkward to have a child weeping incoherently in a supermarket or on a social occasion, there is at least a physiological situation underpinning the hissy fit, which can be quickly resolved once you discover it. Also, when you do your best to be in control, you will ultimately be.

The second category of tantrum is like any conflict overpower. It is less than an articulation of your child's way of trying to proclaim some authority in a circumstance in which she feels powerless. Know when kids say, "No!" Also, they are attempting to convey something to you or throw a temper tantrum. You have to be calm, stand back, and try to find out what the secret meaning it could be that all you need to listen to. Children occasionally feel frustrated, just like grown-ups, as they think nobody is paying attention to them.

Resolving Them

Often it may be tough to say for sure what a temper tantrum is mostly about because small children are unable to describe the question. Most parents, however, learn to identify symptoms and may make a prediction. If your child's behaviour is the product of being starving, get some nutrition for her to consume as quickly as practical, even though it is not her regular mealtime. It is an excellent idea to bring with you some quick lunch just for such emergencies. If you think your child is tired, reduce your conversation and talk in a smooth voice, keep or rock her, as well as end up taking her to her bedroom or anywhere she can relax as soon as possible. If you know your kid is ill, speak with a sweet voice, reassuring her quietly. See if someone near the area can get you an empty crockery or trash can, and a warm washcloth, if you think she will vomit.

Make arrangements as patiently as possible if she needs medical help. If you have been otherwise involved, talk with a friend at the breakfast table or on the phone for a long time; make sure you pay a lot of attention to your toddler when you are done. Some kids struggle with transformations, and this can give rise to a tantrum in itself. If you are in the play area, for example, let your kid know ahead of time that you will leave soon. "We are going to have to return in 15 minutes. Would you like to go down some more of the slide or swing? "The reminder and the choice in advance will allow your baby better manage moves." If your kid tests the limits, stay calm, and resist getting into a fight. Speak in a soothing voice; let her know gently that this is still the law while you understand she gets mad. For starters, "I know you want to still linger at the playground here, but we've got to get home to have lunch."

Avoiding Drawbacks

Family life often has patterns. Recognize if you can pinpoint any frequent tantrum triggers, then try avoiding them. For example, if when you go shopping, your child appears to get tantrums, leave her with your spouse or a sitter. Children often act when plans abruptly change, and if this is the situation with your child, plan ahead of time so and stick to it. Illustrate the boundaries already when you do anything to your kid. For instance, if you go to the supermarket and your child wants to purchase a toy, inform her in advance what you will agree to and adhere to it. Do not give in to children's attempts to get you back down, if they are complaining, demanding, or trying to trick the situation. It may work to distract an infant with a match at the first indication of a tantrum. However, if she does not calm down, detach by sitting down to read or move outside the entrance, letting her know you're waiting to cuddle as soon as she's ready for it. Even people are attempting to overdo it. Young children prefer habits and get upset and weary when they were sweeping from one exercise to another. It is unavoidable occasionally, so consider hard and long before you sign up for baby yoga, dance classes, or some other prearranged courses. Racing from one action to the next raises stress levels for everyone and sets the stage for emotional outbursts.

Tips for Coping

There are many things you should take note when you have a tantrum at your child:

> • Do not turn to violence by hitting your child or spanking her. That is the surest means of training her to be abusive against others.

• Do not try to physically stop a child unless it is about to run out of traffic or harm itself in some other straightforward and tangible manner.

• Should not respond to intimidation or prohibitions. These do not work when children are also unreasonable. They only spiral out of control the already started emotional turmoil.

• Don't argue. You cannot win a debate with an irrational person.

• Do not try to make your child embarrassed or ridicule her behaviour. In the future, this will teach her to cuss out at others.

• Don't attempt to handle the temper tantrum in general. Take your child to a place where you can be isolated, and speak privately. This is polite to others and makes the situation more comfortable for you to handle.

CHAPTER 19:

Tantrums for One and Two-Year Toddlers

A ll humans have emotional outbursts. As we age, we can learn how to manage our frustrations, grief, or anger by channelling that negative energy into more productive outlets. But 1-year-olds do not have this ability yet. It is a life skill that comes from time, experience, and the gentle guidance of others.

In this book's context, a "tantrum" is simply a significant expression of big emotions. Your child trusts you enough to express his true feelings in front of you rather than keeping them bottled up inside. Your job is to help him learn better ways of managing his emotions. You can also use your compassion and gentle reassurance to connect with him emotionally, strengthening your future relationship. When you help your child make it through to the other side of a tantrum, you give him a life gift.

Prevent Tantrums From Starting

The good news: With some preparation, techniques that help you think on your toes, help your child avoid a tantrum. The trial starts with your routines. Young children thrive on predictability and often are distressed by disruptions or the absence of objects in their usual place. By providing consistent practices and an organized environment at home, you are helping your child feel safe physically and emotionally.

The next step is to make a habit of regularly pausing to observe and evaluate your child's practices and emotional states. Is he getting enough sleep? Does he seem to get hungry at the playground after about an hour, or does he prefer to snack at home? What does he find most entertaining while waiting: verbal games, songs, toys, or books? Deterring a potential tantrum may be as simple as packing your diaper bag with a snack or toy or helping your child locate his shoes.

Most 1-year-old tantrums happen because your child lacks the communication skills to tell you what is wrong. If you can figure it out quickly and provide an immediate solution to fix the problem, tantrum prevention is the best form. Besides, if there is an unexpected event or you need to deviate from his usual routine, make sure to take the time to tell him what is going to happen. He will likely reward you with a calmer disposition.

Stop Tantrums

Let's face it. Because life is sometimes spontaneous, and we must have reasonable boundaries, we can't always cater to our child's every need or desire. Children can get frustrated or upset, even when we try our best to prevent it. If the tantrum is the result of a boundary you enforced, do not try to explain or reason with your 1-year-old. At this age, she cannot understand the logic, so this will only complicate things further. You might not be able to prevent your child's tantrums altogether, but you can reduce their frequency and severity by handling these emotional expressions with compassion and consistency. What you need is a plan.

Find your calm. The first step in handling any behavioural issue is to keep your own emotions in check. Remember that you are an adult. If you feel angry or upset, pause to breathe deeply and get your own emotions under control. At this moment, your child is unable to manage her feelings, and you have all the power; before you can offer support and guidance, you need to be calm.

Empathize. Can you imagine how she is feeling right now? What is her body language communicating? Tell her in simple, clear-spoken words that you understand how she feels. If you can determine what it is she needs and supply it, the tantrum may end abruptly and with gratitude from your child. However, if she is in the middle of an outburst, she might not hear you.

Comfort and reassure. Many 1-year-olds will calm down with physical reassurance. Try putting her in your lap to cuddle, gently rubbing her back, or offering a hug. Breastfeeding toddlers may find nursing a natural technique for self-soothing. Singing a lullaby or murmuring reassuring phrases like "I love you so much" can also work wonders. However, some children prefer not to be touched during an outburst. Try not to take offense if your child rebuffs your efforts, but don't walk away. Stay close.

Wait. Carry your child to a more private space to ride the tantrum out, go ahead and do it, but it is important not to rush this part of the process. Trust that this wave of emotion will rise and fall back down naturally.

Use Your Words: Everyone needs to feel understood. When empathizing with your child during a tantrum, try this simple phrase to get the message across. "You are feeling [state the emotion] because [state the cause]." For example, "You are feeling angry because you wanted to play with that lamp."

Recover From a Tantrum

When the big emotions subside, it's time to reconnect and move on. How you choose to recover will depend on your location, the time of day, and your child's personality. After a short-lived tantrum, you may have good results with the "distract and redirect" technique. If the tantrum occurred in a grocery store, for example, the natural next step might be to continue shopping. If you are at home indoors, you can go outside for a change of scenery.

However, your child might not be ready to move on yet. Making it through a long and challenging tantrum can be exhausting. A slower transition back to normalcy will allow both of you to process what happened and regain emotional balance. Cuddle while you hum a tune, read a story, or fiddle with a toy. This special bonding moment after a tantrum can be an opportunity for honesty and affection. Reaffirm how much you love him, recount the lessons learned, and even apologize if you feel it's necessary. Suggest moving on with the day.

Remember that taking the extra time to fully heal any emotional wounds and focus on a loving connection will pave the way for shorter, less time-consuming tantrums.

CHAPTER 20:

Tantrums for Three-Year-Old Toddlers

Since 2-year-olds are renowned for terrible tantrums, you might expect your 3-year-old to sail through the year. Most 3-year-olds do continue to struggle with emotional outbursts; however, in the previous year, your child had very little control over his behaviour. Still, now he is becoming more self-aware, making a connection between action and outcome. Some tantrums at this age may be bids for your attention. This does not make them any less real, but how you evaluate the situation and respond may be a little different. Patience and compassion remain the essential strategies, but you will also need to teach your child problem-solving skills directly.

Determining What to Teach

When your child throws a fit, specifying the real reason why is the key to helping her find a different way to express her feelings in the future. Acknowledge her feelings and offer comfort, but don't over sympathize. As when she was little, wait patiently for the storm to pass, and do not give in to her demands. Now that she is 3, she will be more receptive to your instruction, so think about what life lessons you might impart both immediately afterwards and in daily life.

Here are a few common reasons 3-year-olds throw tantrums and suggestions for teaching practical skills:

Frustration: You said "No" to what she wants. She is just letting you know how disappointed and angry she is and hopes you will change your mind (don't give in). At another time, teach her the right words to say to express emotions and practice them. You can look at books or pictures of facial expressions and name them together, using a mirror to mimic them. You can give her a one-liner to say when she feels frustration, such as "I'm not happy!" or "I want that."

Delayed Gratification: You said "Yes" to what she wanted, but it's not coming fast enough. Tell her that you understand. Teach her how to wait patiently by giving her specific body actions to perform, such as having a big breath and relaxing her body. You may even regularly suggest that she sing a song or read a book to herself as she waits. Children can also be emotionally on edge when a big holiday is coming up, causing more frequent tantrums. Help her by making a visual schedule so that you can count off the days together and do your best to keep any extra stimulation to a minimum.

Attention-seeking: She feels bored or ignored, and she wants your attention. When you don't give it to her right away or in the way she expects, she tries in more prominent, louder, and more disruptive forms. First, evaluate whether you are giving her enough of your undivided attention daily. Screen time and other hobbies can be a severe distraction from parenting, taking up more time than you realize. When she needs you, make a habit of completely stopping what you are doing and tuning in. Then teach her more appropriate physical ways to get your attention, such as tapping on your shoulder or placing a hand on your upper arm. Practice this method several times so that both of you understand your roles.

Stress-Induced Meltdowns

The noise in a bustling store during the holiday season or a crowded playground may be too much for your 3-year-old to handle. Some children are more sensitive to external stimulation, so be mindful of your child's sensory thresholds. Teach him how to go to a calmer space to get away from the noise, or offer a comfort object to ground him when he can't leave. Children with special sensory needs also may benefit from therapeutic interventions, so if meltdowns are predictably explosive and consistently sensory-related, talk to your child's doctor.

If the tantrums have suddenly increased in frequency and duration, it may be a reaction to a stressful experience. For example, you notice that a few weeks ago, tantrums were rare, but recently you changed his nighttime routine from sleeping in your bed to sleeping on his own. It seems successful to you, but it may have raised his overall stress level and reduced his ability to cope. In other words, his cup is full of enough stress already, and additional frustrations are causing it to spill over, resulting in meltdowns.

Avoiding stress altogether is not an option. Learning how to face and cope with adversity is a skill your child needs for life. Other common stress-inducing triggers may include a recent significant injury, moving, an unemployed parent or a parent who suddenly returns to work, or witnessing his parents argue. Please describe what you see in his behaviour and teach him how to verbalize his worries. You might say, "I wonder if you are feeling extra sad because I had to go to work yesterday. I missed you. Do you want to talk about it?" Finally, be flexible so that he isn't taking on so much frustration at once, even if you need to let some minor things slide for a while.

Quick Tip: Although your 3-year-old may start to look more like a small version of an adult, he cannot still regulate his own emotions. You may notice that your child can "hold it together" when at preschool, on a play date, or with a different caregiver, but as soon as he returns home, he is suddenly non-compliant, whiny, and prone to tantrums. This is normal behaviour for young children, who often see the home as a safe place to let out all the frustrations bottled up during the day.

CHAPTER 21:

Handling Tantrums

Not every toddler has tantrums, but most do. They are most common between ages two and three when there can be as many as one to two days for several weeks, and others intermittently. Not all tantrums were created equal. Telling them apart can be tricky.

Stress Tantrums

The toddler is stressed (tired, hungry, ill, or cranky due to several small disappointments, changes, and defeats) when some unpleasant thing happens. Perhaps he hates to have his diaper changed, and Dad insisted on it or Mom kept her hands on the grocery cart when he wanted to push it himself, or his toy broke. That one small incident becomes the straw that broke the camel's back, and suddenly the toddler loses control. The screaming and carrying-on are out of proportion to the problem because the upset isn't about a single event. It's the result of an accumulation of stress that has taken its toll on a tyke who, because of his age, doesn't have a lot of emotional control, to begin.

Trying to sidestep a stress tantrum may merely be postponing the inevitable. As things heat up, it becomes increasingly clear that the toddler is trying to provoke a struggle.

To manage stress tantrums:

1. Hold the child firmly but lovingly and reassure that she'll be okay in a bit. This assumes you can hold her. Children may thrash too wildly to be safely stored.

2. If she's endangering himself, other people, or property as she rolls about the floor, clear the area if you can. Otherwise, move her to a safe place, like a carpeted floor.

3. Let her cry it out. Tears are an excellent tension reliever.

4. Empathize with the fact that she's having a hard day.

5. When the tantrum ends, ask if she'd like to sit on your lap, rock her, lie down, and rub her back.

6. Provide reassurance that things will get more comfortable for her when her new tooth comes through, she's rested, she's adjusted to her new daycare centre, or the stressful situation has passed.

When it comes to stress tantrums, the best cure lies in prevention. Consider them a signal that your toddler is under more pressure than she can manage and see if there's a way to help lessen it. Remember that toddlers are already under a lot of stress because they struggle with their sense of inadequacy from wanting to do things and being unable to do them, having lots to communicate and being unable to say much, and wanting to be independent emotionally needy.

In a stress tantrum, the child isn't trying to get somehing; instead, she tries to get rid of the unpleasant feelings. Having a momentary whim gratified helps a stressed toddler feel better, but not for long. The next small crisis produces another upset of similar or even greater intensity because the real problem — feeling generally overwhelmed — remains.

Manipulative Tantrums

Once their end is achieved—freedom to run around the store, liberation from the car seat, permission to eat the cookie, or a toy—they settle down. Tantrums in public are common because many children have learned if they stage a big one, they will immediately be taken home, which is what they want.

But of course, every time you appease the child by giving in, you drive home the lesson that screaming, hitting, kicking, thrashing, breath-holding, fainting, and even head-banging and vomiting are workable ways to achieve goals.

If the behaviours during manipulative tantrums are particularly dramatic, discuss the problem with your paediatrician to satisfy yourself that—ignoring it—is a safe option. Actions that warrant a professional opinion include banging his head or other self-injurious behaviour, passing out, precipitating an asthma attack, or vomiting.

To end manipulative tantrums:

- If she's a raging puddle on the floor, tell her you'll talk to her when she's settled down.

- Carry her to an open space where she can't harm herself or anything else, preferably with carpet to soften the blows, if she's flinging herself around.

- Step over her and make sure you are close (but out of kicking range) by studiously ignoring her.

- Remain alert to what is happening so you can intervene if she tries to hurt herself or something else.

The challenge is not to take manipulative tantrums personally. See them for what they are: a child's rage at rules and limits. By failing to give in and not paying attention to her, you're showing what happens when people are assailed by crushing disappointments: life goes on. When a tantrum ends, and the child has settled down:

- See it as the victory it is—the child regained control on her own.

- Don't attempt to discuss what transpired before or during the tantrum—let the subject drop.

- Be warm enough to show her you're not angry with her—respond to her desire to be held, hear a story, or participate in another quiet activity once she's settled down.

- Don't try to compensate for having held firm by being overly solicitous.

If throwing a tantrum has worked in the past, the predictable short-term result when parents don't give in is an increase in both the intensity and frequency of tantrums. Confused youngsters work harder to employ the strategy that has worked so well in the past to get their way. It may take several scenes before they grasp that tantrums are no longer a useful method for getting what they want.

Communication Tantrums

Sometimes toddlers throw tantrums out of sheer frustration over their inability to communicate their needs. For instance, your toddler wants something. It's clear to your toddler that you have it. Try as you might, you can't figure out what your child is asking. Get the message across, and then dissolves it, or it is all too clear what your toddler wants: ice cream. He is sure it is in the freezer because that's where it's kept. Except that there isn't any ice cream there or anywhere else because you're fresh out. He's sure you're withholding it, and you can't find a way to explain it to him. Maybe she wants to watch a particular video, but the tape is broken, or he wants his pacifier, but it's lost. The only recourse is to provide reassurance that you would give him what he wanted if you could and let him rage at the injustice of it.

It's not easy being any age, but it can be incredibly hard to be a toddler. Parents who remain sympathetic as children struggle through these trying moments may also feel helpless. Remember that by demonstrating your love for your youngster when she is at her very worst, you are helping a lot.

What to Do During Tantrums

There are many ideas about the best way to intervene during a tantrum. I am going to spell out some general truths about tantrum intervention quickly. There are many exercises in this book, divided according to the age of your child, to help you create meaningful interventions that work for you. But for now, here are a few quick and easy rules that always apply:

- **Stay calm**. The key to all successful parenting—and most certainly to effective intervention during tantrums—is parental **self-control**. We will review some more practical steps to make it easier for you to keep your cool in the following *part 2*.

- **Ask yourself why**. Considering the motivation for behaviour can be very helpful. It might be useful to reframe the question as "What is my child struggling with?"

- **Empathize with the child's feelings.** The feelings are never the problem; it is what the child is doing with those feelings that can become problematic. Acknowledging the emotions, without judgment, is a significant first step.

- **Ignore the behaviour, not the child.** A lot of times, it is very useful to ignore the tantrum. The trick is first to communicate that you are available, loving, and patient but that you're not going to participate in the temper. The connection is the key. "I can see that you're outraged. I am sorry. I will make dinner now, and I hope that you will help me once you have calmed down."

- **Be consistent.** Many parents create rules on the fly and react quickly when things go wrong, which leaves little room for forethought and makes consistency very hard. The goal, however, is to try to make similar choices in similar situations and to hold relatively consistent boundaries. Trust that creating space for planning and forethought is a priority because consistency is a beneficial intervention (and prevention) for tantrums.

- **Offer alternatives.** If your toddler's goals are acceptable, help them find more appropriate means to achieve them. If your child is full of energy and won't stop running in the house, let them run outside with your supervision. If they are angry and throwing things, help them find safer ways to express the anger in their bodies, like stomping their feet or throwing pillows. There are healthy, non-hurtful ways to express emotions.

CHAPTER 22:

Tantrum Checklist

G o through the list of steps. Start with the external environment you've created. Ask yourself, "what caused this tantrum?"

1. Planning and Preparation

- Is it planning? If you could've planned better, you've learned for next time.

- Does my child have engaging activities?

- Did I stop my child's activity without warning?

- Are you using a transition timer?

- Did the tantrum occur when we were not home?

If the problem was not in planning and preparation, move on to trust and security.

2. Trust and Security

- Is my child feeling secure in his external environment?

- Do I have clear limits?

- Are they too rigid?

- Do they allow for playfulness?

- Did I take away my child's control by taking him out of his routine?

- Was this a hungry or tired time for my child?

- Was this a problem at bedtime?

- Do I have an exact bedtime routine in place?

If you have not been able to identify what created the tantrum, go through the next set of questions.

3. Am I present for my child? Am I kind when I speak to my child?

Is the problem me?

- Am I distracted when my child is trying to speak to me?

- Is my mood consistent with my child?

- Am I sending my child mixed messages?

- Is this a discipline or conscious parenting issue?

- Is it more proactive in preventing what occurred, therefore alleviating the need for discipline?

If you are sure you are staying present and being kind, check the following.

4. Going Within

- What are my thoughts?

- Do I have momentum in a negative direction?

- Would meditation help clear my mind?

- Am I worried about something?

If you've identified negative thoughts or momentum, it's time for energy changing ideas or meditation. If you have not been able to identify negative thoughts or emotions, ask yourself the following questions.

5. Self-Awareness

- What is my vibrational nature?

- What is showing up in my experience? Is everything light and easy? Remember, you attract everything to you. If you see anything in your current reality that is not pleasant, you emit a vibration that allows it into your experience.

- Is it all ease and flow?

- Did I let a negative experience gain momentum?

- Have I tried to change my energy frequency?

If you've identified that the problem is your vibration, you must snap out of it. Start with your emotional guidance system. What emotion are you feeling?

You cannot get from worried to happy immediately, but we have to turn the direction of your thoughts.

Pick any subject that feels better and purposely guide your thoughts there for one minute, until they gain momentum.

With that new thought, after one minute, pick another idea that feels a little bit better. Purposefully concentrate on that for one minute.

A Real-Life Example

I have an example of how to go through the checklist to identify the problem.

I wouldn't say I like the mornings, especially school mornings. Every morning during the school year, I would have my two children, who were eight and ten at the time, who I would need to pack lunches for and get breakfast. In addition to them, I had a two-year-old, a three-year-old, and a four-year-old. One morning, I could hear the three-year-old and four-year-old fighting about a toy. I continued to pack lunches because I was running out of time. The three-year-old then decided to hit the four-year-old, so now, they were both crying. I yelled at my children to put their tablets away and finish getting ready for school.

Let's examine the above scenario. First, going through the list, I had poor planning. I could've packed lunches the night before, but I chose to do it in the morning. Second, young children play in the toy room, but I do not have any engaging activities to interact with it. So, with planning, I have identified two hot spots that I could improve on. I should've packed lunches the night before, and I should've had an engaging table activity.

Now, let's move on through trust and security. Are my limits clear? Not necessarily. For the young children that morning, I have not provided any limitations, nor have I offered any structure to their external environment. For improvement, I could've told them I was setting the timer, and when they hear it go off, it means it's time for breakfast. Then they would have predictability and feel some control.

Was I present and kind? No. If I had been present at the moment, I would not have been distracted by making lunches. It would've allowed me, through conscious parenting, to step in before fighting occurred. I would've been able to anticipate it because of the growing escalation. I also was not kind because I was distracted and rushed; I yelled at my own two children, who I should've been more present and proactive.

Moving on, let's continue to see how my thoughts affected this scenario. I already said I hated the morning. When you open yourself up to views of "I hate this activity," more reasons you hate will add to the first thought. I could've changed my thoughts on how productive mornings can be. Just changing the view about mornings will change my entire experience of how mornings feel.

Lastly, in my experience, I have children who are not ready on schedule, children fighting over toys, and a lack of time. I could tell my vibration is not ease and flow. To get me back to a better frequency, I can try any of the energy changing ideas. To set me up for a better morning, I should've also meditated when I first awakened. This would've allowed me to start at a higher frequency, and I could've avoided a tough morning all together.

CHAPTER 23:

Guidelines in Behaviour Management for Toddlers

Managing your child's behaviour is about properly guiding your child so that she learns to behave the right way. There is a positive approach to teaching your child, and this approach is the best. This positive approach has to do with applauding your child when she is right and giving consequences when she is wrong. It is more than just paying attention to her mistake.

To manage your toddler's behaviour the right way, you will first need to:

Understand the Reason for Their Actions

You have lived in the world for a long time, but your child is just starting. This is when your child figures out how the world works (like what a person should do to be noticed or get what he wants). This does not mean you should overlook a terrible character. It means you should understand how they think so that you can know how to respond the right way. You should also know that your child can act terribly for several reasons, one of them being that she may not be getting as much sleep as required. So before administering consequences to a wrong, ensure your child is healthy. If she is not, take her to a GP and sort things out.

Again, your child may be reacting to the change in the family. For instance, your child may be affected by a family member's death, even the birth of a newborn. Starting school may also be a reason for the change.

Choose the Best Management Strategies for Your Child

There are many strategies for correcting your children and managing poor behaviour. Still, you have to know the one you adopt for your child. Every child is not the same, and what worked for your son may not necessarily work for your daughter. Sometimes, your child may need one of the strategies, and another, a combination of two or three.

Before using a strategy, ensure it has been proven to work. And before adopting one, you should run a stern test on your child to see if it tends to do. It is possible for a strategy that once worked not to work anymore; this is because your child is quickly evolving and will need a change of those strategies. If you realize that the strategies are not working for your child, you may need help. There are parenting hotlines available, but if you do not feel comfortable using them, visit a nurse or GP.

Be Committed to a Change

Raising a child is more than applying what you read. It is about dedicating your effort and time to ensure that your child has a good and peaceful home to grow in. Remember, your child is the reflection of you and the state of your home, and if you have a shabby and shallow home, your child will be the same if not worse. Children that grow in loving and secure families have no severe challenge in developing a good character. A child that believes she is precious will quickly learn and grow. These are the primary keys to raising a responsible child.

Take Care of Yourself

Do not get lost in the search for a better character. I cannot say the journey will be smooth, but I assure you to have a productive one. It is always worthwhile to give yourself in, but do not forget to take some time. Take a nap, eat good food, rest, and exercise so that you will be strong and healthy to notice the changes in your child's behaviour.

Dealing With Persistent and Severe Attitudes in Toddlers

Good kids can show off a poor attitude while they are angry or emotionally unstable, but the defiant kid will always have a bad mood on every occasion. If you notice a trend of attitude in your child that you do not like, follow these steps to change them:

a) Start now

My aunt's toddler gave another kid a terrible bite and then started crying. Instead of my aunt to point out the toddler's mistake, she ran to her kid and begged to stop crying. I was amazed, and out of that, I asked her, "why didn't you do something to tell this kid that what she did was wrong? She said she's barely 3; it will stop as she grows. I know for sure that this is not just prevalent in my aunt; many parents do this. Some parents excuse defiance in their kids as the "children's thing," believing they will out-grow it. Wow! But here is the truth; no one grows into discipline. Discipline is taught, and so as a parent, you must start the right time. Children learn fast, and whatever you show to your kids now will stick forever.

b) Make rules and attach consequences to them

Imagine if kids were born with a manuscript for living in the world. So, they would come in and start regulating themselves. Would there have been a need for parenting? I don't think so. In that case, we would have been giving birth to full-grown men. (Ouch! I can't imagine how pregnancy and labor pain would have been) Still taking advantage of their quick learning ability lets them know what you can tolerate and what you can't. Let them know the boundaries. The earlier, the better.

c) He learns the hard way

A kid with a persistent and severe attitude may need to see the consequence of her actions before stopping. Do you think this will be detrimental to you as a parent? Oh no! it will save you a lifetime of continuous administration of punishment for an attitude you wish can end.

If you tell her not to hit the toy on the floor, but she does not listen, let her. But if the toy breaks, do not let her have another until some time passes. This will teach her the importance of what she had; after all, even we adults do not value what while we still have them.

CHAPTER 24:

Behaviour Management Tips & Tools

These are tips that will aid you in dealing with issues that influence children's behaviour.

1 - Fights can be brutal for a child. It's even worse if this conflict happened between the parents. Understand the importance of maintaining a harmonious home where feelings are accepted and discussed without judgment. Disregarding a situation that has been recognized by your child can be harmful to their emotional development. If your child understands an argument or feels the tension in your home, explain that yes, his feelings are valid but that he is safe and loved.

2 - Letting your child make decisions and letting him dream about the future without fear will help him be a happier and more confident child. Allow self-expression and applaud your child's desires. Reinforce and "I can do it!" attitude.

3 - Getting your child to know, appreciate, and respect other cultures are not only a cool thing to do, but it can also help them in the future. Understanding different living ways will allow them to be more approachable and respectful, allowing for better relationships and success.

4 - Helping your child to feel loved and unique, in addition to his siblings, can shape his identity and present him with a healthy sense of self-esteem in the present and future. Everyone needs to believe in themselves!

5 - Children lie and do not always understand the gravity of a lie. Understanding where they are in development is necessary here. Talking about what harm lies can cause is essential in developing their grasp on how all the world works.

6 - Teaching gratitude to your child creates a happier child and can be fun. People love good news, especially children. What's better than having something to be grateful for about? Teach your children to be thankful for small things such as the weather, their toys, and clothes. The fun they have at the park, or even the hug they receive. There will always be something to be grateful for, and this way of thinking can change their world for the better.

7 - Humour is essential in the individual and social development of your child. Laughing is healthy.

8 - Children are surrounded by issues that can cause anxiety and fear. Fear of the unknown is fear of most everything for young children, not to mention the size difference for a child in an adult world. Explore with your child and teach them to feel capable and safe.

9 - You may have heard about "The Terrible Two's." Be aware of what to expect from the tantrum phase. Most parents would agree that the terrible two's are referring to 2 and 3-year-olds. Remember to practice patience and understanding. Children at this stage are ready to communicate and get around independently, and we are still learning. Make learning fun by giving them jobs as a helper with tasks you would normally do alone.

10 - Each child's actions have a meaning, but it is not always clear what it means. Pay close attention to the context of your child's behaviours, and you will understand what each behaviour of your child means.

11- This may seem like nothing to you, but it can mean a lot: Respect your child's growing emotional skills for your child. Their knowledge of the world is rapidly expanding and can become overwhelming. Never embarrass a child for feeling a certain way.

12 - It is usual for some children to feel uncomfortable in new situations. Giving them the rundown before you leave the house allows them to know what to expect, and it can help with confidence.

Be Aware of The Difficulties of The Child

According to experts, persistent difficulties in performing tasks can indicate signs of hearing problems, vision, or hyperactivity. They should be analyzed before raising the conclusion.

Certain behaviours may alert parents to find out if the child suffers from these disorders. It's essential to pay attention to troubles your child may have and discuss them with your doctor regularly. All children develop differently, so don't jump to conclusions on your own.

CHAPTER 25:

Why Toddlers Misbehave

Befote you blow up when your child carries on an unwanted manner, assess his point of view. He would say he is acting in the way in which he is? When evaluating a situation, always consider the conditions and your child's developmental stage. This doesn't excuse the behaviour çnor imply that you shouldn't respond. In any case, first, ask yourself, "What was that about?" This causes you to shape an increasingly empathic and suitable reaction. Common reasons for acting up at this age include:

Interest. A 1-year-old who continues playing with the phone, or a 2-year-old who can't stop pursuing the feline, is entranced and having a fabulous time, instead of being stubbornly disobedient. Toddlers learn about the world through hands-on investigation. Your child might be intent on finding out how a spoon that's dropped off of a high seat sounds not quite the same as a pea. A toddler lacks the discretion to curb this kind of discovery-by-doing, particularly in the face of another captivating situation. If there's no real damage being done, it's ideal for opposing interceding.

Testing. Indeed, even the best-carried children experience an opposite phase around 14 to 22 months, which can keep going for six months or longer. This is the point at which a child becomes progressively mindful of his force. Inebriated by the discovery, maybe your child is asking himself, "Exactly what am I capable of, and what amount would I be able to pull off?" He attempts to use this newfound force at each chance. This drive to stretch the limits is exacerbated by a high level of stiff-necked determination, a low resilience for frustration, and poor relational abilities. Oppositeness is intensified if the child is approached to make a significant behavioural change during this stage, such as disposing of the pacifier or starting latrine preparation. A craving for attention. A child may be exhausted, lonely, or excited with the disturbing reaction he's learned to make by playing with the catches on the TV set. So unfathomable is a child's desire for attention that he may find it additionally speaking to face the consequences of wrongdoing than to be overlooked.

Frustration. Toddlerhood is laden with constraints, both physical (for example, an inability to stack blocks impeccably) and forced (for example, holding your hand when going across a road). A toddler also lacks the verbal aptitudes that empower an older child to make his desires known or to release pressure. Accordingly, frustration mounts rapidly. It's often vented as hostility, anger, and different types of standoffish behaviour. The quickness and furiousness of these upheavals can startle you. Recollect that even though your child may show up more organized and capable than he was only six months sooner, despite everything, he has a lot of developing to do. It's not always developmentally workable for him to control his temper.

Common Problems

Temper Tantrums

- **Why it happens:** Tantrums flare like so many Fourth of July fireworks. The primary reason is developmental. Your child realizes that things aren't the way they used to be. He still wants to be nurtured and coddled like a baby, but he also craves an older child's autonomy. Along with this sense of push-pull comes a host of other influences that can drive him in the blink of his eye.

- **Each day brings a million new skills to begin mastering**, from pulling off a sweater to finger painting. His speech isn't adequate to explain what he means or needs. He faces many new expectations as well, from potty training to behaving well in a restaurant. Emotions change as quickly as the images on a computer screen saver, and fatigue or hunger intensifies a sense of overload. A tantrum is your child's way of saying, "Enough! Help!" She shows her frustration. She knows how: with screams, flailing limbs, dramatic contortions, or collapsing in a heap. Tantrums are perfectly normal. You're not likely to make it through toddlerhood without experiencing one. Or maybe a hundred.

- **Tantrums peak around age** 2. They taper off as your child approaches 3, as her verbal skills and physical control increase, and she learns more appropriate ways to channel her displeasure and outrage (though they can persist right up to kindergarten).

- **Prevention advice:** The simpler and more pressure-free your toddler's days are, the more calmly they will unfold. Look for ways to streamline the morning rush, for example, such as letting your child go to sleep in fresh play clothes the night before. Keep your expectations realistic, too. Never mind if her shirt isn't tucked in or her hair isn't combed. Don't try to haul her around on six different errands on Saturday morning. Also helpful: increasing your tolerance.

- **Ask yourself if an annoying behaviour (or uncombed hair) makes a difference**. If it's not hurting anything and doesn't set a dangerous precedent, let your child have her way. But don't abandon all restrictions in a misguided effort to circumvent tantrums. It's believed that persistent tantrums are especially common in the homes of overly permissive parents. Firmness lets a child know what the limits are, so he doesn't have to test you as much.

Public Tantrums

- **Why it happens:** In addition to the same factors that fuel a tantrum in the middle of your living room, a few other things may cause those that explode in public. Social pressure, such as when you bring your child to a party, can push a child over the edge, for example. Parents, too, feel added pressure in some social situations (a baptism, visiting a new school) when they sense, rightly or wrongly, many judgmental eyes are upon them. Or you may want so badly for your darling to act sweetly in front of Grandma that you unconsciously telegraph your anxiety to your child—maybe you fuss about his clothing or dirty face more than usual, or cluck a few too many warnings ahead of time. Kids also act up in public to get your goat. They know that you respond more quickly or feel less sure of yourself when there's an audience—meaning they may have a better chance of winning their way.

- **Prevention advice**: Prep your child before you go somewhere to make the experience is not unnervingly alien. If you're going to a friend's house for dinner, for example, let your child know who will be there. What sorts of things he'll be able to eat. Before you enter a toy store where you must pick up another child's birthday present—always a dangerous mission—remind your child that you won't be buying him a toy that day.

Biting

- **Why it happens:** Whether your child is the biter or the bitten, it's small comfort to know those sinking little teeth into a friend's soft flesh is widespread toddler behaviour. Because it's so primitive and painful, however, most parents worry. Rest assured that biting doesn't mean your child is antisocial or a Dracula in the making. Children begin to bite people soon after their first teeth appear. The behaviour is most common among 1-and 2-year-olds. Sensitive children who are impulsive or easily upset are especially prone to biting. The practice is usually outgrown during the preschool years, as children learn more socially acceptable ways of expressing themselves. The first bites may be accidental. Babies often gnaw to relieve teething pain.

- **They also use their mouth to explore the world**. If you are breast-fed, you may remember your baby's shock biting your breast when her new teeth came in. She, in turn, probably noted your response, whether it was an exclamation of pain or a surprised "Hey!" Early biting persists when children discover they can use the behaviour to rise out of their parents. It's fun. One-year-olds often bite out of excitement, such as when they get too worked up during wild play. As with a baby's first curious nips, biting can escalate as a child learns that it inspires an instant reaction, and often a ruckus when another child is involved. Remember that negative attention appeals to a toddler just as much as positive.

- **Older toddlers bite others out of frustration**. Lacking language skills or social skills, they resort to their teeth to say "Stop!" or "Enough!" The typical target is a playmate of similar age. Biting acts as a kind of defence mechanism, too. A friend may have crowded a child into a corner, such as in a tussle over a toy. Feeling threatenedm but unable to summon the right words or another form of physical force, the cornered lad lashes out with his handiest weapon, his teeth. Rarely premeditated in young toddlers, biting takes the perpetrator by surprise almost as much as the victim. Stress may intensify the impulse to bite. For example, a child may be in a new care situation or tired by an overscheduled day. Some experts believe that biting is on the rise among toddlers because they are under increased amounts of stress from long days at child care, sometimes without adequate stimulation or guidance.

- **Prevention advice**: You can't entirely prevent bites, but you can reduce their frequency. Avoid sending your child mixed messages by nibbling his fingers or toes in play. Roughhousing, in general, is not a good idea for a child going through a biting spell. Try to minimize the odds of your child feeling overwhelmed, for example, by providing age-appropriate toys and keeping an eye on things when he's with a playmate.

If your child becomes a chronic biter, take a step back to consider his overall day. Is he spending more hours in child care than you think is optimal for him? If he's in a large centre, would he thrive better in a family-oriented care situation where he might get more individual attention? Are there extenuating circumstances, such as a new baby or the death of a pet, putting him under stress, and if so, can you and your caregiver think of ways to provide extra TLC? Give your child ample attention when he's right. On occasions when you notice that he's channeled feelings of anger or frustration in more socially acceptable ways, be sure to comment and congratulate him. The long-term goal is to teach your child self-control so that he can resist the urge to lash out by biting.

CHAPTER 26:

How to Discipline Your Toddler?

Frustrated with your kid's antics? Disciplining toddlers can be tricky. Here are some discipline tricks that actually work.

"Parents need to understand that children are built to explore and experiment. And some of that behaviour parents may call misbehaviour. They are trying to be independent, but they don't have the skills and get frustrated," says Linda Gilbert, manager of training, youth and family development at the YMCA of Greater Toronto. She adds that the focus at this age should be on managing behaviour, not discipline as such.

All our experts agree that children will "misbehave" when our expectations are beyond their abilities. For example, it's not realistic to expect a toddler to follow a string of instructions, or to remember a rule after being told only once.

To keep expectations realistic, it's helpful to understand the developmental aspects that affect toddler behaviour:

1. Social skills

At 18 months, toddlers are just starting to be interested in interacting with other kids, playing with them rather than side by side. But the rules of social play are not instinctive—kids need to be taught about taking turns and being gentle. In fact, aggressive behaviour, such as biting, is normal, says Gail Szautner, chairperson of the Saskatchewan Early Childhood Association and executive director of Children's Choice

Child Development Programs in Prince Albert, Sask. "It's developmental. It's how they react."

Also normal is the reluctance to share. "Developmentally, they are just not ready for dealing with only one truck or always taking turns," says Connie Delorey-McGowan, executive director and owner of Cobequid Children's Centre in Lower Sackville, NS.

2. Self-control

A lot of the defiance that we attribute to toddler behaviour stems from their limited ability to control their impulses. Your daughter may know that chucking food off the high chair is a no-no, but try as she might, the urge to see her mac and cheese go splat on the floor can be overwhelming.

On the other hand, when a toddler's impulses and desires are frustrated, the reaction can be intense (here is so much frustration in a toddler's world: from the noodle that won't stay on the spoon to the grown-up who doesn't understand what she's trying to say.) It's very difficult for her to rein in her anger and resist the urge to hit, throw or have a tantrum.

3. Emotional Regulation

Toddlers have a hard time understanding their emotions, let alone controlling them. And they don't have the perspective or experience to realize that the deep sadness they feel over a broken cookie will soon pass. "Toddlers need help to identify and cope with their feelings," says Delorey-McGowan. Along with your own reassuring cuddles, it can be helpful to introduce self-soothing techniques, such as hugging a favourite toy, sipping water or breathing deeply.

4. Empathy

"Toddlers have a budding awareness of others, but are self-centred," says Delorey-McGowan. It's for this reason that they struggle with empathy — they don't understand that others react negatively to pain or frustration. This also explains why a toddler may react inappropriately to another child's emotions, like laughing when a playmate pinches his hand in the toy chest.

5. Comprehension

How can a child follow instructions if he doesn't understand what's being asked of him? Language and attention skills are just developing in toddlerhood, so it's important not to overestimate what kids can comprehend—that will just lead to frustration on both sides. Says Marshall: "Children can often understand what parents are asking, but it's hard to follow directions the way we want them to. Adults need to guide them."

What's the best way to discipline a toddler? And what do you do when your kid won't listen to you? Here is an age-by-age guide to disciplining your child.

As kids grow and change, so does their behaviour. The child who doesn't throw tantrums at two may sass you at seven, and give you major attitude at 12. The best way to understand your children's behaviour is to understand what they're going through developmentally, say the experts. This knowledge will help you discipline them without resorting to yelling, threatening or having a meltdown yourself. "Discipline is about guiding and teaching our children—it's not about punishment or anger," says Scott Wooding, a child psychologist in Calgary and author of The Parenting Crisis. "It's simply a way of helping kids learn right from wrong, and keeping them safe." Here are some strategies to keep your kids on track at every age and stage.

How To Discipline Your Toddler

Where they're at: Your little guy isn't whining, fussing or having temper tantrums to manipulate you or make you angry, says Elizabeth Pantley, author of The No-Cry Discipline Solution. "Mostly toddlers misbehave because they can't express or control their emotions. They also tend to be very demonstrative. So when they're happy, they're very happy. And when they're upset, they've very upset." Your tot is naturally inquisitive, so it's only normal for him to get into everything. His job is to test his new sense of independence; yours is to set limits.

Typical Trouble Spots

Tantrums: These emotional blow-ups are usually the result of your child's anger and frustration at not being able to say, do or get what he wants, says Pantley. He also has a very short fuse when he's tired, hungry, bored or frustrated. Tantrums are a surefire way of letting you know: "I really need a drink/snack/toy/nap—right now!"

Contrariness: Offer your two-year-old an apple and she wants a banana. Dress her in pink and she wants to wear brown. Your toddler is in the early stages of forming an identity separate from you, and part of the process may be deciding if you want it, she doesn't. Her favourite word: NO!

Discipline Tips Worth Trying With Toddlers

Offer choices: Toddlers are all about independence and control, so you can avoid a lot of problems by giving them a little more say in their lives, says Pantley. Two choices are enough for this age group, for example, "What do you want to do first: brush your teeth or put on your PJs?"

1. **Keep your cool:** Toddlers thrive on attention—positive or negative—so if you overreact when your child intentionally dumps her cereal, or has a meltdown in the grocery store, you can bet she's going

to do it again. Calmly let her know that we don't pour our food on the floor or scream when we can't have another cookie. Keep it short and simple (no lectures, please) or you'll just confuse her.

2. **Nip tantrums in the bud:** Minimize meltdowns by finding out what triggers them. If your tot always loses it when she's hungry, make a point of having lots of healthy snacks on hand. If she gets upset when she has to leave the park, give her lots of warning (10 minutes, five minutes, two minutes) before you start packing up. And limit visits to notorious trouble spots, such as the toy store.

3. **Take a time out:** By the time your child is two, time outs can be an effective discipline tool, say the experts at the Canadian Paediatric Society. If your tot angrily whacks his playmate over the head, take him to a designated time-out area where he can calm down and get control of himself. Explain to him what he's done wrong, using simple words like "no hitting." Time outs should only last for one minute per year of age, to a maximum of five minutes.

Typical Trouble Spots

Whining: "It's as painful to listen to as nails being scratched on a chalkboard — and it's effective because you just want the noise to stop," says Ari Brown, a paediatrician and author of Toddler 411. When whining becomes a habit, your child may not even realize she's doing it.

Not listening: Your preschooler is glued to the TV, ignoring your repeated attempts to call him to dinner. "Asking a child something three, five or 10 times makes raging lunatics out of all of us, and a child learns he doesn't actually have to respond until you're hysterical," says Sarah Chana Radcliffe, Toronto author of Raise Your Kids Without Raising Your Voice.

Discipline Tips Worth Trying With Preschoolers

1. Never ask more than twice: Here are how it works:

- Ask once nicely ("Please put your toys away").

- Ask a second time, but warn of a negative consequence if your child doesn't listen ("I asked you to please put your toys away. If you haven't done it by the time I count to five, I'll have to keep them from you until tomorrow evening"). Avoid making unrealistic threats like "Slam that door and you'll never watch TV again!"

- Apply the negative consequence, if necessary. "If you don't make good on your promise of discipline," says Radcliffe, "you lose credibility."

2. Catch them being good: Your preschooler really does want to please you, so make a point of encouraging him when he answers the first time you call him or shares a favourite toy. "We often pay attention to the behaviours we dislike and pay very little attention to the behaviours we want to see more of," says Terry Carson, a parenting coach in Toronto.

Model the behaviour you want to see "Children learn a lot more from what we do than what we say. If you lose your cool when you're upset, expect your preschooler to do the same. If your child is a champion whiner, he may just be mimicking how you sound when you ask him to clean up his messy room.

Five (5) Golden Rules of Discipline

1. Stand Firm

We all hate conflict, but if you don't stick to the rules and consequences you set up, your kids aren't likely to either, says Wooding.

2. Pick Your Battles

Give the small things small attention and the big things big attention, and you'll be happier and calmer—and (bonus!) your children will be happier, calmer and better behaved too, says Pantley.

3. Praise, Don't Punish

Try to practise "good feeling" discipline most of the time, says Radcliffe. "Simply put, your tone of voice, your behaviour, the words you're using, should all feel good to your child 80 percent of the time. If you can do that, you can do no wrong."

4. Set Clear Rules and Expectations

A carefully selected bunch of age-appropriate rules can make family life a whole lot smoother and easier, says Radcliffe. For example, the "no cookies before dinner" rule prevents regular arguments about snacking before supper. The "no computer after 10 p.m." rule stops a nightly dispute about shutting down the PC.

5. Provide Unconditional Love

Yes, it's a no-brainer, but children need to know you love them, every day, even when they've done something bad.

CHAPTER 27:

Suggested Approaches in Dealing Tantrums

Whis en your toddler misbehaves, instead of immediately moving to negative discipline, do what Denise does. She always tries to ask herself, "Now, why did Selman do that?"

She comes up with an answer: He was tired, hungry, needed some alone time. He needed more Mommy-time.

Sometimes, there is no answer—or at least not one she can come up. Sometimes, due to toddlers' undeveloped emotions and lack of impulse control, they're not even sure why they do some things. But hey! Occasionally, neither are we!

Once she knows the "why," she chases it with, "How can I train him so that this doesn't happen again?"

Suggested Approach #1: Play Detective

If you can't figure out the "why" to the meltdown, play "Detective." Asking your toddler, "Hmmm, what is it that Johnny wants? Is it a hug?" Then, hugging him tight might elicit a reaction—either good or bad, depending on your child and the tantrum level. "Is it a tickling?" These first two help him calm down enough to get him to answer the rest of your questions.

"Is it a drink?" "Is it a snack?" Begin to search. There's some reason he's having his tantrum. "What does Johnny want? Can he point to it?"

Johnny will get to the point that he'll begin pointing to what he wants. At times, it may still take some detective work. If he means at a bookshelf, you know he wants a story read to him, but what if it's a specific book he wants? Maybe Suzie hit him if he points at his sister, or perhaps she took a toy or looked at him cross-eyed. It may take some more investigating.

If you already know the reason and it's due to something he can't have, this approach won't work. Try another.

If it is due to something he can have, help him learn to ask for it nicely. It is where the "How can I train my toddler so that this doesn't happen again?" comes in. If he's still worked up, speak to him in a whisper to know you have his attention. Then, teach him how to ask for what he wants in sign language. You don't have to learn the proper sign. Make up your own.

Suggested Approach #2: Let Your Toddler Be the Teacher

Our goal as proactive parents is to train our children to understand why things are wrong to control themselves. Many toddlers throw tantrums because they don't know what to do with their feelings otherwise. They don't know how to express themselves. However, this in no way validates their behaviour. We must be careful not to allow them to feel comfortable in their misbehaviour.

Instead of yelling at Johnny when he hits another toddler for stepping in his sand creation, call him over and say, "Johnny, that was bad. You're mad. And that's fine. But what you did is not okay. What did you do that was wrong?"

I did three things there. I told Johnny what emotion he was feeling, I told him it was okay to feel that way, and I appealed to his conscience. "What did you do that was wrong?"

After Johnny tells you what he did wrong (hitting the other toddler), repeat what you said earlier, along with what he said: "It's okay to be mad, but it's not okay to hit. Hitting is bad. Instead, you should tell the other kiddo, 'I'm mad.' You shouldn't hit other people."

If he can't tell you what he did wrong, then tell him. Then, give him the spiel I just laid out in the paragraph above.

Next, act confused. Tell him, "I'm having a hard time remembering. Can you help me remember? Can you be my teacher? Why is hitting wrong?"

- It hurts other people.

- It hurts his friendships.

- It makes him madder.

- He'll get into trouble.

After he tells you that, it will take you to guide the conversation. Have him teach you what happens when we hit.

- We have to apologize.

- We get a consequence. This consequence will differ by family, but make sure you're consistent in whatever you choose. The result might even be that they lose whatever they were working toward on their chart if you're charting.

Have him apologize to the toddler he hit. Now his "friend" might not accept his apology and might not even recognize his presence. Still, Johnny tried and learned a valuable lesson.

Then, ask him to please tell you what the consequence is. If you're consistent in your discipline and must be a proactive parent, Johnny will know what that consequence is.

Ask him what alternatives he should have taken. If your toddler has other things he can do instead of hitting, he may choose those alternatives instead. He should know to:

- Come tells you what happened.

- Tell his friend, "I'm mad."

- Use his words, "That was my truck. Please give it back."

- Find something else to play.

You will have to guide this part of the conversation until your toddler gets enough practice to know the answers.

Make Sure To Praise Good Behaviour

If you practice doing those alternatives, it will work it into his muscle memory and make it easier for him to implement them when they're needed. Try having a teddy bear steal his truck. Have a baby doll knock the Barbie from her hands. Roleplay, too. You can be "Bratty Billy" or "Betty, the Bully." Have fun with it!

After you have had a few chances to talk about alternatives with him, start asking Johnny why he should have done instead of hitting his "friend" rather than telling him the other options yourself. Asking him will help work it into his memory.

Take a Moment For Yourself

If you're still having a hard time cooling down, here are some steps you can take to help yourself be that positive role model your toddler needs to be a proactive parent.

- Breathe deeply. In and out. In and out from deep within your diaphragm (your deep inners). Purse your lips and slowly suck in air as you would through a straw.

- Visualize. Imagine a beautiful scene. Mine is a waterfall in a jungle with an orange butterfly fluttering about me. I can almost feel the cold water splashing on my face and smell the freshness of the air. I hear the roar of the fall, the birds' chirping, and the croaking of the frogs. Pick what works for you. Lose yourself in it.

- Ground yourself. No, I'm not talking about grounding yourself to your room. Grounding is a therapeutic technique used with anxiety attacks, but it works well when dealing with frustration.

- Take a timeout. If you've been dealing with tantrums all morning and half of the afternoon, your nerves can get worn pretty thin! You often wonder why you still have hair, and smoke isn't rolling out your ears. Before your heart starts beating out of your chest, make sure the stove is off, and the doors and windows are locked, put your toddler in a safe place, and lock yourself in your room for five minutes!

- Do something you love. "But I don't have time!" you might argue. Yes, you do. Involve your toddler.

CHAPTER 28:

Tantrums Triggers

The sad truth about temper tantrums is that once it has begun; there is no chance of reasoning with the screaming toddler. He/she cannot hear you, according to some recent neuropsychological research. Once again, try to remain calm because you will only add fuel to the already frenzied state of your child.

Your sweet little dumpling has turned into a demon and is in total meltdown mode. Some children are more prone to tantrums, particularly hyperactive children, moody, or those who don't adapt well to new environments. These are a few of the trigger points you can use to spot the signs of an impending tantrum.

The Toddler Believes

This is just a short version of all of the things your toddler believes is wrong in his/her world:

- That car seat is peculiar.

- He/she doesn't want to get in the car.

- He/she wants to get out of the car by his/herself. Go away, Mom/Dad.

- A sibling looked at him/her.

- A sibling won't look at him/her.

- The socks don't work right.

- The shirt has a tag stuck on it: Why?

- Why are his/her lips salty?

- Why is everything 'too hot?'

He/she also asks some of craziest questions. Of course, you don't understand: 'jabajojo'; it must be a foreign language. You think; gee he/she is so smart. These are some of the things the toddler seems to think is entirely wrong in his/her space and time:

- Someone touched his/her arm.

- He/she isn't allowed in the oven to play! Why? It is big enough for me to fit.

- Why can't they understand "I" am Hungary? Maybe that is why "I" spelt it wrong. "I" forget it is called hungry.

Parental Mistakes (According to the Toddler)

- You chose the wrong pants. He/she threw them in the corner and refused to wear them!

- You threw away his/her favourite birthday balloon from a birthday six months ago!

- You gave him/her the wrong brown crayon.

- You gave him/her milk, not the yummy soda.

The Real Trigger Points

Studies have revealed between 60 to 90% of the two-year-old will throw a temper tantrum. The numbers peaked between the ages of 2-1/2 and three years when many toddlers had one daily. Don't worry; by five, most children have ceased the process except for the occasional doozy. Watch out for that one!

The fatigue button can be pushed if your toddler hasn't reached the verbal and emotional capacity to identify what his/her fatigue points might be at a given time. You cannot control his/her emotions, but you can watch out for some of these trigger points:

- **Beware of the 'I Want It' Mode:** Many times, toddlers act out merely because he/she wants something that isn't on the list of what is allowed. An outcry via temper tantrum is usually the result. This is one of the few issues that is best ignored. One of the times that the 'fit giver' cannot have things his/her way.

- **Distracted Parent Trigger:** Children—especially toddlers— crave the parent's attention. He/she cannot understand why Mom or Dad isn't giving 100% of the attention to what he/she wants. Unfortunately—sometimes—the world doesn't coincide with the opinion of what your child believes to be true. Ignoring makes the problem worse. The plea must be answered by distraction.

  This is a repetitive action that will be needed during many forms of discipline. While you take care of your bank business or other chores—simply—provide a picture or colouring book for the contentment of your precious bundle of overactive energy.

- **Too-Fast Trigger:** Sometimes, you don't realize your child cannot process too many new activities in one day. Toddlers take a little extra time to move from one activity to the next.

However, you probably don't realize it because of the path of destruction left by the toys!

- **Give your child extra time to do things on his/her own:** Try not to rush the process. If your child has learned how to dress him/herself; lay out a couple of sets of clothing for the day (Setting them out the night before is better).

Give your child an extra ten to fifteen minutes warning time before you are ready to walk out of the door. This will allow the initial shock of changing patterns/routines to register. It also won't rush the progress already accomplished such as a matching pair of socks. You know how toddlers see a mixed wardrobe!

- **Too much of a Good Thing**: Picture your child at his/her third birthday party. The fun rides, games, food, and prizes have all been prepared and served to the room of toddlers and other friends. When it comes time to blow out the candles, a tantrum erupts. The change of command was too much information at once. He/she was already involved with playing and not concentrated on the cake.

- **Hunger Trigger**: Hunger will give your child an anxious feeling which can undercut the child's sense of security. You need to remember toddlers eat smaller amounts of food at one time which means he/she might be hungry before you.

Hunger will reduce the child's ability to cope. Nutrition is a huge reason for a child to become angry, exhausted, and irritable. His/her blood sugar fluctuations and inadequate iron intake can also be triggers for a tantrum. So; don't forget the goodies when you leave the house for errands.

- Tired Trigger: The depraved part is children don't understand why they are feeling crummy; they just lose it. For example, your toddler might love juice, but you offer him/her a glass of milk. The tired mode kicks in with a total meltdown.

- **Long Times to Wait:** Your curious youngster hasn't comprehended the concept of time. So, ten minutes might as well be ten hours to an active kid. Hopefully, you will see the signs and have a favourite item ready. After all, maybe that is probably what the fidgeting was from the start. Long waiting times is one of the biggest trigger points for a toddler. Think about it!

- **Sibling Rivalry**: If you have another child, do you ever notice a tantrum can ensue if the older sister/brother has a favourite toy? It all amounts to confusion and frustration when a fit is thrown. If sharing is a problem, try to spend equal time to eliminate any identity issues. Let him/her understand how fair it is to share and love as a group. Be firm and calm and provide the all powering distraction.

- **Boredom:** Before a tantrum, do you notice he/she has lost interest in the current activity? He/she might be stuck inside without many new stimuli. This reaction happens more on a rainy day or when he/she doesn't feel well. Once again, try to plan and have a play date with other friends' children. It will bring new energy to the room and possibly prevent a meltdown.

- **Emotional Challenges:** Your bundle of joy can be more observant than you think. Toddlers can become tuned-in to the emotional climate involved around them. If he/she has observed an emotional outburst from a family member or other loved person –including crying or arguments—he/she might act out.

The most obvious way to get attention is to kick and scream for acknowledgement. You need to be there with emotional support and comfort while he/she deals with the stress. It takes time, but your toddler will use the experience to develop a more refined coping skill. It's part of the overall plan of toddlerhood; learning.

- **Pain**: Tots can cry in response to an illness or discomfort, but parents cannot always tell what the culprit is for the outbreak. Common ailments can come from a stomach ache, earache, headache, or teething pain. They can be the leading cause of irritable and irrational behaviour. Your child might not be old enough to display the reasoning. It's up to you to figure it out.

- **Fear**: Hopefully, your toddler doesn't have to experience 'grown-up' fear. For a youngster, it can come from insecurity issues (such as being left at the baby sitter's house). Watch out for the plea of him/her wanting to show you something. That is a good clue. This is also normal but can happen when you are leaving your bundle of joy behind.

  Just ensure your toddler you will be back and let him/her know many things will be fun at the sitter's house. It is best to leave calmly but quickly to eliminate any additional stress.

- **Allow a Quick Nap:** You might need to find a place for your child to rest his/her head for a few minutes if you have to leave the house close to nap time. Just remember to bring your favourite toys and snacks. Try to stay ahead of the game plan.

- **Overnight Excursions**: If you know you are leaving the house for an overnight stay, be sure to bring his/her favourite pyjamas too. Try to cover all of the essential basics of which might be the most favourite items.

- **The Old Motto is Being Prepared**. When you leave the house, have something to occupy your time as well. Have a favourite book or a tablet to write a note to your friends. Take advantage of the time since you don't know how long the quiet will last.

CHAPTER 29:

More Issues of Tantrums

After you have learned different discipline and parenting techniques, it is now time to practice. How will you manage an uncontrollable child doing her theatrical performance in the house? Or those behaviours he intentionally did to get your attention? How about that spectacular tantrum at church and in the cinema?

This chapter will help you put practical discipline into action. Treating tantrums would be dependent on the age of your child, where the temper is being staged, and the reason for such activities. Although this is considered the main attribute of a toddler, there are still those children aged ten years and above who still have tantrums now and then. Wherever possible, it is still best that parents' guide their children and be gentle in dealing with them. Note that as parents, throwing your tantrums in front of your child would defeat the purpose of discipline. And so, when your authority is challenged, you must learn the importance of being consistent and firm in every decision.

The following are some situations where discipline is required and the possible solutions and techniques that you can do:

Tidying Up Toys

Maria often wakes up to a messy house because her children won't tidy up their toys. What should Maria do?

- Do not stress yourself. Children aren't born tidy. They are entirely unaware of the disaster area where they live. They should see it in you, and it should be modelled to them.

- You must have sensible expectations for your children. An orderly house cannot be expected from toddlers under three years old.

- If you have a five-year-old or older, you can train him to be neat and orderly. Please do so by allocating a big box meant for his toys. Once he is done playing, he must put all his toys in there. Make sure you demonstrate how this should be done.

- If he seems to be hard to control, the best thing to do is restrict the toys. You may have overindulged your child with so many toys that the house seems like a warehouse of playthings. So, keep some away and only bring out those toys that he often plays.

- Steer is clear of toys that come apart into tiny pieces. If you don't, you sure will spend a big chunk of your time looking for lost components or parts.

- If it is time to tidy, make sure you say it excellently and reward their efforts.

Intentional Deafness

"Could he be deaf? If you complain about the same thing, then there is nothing to worry about these. Your child does not hear because, yes, he refuses to listen to things from you, especially if you are asking him to do something such as eat his veggies, do his homework, or tidy up his room. Although he does not hear, there is no difficulty picking up the hiss and doing some simple behavioural boost.

- Parents should learn proper communication in the true essence of the word. Do so by not shouting at your child. Gain his attention and make sure to get eye contact. Do not nag. If you need to call him from a distance, make sure he is informed that he must answer back when you get his name. Impose a rule and make sure you both follow it by the book.

- As much as possible, do not let petty things get in nurturing your relationship as parent and child. Arguments and debates are a waste of your precious time when you can both bond, help, and encourage your child.

My Child Doesn't Listen To Me

"My child continues to do what displeases us as parents. I would often tell him to stop; he would for a moment, and then go back to his business once we turned our back."

This is a classic. Children will often do this, and you must be fully aware of it. This is a perfect example of a toddler who will do everything to stretch the limits and patience of his parents. Remember, they can be as creative as that. And, if you lack insight, you may easily fall into the trap. What should you do?

- Ask yourself if you can just let it pass and if this behaviour can be left ignored. If you think this isn't a threat and your child immediately shifts into obeying your commands the moment he sees that no one is paying attention, then you can just let it slide.

- Let your child know and emphasize that you do not like the idea of him not listening to you. Warn him and make sure he listens. Move your child or yourself out of the situation. Sometimes, it is best to shrug things off and keep yourself busy with other important things.

I Am Playing With Dangerous Objects

"He likes playing with forbidden things in the house, such as electrical cords, remote controls, and cellphone chargers. What should I do?"

Children see adults fiddling with their gadgets and other electronics in the house that make them more curious about these things. The moment they get the chance to touch them, they will. To prevent breakages, tripping over cords, or worse, electrocution, adults must keep these valuables out of the children's reach and sight. Also, this must be discouraged the moment you see them about to touch these things. When it is not possible, you may try the following:

- Hold his hand and gently tell him that it is not okay to touch them. "Honey, these things are bad. They are not to be touched by kids like you."

- If the number one fails, you may need to be tough. If touching comes down to a challenge or to get your attention, be firm enough to say "No."

Handling Meal Times

"During mealtime, my child usually throws food on the floor."

Again, another common problem among children. Either they throw their food or eat their food but immediately spit it out. If this is one of his attention-seeking antics, immediately tell him that it is not right to throw away food. You may also tell him stories of children not being able to eat. If these don't work, try the following:

- Make him sit comfortably in his chair and watch as he eats. When he spits food or throws it on the floor, say a firm, "No."

- If he does this again, wipe his hands and set the food aside for later. You cannot force a child to eat if he does not want to. You will only end up disappointed and angry.

- If, after a few minutes, he asks for the food, give it to him, but this time, warn him that it will not be given to him again if you catch him not eating.

You Are Playing Parents Against Parents

"The moment I say, "No," my child will immediately rush to his father to get his "Yes."

If both parents are united in disciplining their child, this particular scenario will not crop up. It will never even exist if both of you have the same goal of disciplining your child. Remember, you may have different opinions, but it should be left to discuss privately. You must always appear to be incomplete unity with your partner in public, especially if your child is present.

My Child Does Not Like To Share

"My 2-year old does not want to share toys with other kids visiting us."

- Young children are not gifted in sharing and socialization. Since they do not understand the meaning of sharing at a very young age, they often feel that the sight of another child or children in the house would mean giving up what is his. As a result, he refuses to share his toys. What should you do in this situation?

- First, you do not have to force your child into sharing his toys with someone else. In other words, don't force the issue. If he does not want to share at that moment, let him be.

- Notice that when you intentionally do not mind your child or let him sense that you are not watching over his every action, he will gradually try to do what you wanted him to do, such as interacting with visitors and sharing food and toys. If you see this scenario, do not immediately praise him, just let him do his thing and smile at him when you catch him looking at you. Chances are, he is making sure you see it and is seeking your approval.

- When he reaches for you or runs to you, hug him, and tell him that he did a great job. Sometimes, children need encouragement from their parents. Just as you are tired of the usual arguments, they are, too.

My Child Is Susceptible

"Each time I raise my voice to discipline, he immediately bursts into floods of tears."

Another common occurrence that usually backfires at parents, leaving them guilty and confused. Some children can be treated with gentle discipline, and some will use their talents to win over their parents' battle. They know that if they cry, it is easier to trump their parents. What should you do?

- When dealing with a sensitive child, make sure that you are gentle. Do not just raise your voice in your attempt to hush him. Stay close, hold his hand, stroke his hair, and give him a warm embrace. Since most children are sensitive when they are not getting enough attention, make it known to him that you are there. Assure him of your love for him.

- For children who use these antics for central manipulation, stand your ground and be firm. When he listens to you, talk to him while holding his hand. Tell him that it breaks your heart, seeing him do things you do not want him to do. Give him enough reasons not to do it again.

My Child Hates Going To Sleep

"My 4-year old just refuses to go to sleep when it is time to take a nap in the afternoon."

Many factors contribute to this significant issue, but you could try the following:

- Allow him to watch TV as you put him to sleep. Most parents would oppose this one, but there are those children who get heavy-eyed when in front of the television. Lay him down. Give him a bottle of milk. If he fails to sleep this way, just let him. Remember, do not push him to go to sleep if he does not want to.

- Let him play with his favourite toy. Again, this is another activity that will not put him to sleep in an instant. Still, at least you get to have him do his favourite activity instead of stressing yourself out and scolding him. You can also read him a book if he is not in the mood to play.

- Keep in mind; the child will sleep when he is sleepy regardless of the kind of activity he is doing. And should he allow you to put him to sleep, carry and hold him in your arms, and sing him his favourite song?

CHAPTER 30:

Toddlers Misbehaviours

Sibling Fights

Siblings fighting with each other is another day-to-day experience a parent should expect. Fights can happen for literally any reason at all; kids can fight over toys, kids can fight for space, fights can even occur over who sits on daddy's lap, whatever it is, kids can fight over it.

Fights, sometimes, can be intentionally sparked by one child or the other; children can seek attention by any means possible, even if it is negative. After all, half bread is better than none. Competition is another reason why siblings fight each other; fights can happen over who does what in first place, to have a bath, who gets dressed first, until the end of the world, kids will compete and fight for supremacy. In the twinkle of an eye, playtime can turn into wartime between siblings.

Having a younger sibling can be frustrating for a toddler, which would cause them to express their anger by trying to start a fight. A toddler is yet to understand what it means to have a younger one; all he knows is that one new little creature has come to hijack all the attention, love, and care he's been getting.

It's not an easy job for a parent who, by adding a new member into the family, now has to add refereeing to the long list of parental tasks. Some parents find it hard to the extent that they never even know what to do when the war begins, this war, which happens, at least, about six times a day.

The following are some tips that should be taken for the tackling and reduction of the daily inevitable sibling squabbles.

- **Kids learn from what they see:** Make sure you are not just telling your kids to do as you say, behave how you want them to copy. When your kids see that you handle everything that comes your way aggressively, you are only teaching them to be aggressive as well, how they see you treat and relate to people matters a lot, the kind of relationship your kid notice between you and your partner is another example they will learn from.

- **Calmness in intervention:** When fights erupt, and you want to intervene, be sure to show a high level of calmness; yelling never solves anything, it only brings about escalation, I know it is annoying to see your kids getting in a brawl, but be sure to suppress your anger and not show your frustration.

- **Try not to judge and take sides:** When you hear your kids fighting over something (probably a toy), and you get there, with or without an idea of who had it first, try settling the fight regardless, putting can build grudges in Kids' minds. It's normal to think about fairness but trust me, and the other kid will have the fault to some other time. There you have your balance.

- **Ignorance:** This will be needed at some point, when you find out that your kids start to fight in search of attention, then some amount of ignorance will help make them know that negative attention is not a way of life, because if they are always getting it anytime they fight, then they will keep on doing it anytime attention is needed. Well, a great way to prevent this is to make sure kids have a lot of equal time and attention.

- **Assurance of importance:** This is for an older toddler who is having a younger sibling, they believe that with the arrival of the new little one, their significance goes down the drain, they will do almost anything to make sure that doesn't happen, they'll fight for their right. This also requires a lot of attention to older toddlers to feel secure and not feel threatened by the arrival of the new one. Parents can prevent this by preparing the kid for the new baby, you create a connection even before the baby is born, having them talk to the baby, feel the baby kick, see images of the baby in the belly, can create the desired connection, making them through pictures of their baby days can also help prepare them for what is coming.

- **Verbal lessons:** Try explaining to your kids how bad it is to fight their siblings, show them how they can live together in peace and harmony; you can even encourage them to employ turn-taking, it helps reduce the rate of fighting as they know they will have their turns.

Swearing and the Use of Bad Languages

With all the excitement and joy that comes with your child reaching the speech milestone, there is also a downside. Kids, as they learn to speak, also tend to pick up the negative words, and getting them to stop this habit is not always easy. Kids can copy these words from immediate family members and people around them, from media and the internet, from other kids, even parents can be of influence.

However, you shouldn't be surprised when you hear your kids swearing for the first time. Even if you know you are not the swearing type, you are not the only source of knowledge for your kids. Kids use these bad languages for different reasons such as attention-seeking, for fun, to show surprise or shock, to show frustration and anger. Below are some tips on how to handle or curb this habit.

Tips on handling swearing and the use of bad languages

- **Refrain from this habit:** Parents that do not want their children to pick up the habit of swearing and foul language usage, should also try to watch their choice of words too, you don't want to be a bad influence to your kids.

- **Don't give them what they want:** Kids can seek attention in many ways, even if it is negative, display of annoyance is also a form of attention to them, so parents should try to exercise patience and calmness when kids do this. In the case of kids using this as a medium to get your attention, parents should try to ignore them; kids would stop using this tactic when they learn that it won't get them any attention. Parents should also make sure not to give kids reasons to desperately seek attention, always create time for your kids, and encourage positive ways of getting your attention.

- **Talk to them:** Let your kids know that swearing is unacceptable, explain to them that some words are not allowed and should not be uttered in daily activities, like when talking to other people, words that can upset them should be avoided. Also, try to provide alternative terms that can be used to replace to swear words to express surprise. Make them know the difference between nice and unpleasant words, and you should always let them know immediately whenever they have used an unpleasant word.

- **Deal with the source:** Try to find out the sources where your kids might be getting this influence and try to take care of it. Monitor the media exposure of your child, make use of parental control features in gizmos, so that they will be restricted to only programs meant for their ages. If you find out that your kids are learning from other kids, try calling the attention of the kids' parents to the situation so that all the kids would be corrected. Ask other members of the family to try and caution their speech around the kids.

- Praise for progress: Try showing appreciation by praising your kids when you notice changes in their expressions, it gets them to use the right words more often.

In addition, be careful not to encourage this habit by smiling or laughing when your kids use these words, even if it's funny to you. Make yourself a better person too by limiting the usage of these foul languages.

CHAPTER 31:

Strong-Willed Kids

With all that has been discussed, we can tell that aggressive discipline is not welcome, but when nonaggressive discipline is not working, is it ok to use too aggressive measures? When we have tried every possible way to correct kids, but they are not heeding, it's only normal to think towards aggressiveness, but it's never right to employ methods that can harm the kids (physically, mentally, and emotionally).

Kids like this are called different names by different people, but the most popular is strong-willed. It is kids are kids that stand by what they believe, no matter what you do to try to change them, you can't force a change out them, except if they are willing to. When strong-willed kids say "NO," it means no.

Some Characteristics of Strong-willed Kids

Strong-willed kids show some characteristics that other kids don't:

- **Can be very persistent:** Strong-willed kids never give in, they enjoy power-struggling and battle for supremacy, and it is very convenient for them to argue for a very long time. There will be going and going. They also always want to get what they think they deserve or desire.

- **Question authority:** These kids don't just accept whatever you tell them. They always want you to give them reasons. They always demand to know why they should do whatever you ask them to.

- **Deep and frequent outbursts:** Spirited kids, as they are also called, are quick to display their anger, tantrums in strong-willed kids are stronger, they can go extreme and do things like foot-stomping, throwing themselves, very loud yelling, et cetera, at the floor, in a bid to make their feelings (of anger) known.

- **Can't wait, impatient, but hate to be rushed:** They are terrible at being patient, they hate to wait for something for too long, but the funny irony is that when it comes to them, they like to work at their pace, they never want to be rushed.

- **They like dominance:** They like to dominate and behave in a bossy way. They always want to be in control.

- Don't care about rules: They live by their own rules alone. They like to decide for themselves.

Spirited kids have a bright side to them in the sense that if well guided, which is tough to do because of their independent mentality, they grow up to have influential personalities comprised of very high self-esteem, solid self-confident, high problem-solving skills due to their independent mentality, never give up spirit and leadership ability.

Dealing with Strong-Willed Kids

The following are the general tips in dealing with your toddlers. Different situations require different solutions. It is now your duty as a parent to identify what works for your kids.

- **Acknowledge their feeling:** Show them that you understand their feelings and reason for their outburst that will calm them down.

- **Identify what triggers their anger:** You have to try to identify regular causes for their anger, then try avoiding the "avoidable" ones, be careful not to indulge them, do not avoid corrective measures. Only avoidable things should be avoided.

- **Always follow through:** When rules are broken, or limits are crossed, be sure to follow through with consequences.

- **Give rewards for good behaviour:** they will repeat good behaviours when rewarded until it becomes part of them.

- **Give timeouts:** It gives them time to calm down.

- Stay calm: Parents have to work on themselves, sometimes we let our anger affect our actions, we have to stay calm.

All other previously stated measures will work on strong-willed children but need extra work; just stay calm and keep trying. You will find that patience yields results.

CHAPTER 32:

Practical Applications

You are equipped with the knowledge and the techniques of effective discipline. It is time to learn their application. Having experience of effectively disciplining your toddler is helpful, so you will know how to respond appropriately in situations where your toddler tends to misbehave. Take note that punishing a child takes self-control, perseverance, and even practice.

The following are based on real-life case studies. First, read the situation and then think of a solution. After this, look at the recommended solution, so you will know how your decision matches with the suggested action. Take note that the answers below are merely guided and do not claim to be the best course of action in every situation. After all, the art of discipline is a continuously developing system.

Charles knocked over the building blocks of his sister, Nina:

- Should you scold Charles, lock him up in his room, or maybe ignore it? After all, it was just a toy that he knocked down. What should you tell Charles?

- **Solution:** Tell Charles not to do it again and apologize to his sister by helping her rebuild the building blocks.

While playing a game, Marco keeps throwing the clay around:

- Should you end the game right away and tell him to clean his mess? Should you let him enjoy what he is doing and continue to scatter clay all about the place? What should you tell Marco?

- **Solution:** Tell Marco to "keep the clay on the table so that we can keep playing."

Max is riding the bike and would not let his friend, Sarah, to have a turn.

- Should you encourage Max not to share his bike with his friend, Sarah? Would you tell Max to stop riding the bike right away and embarrass him in front of his friend?

- **Solution:** Tell Max to take two or three more turns, and then let his friend turn.

Nicole and her friend, Jenna, were playing with the dolls. Nicole forcefully took the beauty that Jenna was playing:

- What should you tell Nicole?

- **Solution:** Tell Nicole that it is Jenna's turn to play with the doll and that if she (Nicole) wants to play with it, she should tell Jenna, "Jenna, may I have a turn to play with the doll?"

Max and Peter were running outside. Max pushed Peter:

- Should you tell your kid, Max, to stop playing right away? Should you wait for an explanation before you respond?

- **Solution:** Tell Max, "Max, you hurt Peter. Apologize and tell him you will not push him again."

Instead of stacking his blocks, your toddler starts throwing them:

- Should you tell your kid not to play with the blocks anymore? Can you ask him to stop what he is doing?

- Solution: Say, "The blocks are for stacking."

You saw your child swearing at his friend. After a few minutes, he approached you and explained what happened:

- Should you have him grounded? How can you explain to him in simple terms that swearing is bad? Would it be acceptable to get angry at your child for severe such misbehaviour?

- **Solution:** Tell your toddle that swearing is not a pleasant and happy word and that he should never say that word to anyone. Also, reassure him that you understand him and that you are on his side, but stress the lesson that he should not swear again no matter the reason.

Your child starts breaking his toy:

- Is it a good idea to stop buying him toys? Should you be mad at him?

- **Solution:** Tell him that "You must be nice to your toys. Tell me you will not break your toys again."

Your child, Frank, punched his friend.

- Should you tell Frank to get inside the house and ground him for a day or even a week?

- Solution: Take your kid, Frank, out to the side, and explain to him that it hurts when we get punched, especially by a friend. Tell him to apologize to his friend and say that he will not hit him again.

Your child starts to draw on the table with coloured pens:

- What should you tell your child?

- **Solution:** Tell her to "Draw on the paper." Could you not make a big deal about it? You can also use the logical consequence technique and tell him to erase his drawing on the table and clean up his mess.

Your kid invites his friend at home. They play the computer. Your kid has been playing for a long time and would not like to share anymore:

- What should you tell your child?

- **Solution:** Say, "Two more mouse clicks, and then, it is your friend's turn.

There is a party at your place. Your child is shy to be with a large group of people and runs away into her room whenever you try to bring him to join everyone.

- Should you just let her stay in her room simply because she is shy?

- Solution: Gently tell your child that she looks beautiful. Tell her that she can go to the large group all by herself after some time or hold your hand now and walk over to join everyone and enjoy the party.

You receive a note from his teacher saying that your child is disobedient. Your child says that it is not true and that everybody hates that teacher:

- Should you ignore the letter from the teacher?

- **Solution:** Tell your child that "In school, we need to mind the teachers. I always listened to my teachers when I was in preschool. I will schedule a meeting with your teacher."

While playing with the building blocks, your toddler took his sister's toy without asking for permission, and he is not willing to give it back:

- What should you tell your toddler?

- **Solution:** Tell him, "Your sister was playing with that block. Give it back to her, and let us find some blocks for you."

During a family game, John starts hitting his sister, Melissa:

- What should you do?

- **Solution:** Tell him calmly to keep his hands to himself and apologize to his sister, or he will have to be eliminated for the family activity.

After playing a game with your toddler, she does not want to help in cleaning the mess:

- Should you force your kid to clean up? Should you be upset with her?

- **Solution:** Tell your toddler that the mess was because of the game. If she still wants to play a game with you next time, she should help you clean up the area.

During a family activity, your toddler begins speaking out loud and would not sit still while you are talking, which also disrupts the activity:

- What should you tell your kid?

- **Solution:** Tell him that everyone has a chance to talk and wait for his turn. Also, tell him that he will have to sit still; otherwise, the family activity can no longer be continued.

During a family reunion, your child does not want to join everyone at the table for dinner:

- Should you grab your child's arm and force her to join everyone?

- **Solution:** Tell her that it is time for dinner. You can also add, "Do you want to go by yourself or hold my hand?"

Samantha is building a tower with her blocks, but Liza keeps knocking it down. Samantha is now getting frustrated:

- What should you tell Liza?

- **Solution:** Tell her to apologize and leave Samantha's tower alone, and then offer to help her build her outlook.

Your toddler, Stella, refuses to eat her snack:

- What should you tell her?

- **Solution:** Tell her to finish her snack, or she can start doing her homework.

Marie is dancing on a chair, and you are worried that she might fall:

- Would you explain to Marie the risks of dancing on a chair?

- **Solution:** Say, "Marie, put your feet on the floor."

Gabriel is yelling at his friend:

- What should you do?

- **Solution:** Take Gabriel aside, and then tell him that he must talk to continue playing.

Rose is dancing in the room when it is time for her to sit down and read:

- What should you tell her?

- **Solution:** "Rose, it is time to read. Choose the book you want Mommy to read to you?"

It is time to go home, but your child still wants to play outside:

- How would you say to your child to go home?

- **Solution:** Say, "It is time to go home. Shall we race to the door?"

It might be challenging to discipline a toddler as long as you are ready. You should not use any form of physical. Discipline is made in a kind and calm manner. As long as you use the proper words and say them correctly, they are powerful.

Being able to teach your toddler good manners and right conduct is always possible. Every time your toddler tries your patience, it is a sign that there is a learning opportunity that you can take advantage. When you are disciplining your toddler, always focus on building a positive relationship. Filial love requires sincerity, perseverance, a fair amount of patience, continuing support, and undying love for your child. Last but not least, remember that children are very fragile. You should be careful with their heart.

The Defiant Child Who Refuses Any Food For Breakfast

"Would you like Cereal or a Banana?"

Breakfast is non-negotiable, but by engaging using a question, they will feel included in the conversation. Consider negotiation and possible compromise, but make sure you are still engaging using items rather than telling them what to do.

"You can wear your favourite shoes today if you have cereal for breakfast. Would you like that?"

The Sensitive Child who has a Tantrum at the Playground

Remember that for the sensitive child, everything is overwhelming and scary. Start by socializing with one child at a time, try and keep a close watch on their cues so you can head off any feeling of being overwhelmed and take them away from an overstimulating environment if necessary. Try to make exposure to situations like this in steps rather than all at once.

"I know this is difficult for you. Can you tell me what's wrong?"

Acknowledge the child's fear, and then by engaging them to draw them out. Let them vocalize the problem so you can better understand how to handle it.

The Self-absorbed Child who Wants their Way

"I want to play alone. He will break it!"

For the self-absorbed child, you need to be brief, acknowledge them, but do not engage, or they will continue to drag you in and manipulate until they get their way. Be firm and offer them an acceptable alternative.

"I know you're worried about the toy. Will you let him play with it now, and then we can put it away somewhere safe later?"

By acknowledging the fear but encouraging group play, you're allowing the child to continue interacting with their peers rather than punishing them by taking away interaction. Giving an acceptable alternative will enable them to think about the situation and be involved in the decision, so they do not resent the outcome. If they continue to act out, say a firm "no" and walk away. Make your position clear and that the subject is closed.

Using these methods, you can calm your challenging toddler and teach them better behaviour. Hopefully, you've learned some useful techniques and can handle any tantrum; your child throws at you.

CHAPTER 33:

After the Tantrum Do's and Don'ts

Finally, we are going to look over what to expect when a tantrum has concluded. No one likes dealing with tantrums. When it does happen, people are generally hopeful that they can avoid more in the future. Unfortunately, there will almost always be another tantrum at some point. However, the way you handle the aftermath of the temper can help you learn how to recognize what has happened and begin to move on from it altogether.

In particular, you may find that your child is quite upset or ashamed after the tantrum. Remember, for most children, and it is a matter of their emotions going haywire—they are not trying to misbehave. If you make your child feel like they have failed to do so, they will feel bad.

With that in mind, let's go over what not to do after a tantrum. These should be avoided—after all, you should be treating your child with the tact and grace that he or she deserves. Your child is not trying to give you a hard time. Yes, that point has been reiterated throughout the book—because it is true. Your child is having time but is not trying to give you a hard time intentionally. Remember that when you approach the situation and allow it to colour your response.

- **Don't shame:** Your child is probably already feeling entirely wrong about the outburst, and piling onto that will not help. Children are smart—he or she already knows that there was some problem with the behaviours, and that is enough. Ensure that you do not tell your child that they messed up or try to make your child feel bad.

- **Don't call your child bad:** No children are naughty. They may be bad at self-regulating, but they are not bad themselves. Remember to avoid labelling the child themselves and instead focus on marking the behaviours. This means there should be no asking a child why they are so bad.

- **Don't make the punishment last all day**: Make sure that after a tantrum and after you have gone over the problem with your child, you return to how things were before. It would help if you did not treat your child differently for the day because of their tantrum, causing more problems for them.

- **Don't withhold affection**: You should never use your love as a punishment. Do not withhold your preference from your child. That is a basic need in those tender years, and withholding it will only cause hurt. Your child trusts you to be their safe spot, and if you take that away from them, how are they supposed to respond?

Beyond just what not to do, however, there is a way that you can deal with tantrums after the fact. When the toddler's emotions have calmed down, you can turn everything into a learning experience for your child. Remember, your child is still developing. Your child is still learning how he or she can navigate the world, which is no easy feat. It takes many years to get all of those social nuances down, and you should not blame the toddler for not being able to manage their feelings when many adults still struggle to do so long after childhood. Being a child is challenging, and you need to remember to have that compassion for your toddler, so they do not feel like they will be a failure. Make sure that you do treat your child with that compassion and do the following after the tantrum. In doing so, you can take it from a moment of anger and frustration and help it mould into a healing and learning experience. With that in mind, consider doing the following after a tantrum has subsided:

- **Do talk about it:** When the tantrum is over, your child can stop and think, it is time to have a pleasant, age-appropriate conversation about what has happened. You can do this in many different ways. For example, you could ask your child about how he or she has done something that is not a nice thing. Remember that wording matters here—you tell the child that the behaviour was not friendly, not that your child was not lovely. While you may be able to differentiate between the two, your child cannot. Your child will not understand the nuance between them behaving a certain way and being a certain way. Spend time talking about what went wrong.

- **Ask what they can do next time:** Make sure that after the talk, you ask your child how they may respond better in the future. Younger kids find it hard to be able to articulate this, but older toddlers and preschoolers usually can. They do not have to go into extreme detail—all they have to do is tell you how can change up what they were doing to better cope with the future situation.

- **Encourage healthy and proper apologies**: Remember, this is a learning experience. Your child has done something wrong that has upset someone, whether that was you or someone else. With that in mind, you must be able to encourage your child to understand how apologies work. Apologies happen everywhere, and because of that, you must be able to remind your child how to do so appropriately. Remember to encourage an apology that includes "I'm sorry for doing [insert behaviour here]." You want them to understand what it was that they did that was a problem, why it was a problem, and that the other person saw it as a problem. This is the manner that everyone should apologize—it acknowledges fault and what had happened.

- **Hug:** When you are done talking, and the apology is over, you should always make it a point to hug your child. This reminds your child that you do love him or her—it tells your child that, no matter what happens, you are still there and that you are always going to love them. You do not want them to assume that your love is conditional—something that can produce problems later on in life. Your pet should be freely given, and you should remind your child that it is there shortly after your child is done with the tantrum.

CHAPTER 34:

No Bad Kids—
Toddler Discipline Without Shame

A toddler acting out is not shameful, nor is it behavior that needs punishing. It's a cry for attention, a shout-out for sleep, or a call to action for firmer, more consistent limits. It is the push-pull of your toddler testing his burgeoning independence. He has the overwhelming impulse to step out of bounds, while also desperately needing to know he is securely reined in. There is no question that children need discipline. As infant expert Magda Gerber said, "Lack of discipline is not kindness, it is neglect."

The key to healthy and effective discipline is our attitude. Toddlerhood is the perfect time to hone parenting skills that will provide the honest, direct, and compassionate leadership our children will depend on for years to come. Here are some guidelines:

1) Begin with a predictable environment and realistic expectations. A predictable, daily routine enables a baby to anticipate what is expected of him. That is the beginning of discipline. Home is the ideal place for infants and toddlers to spend the majority of their day. Of course, we must take them with us to do errands sometimes, but we cannot expect a toddler's best behaviour at dinner parties, long afternoons at the mall, or when his days are loaded with scheduled activities.

2) Don't be afraid, or take misbehaviour personally. When toddlers act out in my classes, the parents often worry that their child might be a brat, a bully, an aggressive kid. When parents project those fears, it can cause the child to internalize the negative personas, or at least pick up on the parent's tension, which often exacerbates the misbehavior.

Instead of labeling a child's action, learn to nip the behavior in the bud by disallowing it nonchalantly. If your child throws a ball at your face, try not to get annoyed. He doesn't do it because he dislikes you, and he's not a bad child. He is asking you (toddler-style) for the limits that he needs and may not be getting.

3) Respond in the moment, calmly, like a CEO. Finding the right tone for setting limits can take a bit of practice. Lately, I've been a encouraging parent that struggle with this to imagine they are a successful CEO and that their toddler is a respected underling. The CEO corrects the errors of others with confident, commanding efficiency. She doesn't use an unsure, questioning tone, get angry or emotional. Our child needs to feel that we are not nervous about his behavior, or ambivalent about establishing rules. He finds comfort when we are effortlessly in charge.

Lectures, emotional reactions, scolding and punishments do not give our toddler the clarity he needs, and can create guilt and shame. A simple, matter-of-fact "I won't let you do that. If you throw that again I will need to take it away" while blocking the behaviour with our hands is the best response. But react immediately. Once the moment has passed, it is too late. Wait for the next one!

4) Speak in first person. Parents often get in the habit of calling themselves "mommy" or "daddy." Toddlerhood is the time to change over into first person for the most honest, direct communication possible. Toddlers test boundaries to clarify the rules. When I say "Mommy doesn't want Emma to hit the dog," I'm not giving my child the direct ('you' and 'me') interaction she needs.

5) No time out! I always think of infant expert Magda Gerber asking in her grandmotherly Hungarian accent, "Time out of what? Time out of life?" Magda was a believer in straightforward, honest language between a parent and child. She didn't believe in gimmicks like 'time-out', especially to control a child's behavior or punish him. If a child

misbehaves in a public situation, the child is usually indicating he's tired, losing control and needs to leave. Carrying a child to the car to go home, even if he kicks and screams, is the respectful way to handle the issue. Sometimes a child has a tantrum at home and needs to be taken to his room to flail and cry in our presence until he regains self-control. These are not punishments, but caring responses.

6) Consequences. A toddler learns discipline best when he experiences natural consequences for his behavior, rather than a disconnected punishment like timeout. If a child throws food, mealtime is over. If a child refuses to get dressed, we don't go to the park today. These parental responses appeal to a child's sense of fairness. The child may still react negatively to the consequence, but he does not feel manipulated or shamed.

7) Don't discipline a child for crying. Children need rules for behavior, but their emotional responses to the limits we set (or to anything else for that matter) should be allowed, even encouraged. Toddlerhood can be a time of intense, conflicting feelings. Children may need to express anger, frustration, confusion, exhaustion and disappointment, especially if they don't get what they want because we've set a limit. A child needs the freedom to safely express his feelings without our judgment. He may need a pillow to punch—give him one.

8) Unconditional love. Withdrawing our affection as a form of discipline teaches a child that our love and support turns on a dime, evaporating because of his momentary misbehaviour. How can that foster a sense of security? Alfie Kohn's New York Times article, "When A Parent's 'I Love You' Means 'Do As I Say',", explores the damage this kind of "conditional parenting" (recommended by experts like talk show host Phil McGraw and Jo Frost of "Supernanny") causes, as the child grows to resent, distrust and dislike his parents, feel guilt, shame, and a lack of self-worth.

9) NEVER Spank– Most damaging of all to a relationship of trust are spankings. And spanking is a predictor of violent behaviour. Time Magazine article, "The Long-Term Effects of Spanking," by Alice Park, reports findings from a recent study: "the strongest evidence yet that children's short-term response to spanking may make them act out more in the long run. Of the nearly 2,500 youngsters in the study, those who were spanked more frequently at age 3 were much more likely to be aggressive by age 5." Purposely inflicting pain on a child cannot be done with love. Sadly however, the child often learns to associate the two. Loving our child does not mean keeping him happy all the time and avoiding power struggles. Often it is doing what feels hardest for us to do saying "No" and meaning it.

Our children deserve our direct, honest responses so they can internalize 'right' and 'wrong', and develop the authentic self-discipline needed to respect and be respected by others. As Magda Gerber wrote in Dear Parent—Caring For Infants With Respect, "The goal is inner-discipline, self-confidence and joy in the act of cooperation."

CHAPTER 35:

Tips to Decrease Tantrums

Keep Your Cool

No matter how upset you may be, you must keep your calm and keep your emotions even and calm. Your toddler will pick up on your demeanour. If you are collected when you administer discipline, they will respond more favourably. If you feel angry, step away a few minutes before disciplining your toddler. Keep emotions in control.

Give them a Break

Sometimes disciplining a toddler means you need to give them a break. Instead of punishing them for something, pull them away and put them safely to take a break from the situation. Explain to them why you are forcing them to take a break from it. Please help them understand why they need to change what they are doing to make it better.

Diet Affects Children

Feed your child sugar and watch them become excessively hyperactive, then watch them become very lazy. Eating the wrong foods can affect the behaviour and cause behavioural issues increasing the need for disciplinary actions. Feed your toddler nutritious foods. Watch their behaviour and health improve. Prevent giving junk food and replace it with fresh fruits and vegetables. Stop the sugary drinks and serve plenty of water.

Keep a Daily Diary of Their Behaviour

To understand what makes your toddler tick keep a daily journal of their behaviour. Record whether or not they have had enough rest. Record the foods they eat, record how they act right after eating and record their behaviour a couple of hours after eating. By viewing your child's routine, you can pinpoint the things that may spark behavioural issues. Record their moods, their diet, and their rest.

When You Administer Discipline, Never Keep Threatening to Do It

Do not ask and ask over and again without action. Make the warning a one-time thing and then, if needed, get up and administer the discipline. Ensure they are aware that if you say you will discipline their bad behaviour, you will carry through with it. If you do not, they will not listen to you.

Put Them Into a "Time Out"

Sometimes the best way to get a toddler's attention and change their behaviour is to put them into a "time out." Doing time out allows them to think about why you did this. Before you put them, there explain what they were doing wrong and why you have them sit down. Do time according to their age, one minute per year.

Praise Them When Appropriate

One of the best ways to get your child to behave is to praise them when appropriate. When they do something right, you need to let them know. When they may have had an issue before and have corrected it, let them know you are proud of them. Praise them verbally in front of others. Offer them little rewards for good behaviour. Give them incentives to behave right.

Listen

Sometimes parents lose their ability to administer discipline because they refuse to take the time to listen to their toddler. Even toddlers have something to say. Parents may think it is gibberish or do not know better, but sometimes they talk gold nuggets. Take the time to listen to them. Give them the respect you give to any other person and listen to them.

Both Parents Need to Agree on The Type of Discipline

Never pit against your spouse (or their other parent). If you do not agree in discipline, then take the time to discuss this and come to a good agreement with it. Children need to see a united front with their parents. If agreeing is difficult, you may need to compromise. Do what it takes to settle.

Be Consistent With Your Toddler

Toddlers thrive on maintained routines. If you have a specific bedtime, stick with it. If you have certain foods you allow eaten for breakfast, stick with it. It is when routines are disrupted that children may act up and display bad behaviour. Keep this in mind when disciplining a misbehaved toddler. Has your toddler's routine been interrupted, causing bad behaviour change?

Daily Habits

Sometimes toddlers may display behavioural issues if you have changed something significant in their regular daily routines. One of the significant changes that may disrupt good behaviour is moving a toddler out of their crib before they are ready. Before you get rid of the crib, make sure your child is prepared to sleep in a big kid bed.

Provide a Good Distraction

An excellent way to prevent bad behaviour from taking full effect is to provide a good distraction for your toddler. It could be there focusing on a particular thing that causes them to act ill towards others. This behaviour crop up, try to offer a distraction to pull their attention elsewhere. This helps to keep your toddler focused on good behaviour.

Sometimes a Child Will Act Out if They Want Attention

Try to assess the situation and discern if this is the case. A child who acts out for attention may be scared or distressed instead of punishment as a discipline that offers comfort. It could be all your child needs is some reassurance. Sometimes a friendly hug and a kind word will help to turn them to good.

One of The Worse Things You Can Do to Your Child is to Bribe Them Into Behaving

This sends a signal that all they have to do is act up or misbehave, and they will get a neat reward out of it when you tell them to stop misbehaving. Instead of bribing them, offer a bonus before they act up for good behaviour. That is better and makes sense.

Taking Care Of the Small Tantrums

If your child is accustomed to throwing little tantrums without any consequences, you can rest assured they will someday result in a big huff. Remedy this by taking care of the little tantrums. Excellent and proper discipline means you operate with this regardless of how major or minor the tantrum. If you discipline the little tantrums from toddlers, you may help avoid them boiling over into significant tantrums.

One Choice is the Best One

Sometimes behavioural issues occur when the child is offered too many options, and only one option is the best. Never provide your child with more options if you are set on just one way to do it. This may take longer to convince, but in the long run, you will avoid behavioural issues. Always be honest, and if there is only one option, never offer other choices for them.

Please Help Them to Realize Their Limits

Behavioural issues may stem from the toddler becoming frustrated. Toddlers are just little adults with immature brains and lacking in physical strength. This can frustrate a child if they wish to do something beyond their mental or physical level. Guide them in dealing with their frustrations by showing them different ways of thinking and doing things. Please help them to realize their limits until they are older.

If You Tell a Child No On a Situation, You Must Stick to Your Answer

Sometimes adults find it easier to go back on their "no" response to keep a child from throwing a tantrum. Stick with your no answers and hold to them regardless of how your child is acting. Soon they will learn.

Get on Their Level

Sometimes when you find your toddler misbehaving, and you have to administer more discipline, you need to get on their level. Try to think as they do. Look around and see their frustrations and temptations. You may discover the issue and then can better deal with the situation. Try to realize what your toddler wants and what makes them tick and then proceed accordingly with them.

Your Toddler May Be Frustrated With the Foods you Feed Them

Today it is easy to get ultra involved in all the offerings for babies and toddlers in the grocery store. Everything is tiny sized and babyish. Your toddler needs a chance to eat regular food too. Try offering them a standard plate of food, make smaller portions, and see if it will help with their behavioural issues.

CHAPTER 36:

Preventing Issues With Behaviour

P revention is better than cure. Hence, learning how to prevent problems with children's behaviour seems far better than knowing what to do when you have a problem. Prevention has two main components: trying to learn to anticipate your children. Work out how to prevent the possible issue.

Expectation includes learning by watching him about your child's behaviour. See just how he plays with any toy, and how long he might last. What drives him into handling objects and playing with them? Are they giggling? Are those new ones? Require your guidance and support to make him play? Does he become frustrated by his incapability to do anything? Try breaking things and taking them apart? How fast does he become bored? Observe how he responds in different situations: in the grocery store, in the house of another. Even before you understand how your kid will behave, you can begin anticipating what will occur, and you will be ready. Anticipation is also assisted through constant monitoring of your preschooler. If he has been out of your eyes for ten minutes, he will probably be exploring and is likely to get into trouble. The expected lack of child monitoring (Patterson, 1982) is among the most notable characteristics of families with the most challenging behavioural issues. If you cannot watch him, make sure your spouse knows they are responsible for monitoring him. It can be exhausting because you feel you have to have eyeballs in the back of the head, so you never feel you can concentrate entirely on anything. That's why having your first child can be so exhausting because the older child will often disclose to you when you have more than one if the kid does something he shouldn't do.

Just use the knowledge you gained by watching your child and awareness of their developmental stage to prevent issues. Make the home environment safe; start by removing from the floor plants and electronic devices once your baby crawls. Use stair gates to stop him from going up and down the stairs when you do not look. Put child-resistant locks on kitchen cabinets. If your child gets bored sitting in the stroller, have toys and meals and drinks to use as interruptions if you are out of the home. Talk to him to get him involved in your activities; sing a song to get him involved and keep him happy; Go to the grocery store, which shows no sweets. Keep trips brief, and do not expect him to sit gladly in the buggy for an hour while you are watching dresses.

There is an old study about watching mothers in supermarkets with their kindergartners (Holden, 1983). It showed that three different types of mothers. Some moms would scream at their kids and tell them off when they began misbehaving. The second group would divert the attention of their kids once they got tough. While the third group would escape problems, talking to their kids, and getting them involved in shopping. The least problem had been for the mothers who could foresee the issues and reduce them before they even started. However, the moms who hollered had the most challenging time, and their kids made the most requirements. This study helps us to recognize how parenting style has a significant impact on the behaviour of children. Their training is quick, and your kid should be well conscious that if this is a diversion strategy that you used previously, you have everything in your pocket for him. He will scream and desire candy and biscuits if you have once quieted him with all those. If he believes he can get you to start chasing him down and have a game, he will runoff. Therefore, if you see shopping as part of a social venture your kid is interested in, you will notice he will be quieter for longer than waiting as you are moving home. He will eventually get bored, of course, as he does not want to look at the things you would like to look at, but you can purchase yourself for some time without crying and whining. This is a robust positive parenting method, as it provides a strong relationship between your child and you. You think about your child's needs and interests while doing what you wish to do as well.

He starts to feel involved and appreciates chatting and attention and is trying to notice stuff around him. You can direct his interest, broaden his language skills, and provide experiences of learning. For instance, enabling him to start putting the fruits and vegetables in the supermarket bags results in having to touch and feeling those foods. He learns their initials, feel, and smell. He also gets to practice counting. Having a chat like this can be hard work, and sometimes you feel a total idiot when you have been talking to the kid for the most of the day and when he comes home, carry it on with your partner. This may be an essential difference between men and women. Women generally find it easier to chat about what they are doing than give a meaningful commentary on their activities and emotions. In contrast, men tend to be silent and not verbalize their thoughts to the same degree. To reap the benefits of it, as it will only benefit your toddler.

CHAPTER 37:

The Common Mistakes That Parents Make and How to Fix Them

Disciplining your toddlers alone is not the only thing you can do. It would help if you also avoided the common pitfalls of parenting. Many of these blunders do not just decrease the effectiveness of the discipline that you impose on your toddler but may even encourage your toddlers to misbehave. Here are the common mistakes that many parents make when disciplining their children.

Being Aggressive

Some parents give up and become aggressive. The problem with being assertive is that the children learn nothing except fear. They do not get to understand the value that you want them to know. Instead, they obey you out of fear. Studies also show that toddlers who have experienced aggressive or abusive parents are likely to grow aggressively. Being bold does not mean spanking your kids, but it also includes using highly offensive words and threatening words. It is necessary to note that you are dealing with a toddler, and being aggressive is the worst thing you can do.

Comparing Yourself With Other Parents

Stop comparing yourself with other parents. How they discipline their kids is their problem. If one of your friends tells you that slapping your kid in the face is useful, even if he could prove it, do not follow the advice right away. After all, according to various studies, slapping or hitting your kids is not an effective way to discipline them.

Comparing your Child With Other Children

It seems unfair to compare your child with other children, except if it will be something that will make him feel good and comfortable about himself. Would you like your child to reach you in terms of money with a parent who is much richer than you are? Of course not. In the same way, you should not compare your child with other children. Your toddler is unique in his way, and you should appreciate him as he is.

Lying

Some parents lie to their toddlers to make them obey. Although this may be applied from time to time, it also has terrible consequences. In a case study of a mom from New Jersey with a 2-year-old daughter, it so happened that one day when her child did not want to get in the car, she pointed at her neighbour's house nearby and told her kid that it was a daycare centre full of troglodytes from a scary TV show. She said to her daughter that she had two choices, to get in the car or be stay in the house with a threat of being attacked by creepy cavemen. Of course, her daughter finally gave in and entered the vehicle. Now, if you look at what happened, it will seem that it was successful. There was no shouting or spanking or anything that took place. However, the problem here occurred after the incident. Following the case study, the mom's daughter began to fear daycare centres, thinking that such places have scary cavemen. As you can see, although the mother was able to make her child get into the car, the consequence was worse. Therefore, instead of lying, the best way is, to be honest, and be emphatic.

Yelling

According to Dr. Alan Greene, a paediatrician and member of the clinical faculty at Stanford University School of Medicine, if you lose control and start yelling, your kid will also do the same. Now, this does not mean that your kid is intentionally disrespecting you.

This only proves that your child is having a hard time with you because you cannot understand each other. Therefore, you must keep your voice quiet yet firm. Eyes contact also helps.

Thinking that You Understand Your Toddler

The truth is that you cannot always understand your toddler. This is because toddlers do not think the same way as adults do. You cannot tell precisely how certain things have an impact on your toddler's feelings and thoughts. More importantly, you do not know just up to what degree. Therefore, do not be too hard on your toddler.

Raising the Child, You Want

Do not impose your life or your will upon your toddler. Your child has his own life. Let him pursue whatever he wants. Let him paint his dreams and believe in them. Focus on the child whom you already have and not the idea of a child in your mind whom you would wish to have. Your child may not be wired the way you want him to be, which is normal. Let your child have his chance in life. Let him believe and live his dreams.

Correcting Everything at the Same Time

Many parents try to correct all their children's inappropriate behaviours. They expect a toddler to do it within a short period. This is a very unreasonable expectation. Even you cannot change your bad manners and behaviours quickly, so do not expect your toddler to do it much more than you can. Not to mention, most parents' complaints about their toddlers are normal behaviours (or misbehaviours) for a toddler.

Choose to pick your battles, and do not even attempt to win everything simultaneously. You may start with the behaviour that you consider to be the most serious and requires attention. Once you have corrected it, then you can move to another. Of course, you should discipline your child with every opportunity that presents itself. But, learn to focus on a particular behaviour, so you can also gauge the effectiveness of the technique or techniques that you are using.

Long Explanations

Long explanations do not work on toddlers. You will only seem like talking gibberish after a few minutes. Do not forget that toddlers have a short attention span; therefore, long explanations do not work well. For example, you do not have to lecture your toddler why eating cookies before bedtime is not suitable for her teeth. She will learn that when the right time comes. Instead, say, "No cookies." You do not have to explain so much. Toddlers, as what they are, are not meant to be very logical. They do not care so much about explanations. Of course, this rule is subject to exceptions, such as when the toddler himself wants to know the reason behind something or when giving an answer appears to be the best course of action.

Bribe

Do not bribe your toddler to make him do what you want. Otherwise, he will always ask for it, which could be a problem in the long run. In a case study of a mom in Montclair, New Jersey, she offered her daughter a chocolate piece if she (her toddler) would eat her meal. It worked well. Her daughter finished her meal quickly. However, what happened here was that after that dinner, the daughter would always ask her mother to give her a piece of chocolate so that she would finish her meal.

Instead of bribing your child, the suggested way is to help her realize the importance of food. The better way would be to tell her child that she will get hungry late in the evening if she eats so little and that she will not be healthy, making her sick. If you face a similar problem with your child, you can tell her about the health benefits of the food, like it could make her skin more beautiful, make her taller or smarter, and others— but do not lie.

Not Asking Questions

Toddlers usually have so many questions. As a parent, you tend to answer your query as much as you can. It is worth noting that you should not lie to your child when he asks questions. However, you can make silly answers, but be sure that he knows that it is a joke when you do so. Also, avoid giving creepy answers or those that will tend to scare your child. So, avoid responses that relate to ghosts and other scary stuff. However, parents get too caught up with answering their child's countless questions that they miss another essential thing to do: to ask their child questions. If you can take the time to ask your toddler questions, even crazy and illogical ones, that you might hear. Toddlers have a powerful imagination and are very curious and open to almost everything. By asking questions to your child, you will also get to understand how he thinks, and even appreciate how young he truly is— so all the more reason why you should never be aggressive or harsh on your toddler.

Don't Give Ultimatums

Young children need to see their authority as their parent. It makes them feel secure knowing that there are mature, responsible, knowledgeable, authoritative people around them. However, when you make ultimatums to your children, such as telling them to eat their food or the monster will come and get them, they will want to test your threat. A toddler who does not want to eat will close his mouth, and although scared, he will want to see if what you said is true. So he'll wait for the monster, and when no monster comes, he'll know that your words are empty.

Don't Play Good Cop, Bad Cop

Do you and your partner play the "good cop, bad cop" when disciplining your toddler? Even if it works, your child's relationship with the parent that plays the "bad cop" may eventually suffer. Both parents need to be the "good cop." Every toddler must be able to feel safe with both parents and not just one of them. Also, children look up to their mother and father and expect only the good from them.

Don't Be Divided

When disciplining a toddler, the mother and father need to have a united front. Once your child sees any weakness in any one of his parents, he will use this to get what he wants. Therefore, parents need to talk before creating rules, setting limits, giving rewards, or implementing punishments. Plus, they have to agree on everything. Otherwise, the toddler will sense that one parent does not agree, and he will take advantage of this.

For instance, if the rule is that the child can only have one scoop of ice cream, both parents need to be firm about implementing it. If one parent backs down and gives the toddler another knowledge, then the rule is broken, and the other parent's authority is undermined. For the child to learn discipline and recognize both parents' power, moms and dads need to stick together.

Furthermore, a parent should never say anything to a toddler that disparages the other parent. This will only confuse a young child and affect how he regards the parent who disses and the parent being dissed.

Don't Set High, Unreasonable Expectations

Your child is a toddler. What were you expecting from a child aged 2, 3, 4, or 5? Praise your child for achievements and good behaviour. Allow him to make mistakes that he can learn from here. Don't pressure your very young child to be something that he isn't ready for yet. Treasure your child at a young age. Let him be a toddler.

Conclusion

R aising toddlers is not an easy task. Making it would be the most challenging job you have ever had. Yet, it is also going to be the most rewarding and will give you more memorable experiences and memories than you could ever imagine. You live for your children in many ways; most parents do. We are extremely prideful in our children, and these are amazing factors to have as parents.

The toddler years are, perhaps, the most memorable for every parent. Who can forget the cute, chubby faces, the adorable giggles, and those monstrous tantrums? Every parent has been through a full-blown tantrum. Many have learned to effectively deal with it while others are still struggling with their little ones. Tantrums can be physically and emotionally draining for both the parent and the child. Parents don't want to see their little ones crying and suffering, and some will not know what to do in these situations.

You finally have all the tricks to turn your toddler into a prodigy of modern discipline and success! Parents are exhausted by the tantrums, misbehaviour, and outright meltdowns. We cringe when we hear our kids say, "no." We couldn't understand why they didn't listen to us. All we wanted was to know how to say "no" when they cry for a toy they can't have. Their behaviour has left us reeling when they amplify tantrums in the middle of a mall. They tug our pants and give us hell. No one cared to tell us the full truth about the terrible twos.

Some of us were fortunate enough to expect this stage, but we still didn't know how we survived the last one. Moms and dads are overwhelmed when their two-year-old draw all over their curtains with markers or refuses to eat their food. Who can forget when your child made the neighbours think someone was being murdered when you tried to bathe them? Toddlers bounce around like drops of cuteness until they punch another child or scratch their parents with those unbelievably sharp nails. Toddlers will always be prone to tantrums; it's something natural. They will also demonstrate other behavioural problems as they grow. However, parents need to remember that toddlers are acting this way because they are not emotionally and mentally capable of doing otherwise. Hence, parents need to treat their toddlers with patience and understanding. Moms and dads out there should also remember to regularly assure their tantrum-prone little one that they love him very much, no matter what.

These days are over, and you finally know how to discipline your toddler with expert advice and psychologically-backed techniques. You've learned about the priceless advantage of guiding your child positively through early childhood development to crush those tantrums as much as parents can. You know they can never be erased, but you also learn how to respond to them and decrease them significantly. Age by age, you can use proven methods of regulating your child's moods, aggression, and lack of reason.

I've shared every secret I have with you. I've covered all the most common struggles we face during the various stages. No stone is left unturned, and you can now work on building a relationship that exceeds your expectations. Watch as other parents stare in amazement while you handle your toddler without outdated methods. Your home, family, and child-guidance are now officially out of the war zone. You have what it takes to handle anything they throw at you directly in great detail.

All that you must still do is make a concerted effort to stick to your new discipline strategies and enjoy the peace that comes from them.